"CAS

Understanding the past to know the future

Edited by Carlos Alberto Bisceglia

Carlos Alberto Bisceglia

Homo Reloaded

The hidden history of the last 75,000 years

INDEX

PART 1

1 - Origins   p. 13

2 - Evolution   p. 23

PART 2

3 - The mystery of 'humans'   p. 41

4 - The first "reload"   p. 47

PART 3

5 - The Story of Sulawesi   p. 67

6 - T The second 'reload' of humans   p. 73

PART 4

7 - Ice Age   p. 83

8 - Before the Maya   p. 97

PART 5

9 - The End of the Ice Age   p. 125

10 - The End of Sundaland   p. 139

11 - The Hidden Metropolis   p. 149

PART 6

12 - The great Asian "reload"   p. 165

PART 7

13 - The "Younger Dryas"   p. 177

14 - A tale in a stone   p. 193

PART 8

15 - Desertification of the Sahara   p. 225

16 - The 'Mount Atlas Exiles'   p. 249

17 - Technology of the 'Exiles'   p. 263

PART 9

18 - The "reload" of the Y chromosome   p. 303

19 - The Missing Wonder   p. 311

PART 10

20 - The first "facilitator"   p. 325

21 - The Last   p.356

Introduction

The "Timaeus" is a dialogue written by Plato around 360 BC. At one point in the story, a mysterious priest from the city of Sais, citing information from very ancient scrolls, says the following:

"[Mankind in the past has been affected] by many catastrophic events that have decimated the population in many ways! The greatest catastrophes occurred by means of fire and water. Other minor disasters occurred for many other reasons.

Do you remember the story that is told among you? The one according to which one day, Phaethon, son of the Sun, after taking the reins of his father's chariot, set fire to everything on Earth, and he himself died struck by lightning, because he was unable to drive the chariot like his father? Well, this story is told among you in the form of a myth! It actually describes the motion of celestial bodies revolving around the Earth. At long intervals of time, these cause the destruction of everything on Earth by means of a great deal of fire. Then, those who dwell on mountains and in high, dry places die more easily than those who dwell by rivers and the sea. The Nile, which is our saviour in other things, also saves us from this calamity by means of its waters.

At other times, however, the gods submerge the earth by purifying it with water. With us, the farmers and shepherds who live in the mountains are saved, while those who live in your cities are swept away by the overflow of the rivers to the sea. In our region, water does not flow from the plateaus to the ploughed fields. On the contrary, in our country, water rises from below. Therefore, no one is carried away by the water. That is why the oldest traditions have been preserved in our land.

By us, in all places where excessive cold or too much heat does not prevent it, the lineage of men, though in alternating stages, has always existed. And all things worthy of remembrance that happen, whether by you or elsewhere, are written down and preserved in temples.

But as soon as one of his own people or of a neighbouring people rediscovers writing and all that is necessary for civilisation, after a lapse of time here comes the Flood again, which, like a disease, descends again from heaven. Of you it leaves alive only those who are ignorant in letters and the arts. In this way you become children again, as from the beginning, knowing nothing of what happened from us, nor of what happened with you, and which took place in ancient times." - End quote.

The words of the priest of Sais, recounted by Plato in the "Timaeus," leave no room for interpretation. He says, "As soon as they [humans] rediscover writing and everything else that is needed for civilization, after an interval of time here it is again [destruction], which, like a disease, comes down again [from the gods] from heaven." And one has to start all over again. According to the priest of Sais, therefore, human civilization, throughout its history has been several times "reloaded," that is, reloaded and rebooted, like you reboot an app in a mobile phone, to make it start from scratch.

According to this sage from the past, there is almost a "cyclicity" in human history. This cyclicity sees entire "human families" make their appearance, progress, reach a climax and then disappear. How much truth is there in this statement from about 2,500 years ago? Are there traces of various "reloads" in our history? Will there be more of them? Can we avoid the next one?

PART 1

Dating:

From about 14,000,000,0000 years ago to 2,400,000 years ago

Topic:

Origin of Life

Life propagation

Involved populations:

Every form of life

1 - Origins

How did the Universe originate? For more than fifty years we have heard various scientists express extreme confidence about the "Big Bang," a giant explosion that supposedly gave rise to the entire Universe. As science has progressed, in a great many university centres this theory is now considered totally outdated.

Without wanting to go too deep into this vast topic, we can say that science has produced a new theory on the 'origin of the Universe, the so-called "M Theory." (Edward Witten was the first to postulate such a theory at a conference on "String Theory" at the University of Southern California in 1995.) "M-theory" seems to explain much better the reality in which we are all immersed. What does this theory say? Wanting to greatly simplify, we can list the following key points:

(1) All the matter of which our Universe is composed actually consists of infinitely small, microscopic vibrations, called "strings." These vibrations influence each other to constitute what we perceive as "matter." So the Universe, in reality, would be much like a huge "symphony" of an incalculable number of "strings."

(2) All these strings do not generate a "single" Universe, but theoretically an infinite number of Universes. These Universes are actually three-dimensional membranes, floating in the vacuum, like giant veils. From time to time these membranes, or veils, collide with each other at certain points, giving rise to "collisions." For a long time we

thought that one of those "collisions" was the "Big Bang," the primordial explosion.

(3) Our reality consists of as many as eleven dimensions, in which the Universe-Branes (membranes), which are 3-dimensional, float.

(4) Although individual Universes may have had a beginning, it is not necessarily the case that "reality" in general is subject to time, which is just one dimension like any other. So our reality may have neither a beginning nor an end. Even what we perceive as "time" is probably an illusion of our own. Time, in fact, does not exist.

Of course, we have tried to simplify the description of "M-theory" as much as possible, since this book is not a treatise on physics. Nevertheless, we realize that this explanation of the Universe is quite different from what we are used to hearing in school or in documentaries from a few years ago. However, it is best to abandon old concepts such as the "Big Bang" or the like and keep up with science. This will help us a lot in our journey to find the "reloads" of human history.

Life on Earth

When and how did Life appear on Earth? On the "when," it seems that the first forms of Life appeared on Earth as early as 4,000,000,000 years ago. Regarding the "how," beyond the details that may vary, science has two completely opposite and conflicting theories that try to explain the appearance of Life on Earth. These theories are "abiogenesis" and "panspermia."

Abiogenesis holds that life on Earth arose spontaneously from "non-life." Starting from inorganic materials, at the end of a slow process of assembly driven purely by chance that occurred within hydrothermal vents under the oceans, these "non-living" materials would have combined in such a way as to create material that then became "living."

According to abiogenesis, only the basic elements to create life in water were present on the meteorites and comets that fell about four billion years ago on Earth. No one can explain exactly how these elements spontaneously combined into nucleic acids and proteins so that the formation of the first simpler organisms could be initiated. In fact, in this respect, abiogenesis is almost a new edition of the theory of "spontaneous generation," which was refuted in the 17th and 18th centuries, thanks to some experiments by Francesco Redi and Lazzaro Spallanzani. Yet, abiogenesis is the theory on the genesis of Life on Earth that enjoys the most credit in the scientific community.

The second theory of the genesis of Life on Earth, "panspermia," on the other hand, is strongly criticized by those who teach abiogenesis, but is supported by some of the most celebrated scientists, including several Nobel laureates. Among them we can point to Francis Crick, Nobel laureate in medicine in 1962, one of the two scientists who discovered the helix model of DNA, and thus one of the fathers of genetics. We can count Svante August Arrhenius, Swedish chemist and physicist, Nobel Prize in Chemistry, awarded to him for understanding that electricity diffuses with the passage of ions. Or we can remember astrophysicist Fred Hoyle, the one who produced the theory of element synthesis within stars (a theory now considered a certainty in astrophysics), and his assistant Chandra Wickramasinghe.

What does the theory of "panspermia" teach? According to this theory, it is evident that the earliest traces of life on Earth predate, and by far, the geological time period when the Earth could "spontaneously generate" Life. In fact, in March 2017 a study by Matthew S. Dodd and other authors appeared in the famous journal "Nature" . This article states that in some sedimentary rocks from an ancient hydrothermal chimney in Canada, at a location in Quebec called Nuvvuagittuq, possible fossil microorganisms dating back as far as nearly 4,300,000,000 years have been found. Previously other researchers, including Elizabeth A. Bell, had shown evidence of biological organisms dating back 4,100,000,000 years.

We must specify that we are not talking about "building blocks of life," that is, organic substances that will one day become living organisms. Here we are talking about complete microorganisms, which means DNA, RNA, mitochondria, cell membrane, and everything needed for the reproduction of Life of single-celled organisms. All this existed on Earth as early as 4,300,000,000 years ago.

But it is an established fact that at that time the Earth was little more than a glowing ball of lava, struck by meteors, and struggling to find its equilibrium. Where, then, did those already-formed microorganisms emerge from? Scientists who support panspermia say the only possible explanation is that these microorganisms arrived on Earth from space.

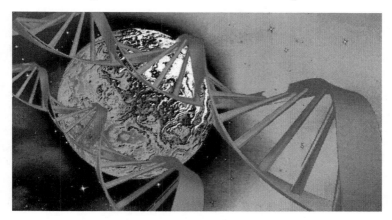

But proponents of panspermia do not just say that. According to calculations made by these researchers, the probability that a perfectly functioning enzyme, with the correct amino acid sequence and spatial form, could assemble itself randomly, through trial and error, is no more than 1 in 100,000,000,000,000,000,000. The problem is that for "Life" to be formed, about 2,000 enzymes are needed. The probability of getting them all through a series of random attempts is only one in 1 followed by 40,000 zeros. This is an absolutely ridiculous possibility.

Proponents of panspermia put the two together, namely, that microorganisms arrived on Earth from space before Life appeared on the planet, and that on Earth it is impossible for

Life to have generated spontaneously. From this they deduce that Life must necessarily have arrived in some form from outer space, according to the principle that Life can only be transmitted from "pre-existing Life."

A "Living Universe"

All this has led many researchers to ask the question, "Do we live in a living Universe or a dead Universe?" Until recently, physicists have treated the Universe as something dead, inanimate, composed of mere minerals and gases moving from side to side without purpose. This model of the Universe derubricates 'Life' almost to an 'accident of the road', something insignificant that may or may not be there without making any difference. In the Universe models of the last century, the "Life" problem was not contemplated at all.

It is now becoming increasingly evident that a gross error has been made in this old conception of the Universe. An article entitled "Discovery of organic grains in comet Halley," which appeared in the famous journal "Nature" on Sept. 6, 1986, tells us something interesting about this. Using infrared spectrum analysis, researchers D.T. Wickramasinghe and D.A. Allen hypothesized the presence of biological material on Halley's comet. Was it bacteria? It certainly seems so. This discovery would be evidence of the presence of Life outside our Earth.

On November 12, 2014, the "Rosetta" probe released the "Philae" lander onto comet 67P/Churyumov Gerasimenko, which landed on its surface. The "Philae" lander was equipped with a "Sample Drilling and Distribution" system, which was responsible for collecting soil samples and transferring them inside the probe for analysis without having to return to Earth. The mission ended on September 30, 2016. The results of the analysis showed the presence of molecular oxygen and water inside the comet. In addition, the comet's "strange" emission of ethyl alcohol was established. Researcher E.J. Steele, in his paper in 2018, wrote in this regard, "Many species of fermentation bacteria can produce ethanol from sugars, so the recent discovery that comet Lovejoy emits an amount of ethyl alcohol equal to 500 bottles of wine per second may well be an indication that such a microbial process is indeed operating."

In May 2001, two researchers from the "Federico II" University of Naples, Bruno D'Argegno, professor of geology, and Giuseppe Geraci, professor of molecular biology, announced that in some 4.5 billion-year-old meteorites there were traces of organisms that may be bacteria or their "cousins," the "archaea." Consider how few asteroids and comets we have been able to analyse, and how little time we have been doing so. Despite this, we have found many traces of bacteria. If we compare this with the billions of billions of meteors and comets floating in space, it is clear that the Universe is teeming with bacteria that use comets as a kind of "hitchhiking."

All this leads many famous researchers to think that in the Universe, Life is anything but an "accident" that happened only on Earth. In the Universe, Life is the rule. So we can no longer speak of a "dead" Universe, but of a "living" Universe. But if the Universe is alive, then all the old models of the Universe are wrong, or at the very least, partial. This is because in these old models, the "Life" element was never taken into account as "fundamental."

Take for example the question, "How does life spread through the Universe?" According to current physics, nothing can move faster than the speed of light. But this would mean that if we wanted to travel end-to-end through our Universe at 99.99% of the speed of light, it would take us about 14,000,000,000 years. Basically we are almost immobile in the Universe. But if we are immobile, then it means that Life cannot travel through the Universe, remaining "alive." In fact, it is highly likely that most living things, such as bacteria, would die during such a long journey. Yet, Life travels in our Universe, and we have evidence of this. How does it do it? Where does it come from? Who or what sends it? Evidently, something about the very way we conceive of the Universe is wrong or escapes us. One thing is clear, however: we cannot explain the origin of the Universe without explaining the origin of Life, because this explanation would not make sense.

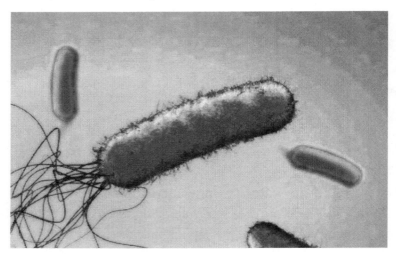

Lords of the cosmos: bacteria

We have come to understand that origin of the Universe and origin and spread of Life go hand in hand. We cannot propose theories that take into account only one of these aspects, omitting or ignoring the others, because that explanation would not make sense. We do not observe a "dead Universe," in which each part is isolated from the rest, and life, if it exists, is only a local "accident." Conversely, we observe a "living Universe," in which despite the enormous distances that separate the various planets, stars and galaxies, Life exists in abundance and travels, probably establishing new connections.

Evidence shows that there is superabundant life in the Universe in bacterial form. Bacteria have an incredible growth rate. A bacterium, if it is under ideal conditions, will reproduce by duplicating itself even every 20 minutes, giving rise to 2 "daughter cells." Within 20 minutes these "daughter cells" will divide in turn, producing two more cells apiece, and so on. In a hypothetical unrestrained growth, a single bacterium can become "billions" in a truly brief time. These numbers help us understand what bacteria are capable of, despite being microscopic beings. Bacteria live with and without oxygen, endure extreme heat and extreme cold. We cannot talk about Life in the Universe by excluding from the topic the true 'lords' of the Earth and the Universe, namely bacteria. But what links more complex forms of life, such as animals or plants, to these primordial bacteria? Let us continue the research

.

2 - Evolution

In reality we are what our DNA is. A horse's DNA will produce a horse. A sheep's DNA will produce a sheep. The DNA of a Homo Sapiens will produce anther Homo sapiens. When talking about species and evolution, it would be a big mistake to talk about body, cells, tendons, and bones. In fact, no variation is possible within a species unless its DNA changes. Therefore, whenever we talk about the evolution of a species, we are actually talking about the "evolution of its DNA." How is it possible for our DNA to evolve?

From Darwin to us

The concept of evolution originated with Charles Darwin (1809 -1882) who was the first to express the theory of "natural selection," in which only the "best" specimens would be allowed to survive and thus reproduce. This selection of the best, according to Darwin, was the driving force behind the evolution of various species. According to this idea, those best adapted to the various changes would survive, reproduce, and then spread their genes, pushing their species toward slow but substantial evolution. More than one hundred years later, although this principle in principle still holds true, it has been realized that things are not that simple at all.

About 60 years after Darwin's death in 1953, professors James Watson and Francis Crick proposed the first detailed model of DNA, our genetic code, and since then the "theory of evolution of the species" has begun to creak increasingly every year. DNA contains all the genes that are activated to regulate any function in our bodies. It is our DNA that makes "us" what we are. Therefore, we have come to realize that human evolution is actually the evolution of its DNA. If we have evolved, then that means our DNA has evolved. But in Charles Darwin's time, the existence of DNA was not even known, so no hypothesis was made about how a DNA could evolve from one species into another. This gap has not yet been completely filled.

In fact, DNA mechanisms present serious problems to coexist with the theory of Evolution. Why? Let us take a "borderline example" to illustrate the point. Two giraffes need to feed. The only leaves available are high up on the top of a branch, so they are difficult to reach in order to eat them. But since there are no other leaves around, only the giraffe that can eat the leaves at the top of the tree will survive and reproduce.

Can one of the two giraffes, by making an effort, become more adept at eating the leaves on top of the tree? The answer is yes. Also, can one of the two giraffes, by trying every day to eat the leaves at the top of the tallest trees, strengthen its neck and perhaps lengthen it a little as the years go by? Once again, the answer is yes. Third question: will the giraffe that has toughened and lengthened its neck a little during its life, pass this characteristic to its offspring as well, who will then gradually have longer and more robust necks? The answer is: no!

Why is the answer "No?" The first reason is that our physical, mental, and whatever else we do normally fail to affect the composition of our DNA. In particular, they do not change the DNA of our reproductive cells. The giraffe with the strong neck will only have strong neck muscles, but he will not have affected his DNA at all. This means that her son will have the same DNA as her and will therefore have to start from scratch with attempts to toughen and lengthen his neck, and so will her grandson and his descendants. (Of course, we have simplified many details to make the point clear).

The only mutations that can be transmitted from parents to offspring are those that appear in the sperm and egg cell from which the offspring will be conceived. No other mutations in any other part of the body will be passed on to one's heirs. This means that unless we expose ourselves to radiation or other chemicals capable of altering the DNA of reproductive cells, there is nothing we can do to trigger the "spring of evolution." Whatever particular skill we acquire by our own efforts during our lifetime, it will not rewrite our DNA, and therefore that particular skill will die with us. We will not pass it on by mere "inheritance" to our descendants.

What then can cause DNA to evolve? From what we know today, only "spontaneous mutations" (in addition to harmful external factors) can change our DNA. But our experience shows us that spontaneous DNA mutations are usually harmful. All spontaneous DNA mutations in the human species are regarded as "genetic diseases," and not as attempts at evolution. This is because, usually, a gene that functions differently than usual can create imbalances that can lead to death.

To hypothesize "useful" spontaneous evolution of our DNA, and not harmful evolution, Japanese biologist Motoo Kimura produced what is called the "Neutral Theory of Evolution," and which is now widely accepted. Wanting to simplify this theory, Professor Kimura calls in "non-lethal micro-mutations," which together with the principle of "selection of the fittest" would act in tandem to modify our DNA. What is meant by this principle? Simplifying the concept very much, we could say that our DNA, in a spontaneous way continuously proposes "nonlethal micro-mutations" in each individual. This would occur because of DNA replication errors. These would be mutations small enough not to compromise our health, but significant enough to introduce a new character into an individual. This would produce "alleles," i.e., genetic "variations" that can exist "latently," and that "come out" only when two similar genes cross paths. In this way, one small step at a time, we would experience over the various generations "small mutations," and the ones that fit best would over time take over.

But according to several researchers this would not be enough for our DNA to evolve. At the same time as these "nonlethal micro-mutations," resulting in the formation of "alleles," a situation must occur in which that "micro-mutation" is useful for that individual at that particular time, making him or her "more suitable" than others who lack it. This would trigger "natural selection" or "selection of the best." It would mean that those who will have had that "nonlethal micro-mutation" should have a better chance of reproducing than others, and thus pass on their modified genetic makeup to others. As the genetic makeup of the "first mutant" spreads through the population, it "recombines" with other DNA. Over time that "mutant" aspect becomes common, is passed from father to son, and thus "micro-evolution" is established.

According to scholars, an exceedingly long chain of millions or billions of "micro-evolutions" that occurred under conditions of complete isolation, that is, while a species could not receive external DNA, would have led to the evolution of one species into another. But this explanation makes several people's mouths twist. According to celebrated geneticists, such an evolution should show that one species evolved into another gradually. However, this is not what is observed in fossils. In the case of Homo Sapiens, for example, it is demonstrable that this species suddenly appeared about 200,000 to 300,000 years ago and does not seem to have any direct link to any of the earlier species.

Moreover, according to other researchers, the combination of nonlethal "micro-mutations" and "survival of the fittest" would require our DNA to ring up a virtually endless series of excellent results in order to succeed in evolving. But to do this would require an almost infinite period of time! Conversely, it would only take one reproductive error to blow everything up. From the standpoint of simple statistics, this does not seem to be likely. It does not look like things could have gone that way.

The "Enablers": viruses

We have understood that if a bacterium is to become a complex being, such as an animal, then its DNA must necessarily mutate, it must "evolve." According to many researchers now, we cannot talk about "DNA evolution" without calling in "viruses." They would be the real "cause" of the "evolutionary leaps" we find in all living species. Let us see why.

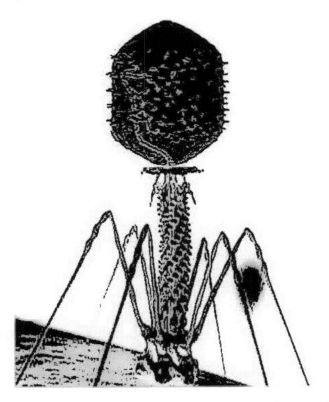

When we think of viruses, we always think of a harmful being. Nothing could be falser. In fact, the virus can be compared to a biological USB stick, which contains within it a "genetic program" that is capable of using the host cell as a "factory" to self-reproduce. The virus connects to the cell, transmits its RNA, and from then on, the cell will "also" do what the virus ordered it to do (normally the virus orders to create many copies of itself). It is true that some viruses turn out to be harmful to the host body. But this is a "secondary"

consequence, not directly intended by the virus. In contrast, theoretically it would be in the virus' interest that the host body does not die. Conversely, the "reproduction system" of the virus itself would be destroyed.

But viruses do not stop there. In addition to using their genetic material to induce a cell to reproduce them, viruses are prime suspects in the phenomenon known as "horizontal gene transfer." What is meant by this term? It means the ability of some viruses to transmit parts of DNA to other living things that are not their own descendants, thus not using the gametes of reproduction. That is, a virus is theoretically capable of taking an entire section of an animal's DNA, "loading it inside," and then dumping it into the DNA of a completely different animal. In this case, the virus does not just use its genetic material to reproduce. Now the virus would even be able to modify the DNA of individual cells in the host body.

If this virus creates a "horizontal genetic transfer" in the gametes, that is, in the reproductive cells of the host organism (such as, for example, a sperm or egg cell), then from then on, all descendants of that organism will be born with that "modification" in their DNA. Viruses, then, are theoretically capable of giving us crazy "evolutionary leaps" that are so abrupt as to be unimaginable with traditional evolutionary theories.

These are aspects that Charles Darwin could not have known about when he formulated his "Theory of the Origin of Species." On the other hand, according to many scholars these are aspects that are becoming increasingly obvious as the research of genetics continues.

2 - Evolution

A new idea

With this new conception of the Universe in mind, on what new principles should a new "Theory of Life" in a "Living Universe" be based? We list some of the fundamental ones.

(1) We should accept the idea that in order to allow for the origin of Life, in turn, the theory of the origin of the "living" Universe cannot be assumed to be a destructive character event. Thus, the Universe cannot have "originated" from a mega-explosion of incalculable power, such as the "Big Bang," the effects of which continue to be present for billions of years. Explosions bring disorder, while life is the triumph of order. In a "Living Universe" model, life appears almost simultaneously with matter, and therefore does not have to be destroyed by the Universe's own creative forces. An initial "Big Bang" is not compatible with the model of a "living Universe."

(2) In a "Living Universe" model, the distances between the various places in the Universe where Life can be transmitted must be attainable in biologically bearable times. Only in this way can Life be allowed to be transmitted without it dying on the "journey." Thus, there must be a way in which matter can move within galaxies, or even between galaxies. Consequently, the limit on the "speed" of light in the Theory of Relativity, for example, cannot be considered absolute. There must be a way to circumvent or get around this limit. Otherwise, life could not be transmitted within the Universe itself.

(3) In this "Living Universe" model, bacteria, and their close relatives, the microorganisms of the genus archaea, are the basic organisms that are transported to planets whose

geological and atmospheric conditions allow the development of Life. Bacteria, therefore, at least in functional aspect, in this model of the Universe would be similar to "spores," which transport life wherever possible. But in a "living Universe" model, bacteria must be able to arrive "alive" at their destination, and not fossilized. So these bacteria probably arrive by safer systems than meteorites and comets, which would probably kill them instantly with their impact on Earth. Someone or something must be able to allow them to make a "soft landing" on the planets where Life will later develop.

(4) In this "Living Universe" model, viruses would be responsible for the "horizontal genetic transfer" that causes a species to adapt to the 'environment or change totally, producing new species. In this way it would be scientifically tenable that one species could change into another at astonishing rates. But, as in the case of bacteria and archaeal organisms, an explanation must be provided as to how these viruses can enter the Earth's atmosphere without being burned by the heat that develops around meteorites or comets. Once again, there must be a "responsible party" for some sort of "soft landing."

A new evolutionary model

Wanting to summarise the evolutionary scenario of a hypothetical 'Living Universe' model, we can imagine that bacteria reached the Earth alive around four billion years ago. Viruses followed shortly after them. When the Earth's environment allowed, a series of retroviruses continuously injected new pieces of DNA into a host bacterium. From being a single-celled organism this gradually evolved into a multicellular organism. These continuous "inputs" of "new DNA" by viruses would have caused evolution to proceed "in leaps and bounds." Other evolutionary mechanisms (nonlethal micro-mutations and species selection) would have taken care of microevolution.

In this model, the evolution of one species into another becomes more credible because:

(1) We start from a base where the DNA and related genes already exist, and they are those of the bacterium or microorganisms of the genus archaea.

(2) Viruses, with their "horizontal genetic transfer," would have allowed for enormously faster evolution than the mechanisms envisioned by traditional evolutionism.

(3) Natural selection and micro-mutations would still retain their role, albeit less incisive than in classical evolutionary theories.

It is obvious that the principles we have stated, and which several researchers are beginning to consider, are little more than postulates. They need to be demonstrated and explained in detail. However, the basis for this mechanism seems to be more solid than holding that by "pure chance" inanimate material became living. Moreover, this innovative approach requires that Life developed in only a few places in the Universe, theoretically even in one. Subsequently, Life simply had to travel. The chances that Life could have existed in this way increase dramatically.

Without a real beginning

However, the basic question would remain: who produced the first bacteria, and from whom or where did the viruses with the various DNA "updates" come? Whatever place in our Universe where Life must have first developed, the "probabilities" that it developed "spontaneously" are similar to those that would be found on Earth. Even in that remote part of the Universe, the probability of Life developing on its own would be 1 to 1 followed by 40,000 zeros. We would be back, then, to square one.

The only possibility of life developing is therefore to assume a timeless Universe, such as that described by "M-theory." A Universe that perhaps regenerates itself with "contractions" and "expansions" of its "membranes," but where time essentially does not exist. Only by having 'infinite' time can we expect that life can try 'infinite times' to generate itself, being certain that it will eventually succeed. In that "eternal present," in the face of infinite time, any statistics lose their value, because no matter how small the chance of success, that event will happen.

Life Couriers?

But even if that were the case, who or what brought the bacteria, viruses, and the right combinations of DNA transmitted by them to Earth? Is it possible that the bacteria and viruses that probably gave rise to Life were brought from space not on asteroids and comets, but through intelligent beings?

2 - Evolution

Let us ask ourselves: are we alone in the Universe? To this question, more than 99 percent of the members of the scientific community today would answer with a dry, "No, we are not alone in the Universe." This statement has now become less and less a personal opinion of a single scientist, and increasingly an objective observation. Indeed, with the advent of new telescopes, including the famous "James Webb Space Telescope," an extremely considerable number of "exoplanets," or planets located outside our solar system, have been discovered. Many of these exoplanets are in a "habitable zone," that is, they travel an orbit around a star that allows the planet to have a temperature conducive to life.

Moreover, several of these exoplanets would have a mass comparable to that of Earth. The force of gravity exerted on any living things, therefore, would be neither too strong nor too weak. In addition to all this, while in the past it was believed that water was the rarest element in the Universe, today we are beginning to realize that perhaps it is the opposite. Several planets and satellites in the solar system contain water, in various forms. So it is entirely likely that water is a fairly common element in the Universe.

All these aspects were observed by peering into a really small, infinitesimal portion of the known Universe. Multiplying the number of "habitable" planets found in this small search area, by the millions of billions of stars similar to our Sun of which the Universe is composed, yields a number of "potentially habitable" planets of several billion. It is likely that in at least a few millions of these exoplanets' life has developed, and it is entirely plausible that in at least a few thousand of them life has reached a development quite similar to that of the human race, if not much more advanced. Thus the probability that there are intelligent, technological life forms in the Universe is infinitely higher than the probability that there are none. That is why the scientific community now virtually takes it for granted that there are other intelligent civilizations out there.

Did they ever come to Earth?

Taking it for granted that these intelligent life forms exist, we ask a further question: are these civilizations exploring space? Again, the answer can only be in the affirmative. Homo Sapiens has existed for no more than 200,000 to 300,000 years. Yet as soon as humans had the technology to do so, they sent satellites and probes to every planet in the Solar System, and even outside the Solar System. Several humans have already left planet Earth to visit our satellite, the Moon, and trips are being planned to send humans to other planets, such as Mars.

If we think about it, the 200,000 years of existence of the human race is a very insignificant amount of time compared to the several billion years of existence of the Universe. Therefore, it does not appear that we are the oldest intelligent life form in the Universe. It is much more likely that we are among the latest arrivals on the scene. It is entirely realistic, even logical, to think that there are intelligent life forms with sufficiently evolved technology, and that they have existed for millions of years before us. And it is equally realistic to think that these intelligent beings began exploring the space around them long before we did.

This obviousness forces us to ask another question: how far have these civilizations gone in exploring the space around them? Have they gone as far as to explore the Earth yet? Indeed, the absolute certainty of the existence of other life forms in space means that the question to be asked is no longer, "Has planet Earth ever made contact with an extra-terrestrial civilization? ". The right question to ask is, "When has planet Earth had or will it have contact with an extra-terrestrial civilization? ". Why do we talk about "planet Earth" and not "human civilization"? Proverbial human egocentrism makes us believe that Earth was born with us, with our civilization. But this is a blatant lie.

Planet Earth has lived quietly without us for more than 4.5 billion years and seems to have fared fine. We, with our paltry 200,000 years of existence as a species, are the latest arrivals even on the Earth scene. This means that, in the past 4.5 billion years, one or more nonhuman civilizations, theoretically, could have safely visited our planet, or even colonized it, while Homo Sapiens simply did not exist. It is a bitter pill for some to swallow, but it is best to start opening their eyes.

Our Universe, or more accurately our "membrane" of the Universe-Brane, has existed for at least 14,000,000,000 years (assuming it had a real beginning, which is not entirely a given). Extremely complex life forms such as dinosaurs existed on Earth as early as 230,000,000 years ago. Is there any scientific reason that prevented any extra-terrestrial civilizations from visiting our planet during the time when humans did not even exist on Earth?

As we said earlier, the only real objection that can be made to the possibility that alien life forms have visited Earth in the past, or in our present, concerns the distances that separate us from other stars or other galaxies. Based on the Theory of Relativity, we currently believe that an object cannot move at or above the speed of light. But even assuming we could travel at this fantastic speed, it would take about 100,000 years just to travel through our galaxy, and as many years to travel back. Relative to our short life span of about 70 to 80 years, even traveling at the speed of light would not be enough to even allow us to explore one of the arms of our galaxy, let alone the Universe.

The planets in our Solar System seem to be devoid of evolved intelligent life. Therefore, if Earth has been visited by other intelligent life forms in the past, or in the present, they probably came from far away. These possible visitors, what transportation system did they use, or do they use to be able to travel the cosmos? If Life has come to Earth through an intelligent life form, then we must assume that there is a Physics that we do not know about, and that allows one to be able to move at a speed thousands of times faster than light. Or even travel through time or other dimensions (time, in fact, is only one of several existing dimensions). If this were not the case, not only the Earth, but every single planet in the Universe would remain virtually "isolated" forever. Therefore, it is more logical to assume that there is a way to move either in our "membrane" of the Universe, or perhaps even "from membrane to membrane," in reasonable time. This is the basic condition to be able to say that Life was brought to Earth not randomly, via an asteroid, but with a definite purpose by intelligent beings.

PART 2

Dating:

From about 2,400,000 years ago to about 75,000 years ago

Topic:

Birth of humanity

First "reload" in the human race

Involved populations:

Homo Sapiens

3 - The mystery of 'humans'

How did humankind appear on Earth? Let us put aside for the moment what many researchers believe to be our "ape-like" ancestors (but not everyone agrees). The main families of "primates" undoubtedly identified as "human" are the following (for the sake of brevity we avoid listing each individual variant):

Homo Habilis - Appeared about 2,400,000 years ago and became extinct about 1,440,000 years ago. What made it "human"? The size and shape of the skull box was close to human. In addition, some remains found suggest that it used stones to crush the bones of its prey.

Homo Ergaster - Appeared in Africa about two million years ago and became extinct about one million years ago. What makes him considered human? Physically he was similar to us. Also, according to scholars, along with the other two variants *Homo Erectus* and *Homo Heidelbergensis,* it was the first hominid capable of articulating language.

Homo Erectus - Homo Erectus appeared in Africa about 1,800,000 years ago. It probably still existed about 150,000 years ago. Compared with earlier species, it had a relatively developed brain and was a skilled "craftsman." In fact, stone axes have been found, probably made by this species. It was the first true hunter-gatherer of the genus "homo."

A great idea is not matched

For a long time, researchers were convinced to find evidence, even minimal evidence, to prove, for example, that Homo Habilis evolved into Homo Ergaster, or any other type of the genus "homo." Unfortunately, after decades and decades of research, not one such piece of evidence has ever been found. Wanting to be honest, what researchers have found is the following: each of the different families of the genus "homo" appeared suddenly. During its existence of hundreds of thousands of years, it never "evolved" in any appreciable way. Each "family" has always remained itself. After a certain period of time, even more than a million years, each of these "families" simply "disappeared" from the scene. It became extinct.

From a scientific point of view, therefore, it is no longer correct to say that modern humans evolved, for example, from Homo Erectus. This was a hypothesis, even an honest one, of many researchers, who were convinced that in time they would find evidence for this "evolution." This evidence, at present, has not been found.

How then can we explain the existence of different families of the genus 'homo' over time? It is undeniable that these "families," as time passed, came closer and closer to what we regard as "modern man." But it is also equally undeniable that this kind of "evolution" is not linear but occurs in "sudden jumps." An abrupt change in the species suddenly appears on the scene, which then stabilizes. Over time, this "new species" does not evolve, but disappears, making way for a "new version."

This truly abnormal way of "evolving," with huge "leaps," really seems to be due to the action of external elements that suddenly enrich the DNA of a species to make it take on new potential. It seems the trace that some viruses periodically act as "facilitators" to trigger a real "evolutionary leap." An incredible discovery that took place in 2012 on our species namely the "Homo Sapiens," seems to confirm this intuition. Let us see why.

The "turbo" gene

Let us talk about the miR-941 gene. What is it all about? To put it simply, a gene is a DNA sequence that enables the construction of individual molecules. Genes, therefore, "build" what we are. Usually, genes are "inherited" from parents. So, normally, we are the "mix" of genes from our parents and ancestors. New genes, or defective genes, usually cause disease and sometimes even death to those with the changed genes. In spite of this, it has been found that in the history of Homo Sapiens suddenly a "new" gene, that is, one that was not inherited from the parents, appeared, and proved to be "exceptionally useful" to the species. Such an event is so rare that it is almost impossible for it to happen naturally. What gene are we talking about?

On October 23, 2012, the article entitled: "Evolution of the human-specific microRNA miR-941" appeared in the prestigious journal Nature Communications. What does this gene do? In part, the article says: 'Human-specific effects of miR-941 regulation are detectable in the brain and affect genes involved in neurotransmitter signalling. Taken together, these results implicate miR-941 in human evolution and provide an example of rapid regulatory evolution in the human lineage'. Elsewhere it says, "We find that miR-941 emerged de novo in the human lineage."

Thus, it is a gene responsible for the evolutionary processes of man, which have modified him to the present degree of mental capacity. In practice, for example, compared to monkeys, this gene (present only in humans) induced anatomical changes that favoured the ability to speak, as well as brain development such that we can develop thoughts, ideas, and concepts. This would be enough to make the miR-941 gene 'suspected' of being a primary cause of our evolution. But there is much more to it.

Simplifying things greatly, researchers have found that we possess two types of DNA. One is 'coding', i.e. it works and produces the molecules our bodies need. The other is 'non-coding', i.e. 'inert'. Apparently this second part of DNA does not seem to do anything. According to some researchers it would just be remnants of old, now useless pieces of DNA. Until a few years ago the term "junk DNA" was used to call this "non-coding" DNA.

The miR-941 gene is currently not in the "coding DNA" area, but in the "junk DNA" area. But if the miR-941 gene has influenced human evolution, it is obvious that at some unspecified time it was part of the "coding DNA." What "turned on" this gene in the "non-coding" section when it was needed? And what "turned it off" when it had completed its task? It seems almost as if someone "turned on" this gene for a time until the desired result was obtained. Having obtained the desired level, he then "turned it off," leaving it "asleep" in the "non-coding" zone of our DNA. Who determined, then, to what extent we were to "evolve"?

Was it a virus that acted as a "switch," "injecting" us with this piece of DNA, and then turning it on or off as needed? Did the same mechanism kick in for other genes? Whose "hand" is it that turns on and off, at different periods of time, the genes responsible for our evolution?

Why, as at least a couple of million years have passed, do the ancient "families" of the genus "homo" increasingly resemble modern humans? In our hypothesis that some species were artificially "influenced" by grafting new DNA using viruses, is it possible that these were "failed" attempts? Yes, this is possible. But if this were true, it would mean that our planet has been "visited" by "facilitators" not since today, but for several million years. This is not a detail, but it would completely turn the tables on our existence. However, we will address this topic later

4 - The first 'reload'

About 75,000 years ago, our "more distant" relatives, namely Homo Habilis, Homo of Ergaster and Homo Erectus, had already been extinct for an awfully long time. What the found evidence tells us is that our species, namely Homo Sapiens, suddenly appeared about 200,000 to 300,000 years ago. But we were neither the first nor the only "humans" who populated the Earth at that time. According to the latest research, at least three "human families" existed on Earth at that time. In Eurasia lived predominantly what we call today "Neanderthal Homo." In Africa lived what we call "Homo Sapiens," to whom we belong. In Asia lived the "Homo Denisova." (There is talk of a fourth species, Homo Floresiensis, who would have lived in Indonesia, but there are conflicting views on this).

About 75,000 years ago, the first "reload" of an entire "human species" that we know of took place in Africa. Sapiens, as we mentioned earlier, lived almost exclusively in Africa at that time. It was they, therefore, who were one step away from complete extinction. About 75,000 years ago, both the northern hemisphere of the Earth and the southern hemisphere were very cold. Probably many areas of northern Europe were frozen. Conversely, the area of North Africa, being close to the equator, was relatively "temperate." This explains why, until they migrated from Africa, Sapiens had pigmented skin, and thus were black skinned. Although they had relatively prospered in their territory, suddenly the Sapiens ran into a "genetic bottleneck."

4 - The first 'reload'

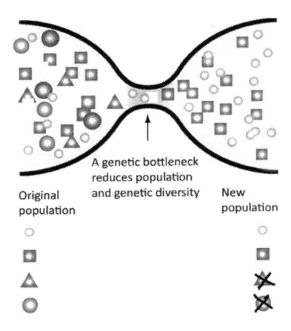

A genetic bottleneck reduces population and genetic diversity

Original population

New population

What is meant by "genetic bottleneck"? This term refers to a drastic reduction in the number of individuals that are part of the same species, to the point where only a small remnant survives. Exactly, a "reload." This population collapse can be detected, with modern genetic engineering techniques, by examining our DNA. This abnormality can be discovered because, under normal conditions, human DNA is "constantly shuffling," as people from different genetic groups join together. When, however, this variation decreases dramatically, or even becomes zero, it is clear that there were no other humans to mix with.

The simplest explanation for this phenomenon is to assume that a good chunk of the population had ceased to exist at that particular time period. This is why a "genetic bottleneck" can indicate a dramatic reduction in population in a given geographic area.

"Genetic bottlenecks" are not a rarity in human history. A 'genetic bottleneck' occurred when Sapiens first tried to leave Africa. Another occurred when this group separated in the Middle East, when some headed for Europe and others for Asia. Another "bottleneck" occurred when Sapiens headed to Australia. The last known "genetic bottleneck" appears to have occurred about 7,000 years ago.

However, several geneticists are convinced that they have found in the Sapiens' DNA, that is, in our DNA, the "bottleneck par excellence," something that has forever changed the history of this "human family." Renowned biologist and popularizer of science Richard Dawkins, Professors Michael Rampino and Stephen Self, and Professor Stanley H. Ambrose of the Department of Anthropology at the University of Illinois, are just a few of the many famous scientists who have dealt with this mysterious event.

According to these geneticists, the "scene" reading in Sapiens DNA is as follows: at some point between 75,000 and 50,000 years ago, there was almost zero genetic reshuffling among our first parents for a period of time. The population that underwent this "genetic bottleneck," and which was stationed in North Africa, included basically the entire group of Homo Sapiens living at that time. Thus, according to many renowned geneticists, the most plausible explanation for this phenomenon is that for some external reason, homo Sapiens at that time came within a step of total extinction.

4 - The first 'reload'

What led to the "reload"

To stay as grounded as possible in scientific facts, we will quote excerpts from the paper entitled "*Late Pleistocene Human Population Bottleneck, Volcanic Winter and the Differentiation of Modern Humans,*" published by Professor Stanley H. Ambrose in 1998. Among other things, the text says that "The earliest truly modern humans from an anatomical point of view, who were located outside Africa, were settled at the gateway to Africa, in the Levant, and date from about 100,000 years ago."

The study goes on to say, "Several nuclear and mitochondrial DNA studies have shown one or more ´significant bottlenecks´ (i.e., a drastic reduction in the size of a population), followed later by considerable new population growth, during the last glacial period." The study goes on to say, "What size was this ´bottleneck´? Jones & Rouhani (1986) suggest that in that ´Old World´ there could have been a total population of forty individuals for about two hundred years, or 4,000 individuals for 20,000 years. Harpending et al. (1993) provide estimates of about 500 to 3000 females. Rogers & Harpending (1992) suggested a population of less than two thousand females. Rogers & Jorde (1995) suggest less than 1,000 individuals."

The study goes on to say, "Later, beginning about 50,000 years ago, there was dramatic population growth. This expansion occurred separately within the various daughter populations, which had since dispersed and were now genetically isolated from each other (Harpending et al., 1993)."

4 - The first 'reload'

As we read from the study, about 75,000 years ago, the world population of Homo Sapiens (found exclusively in North Africa) collapsed, only to recover 25,000 years later, or about 50,000 years ago. The most pessimistic estimates even speak of a population reduced to only forty surviving Sapiens across the Earth, over a period of about two hundred years. Only about ten families at most would have been saved, then. This is a true "near extinction" reload.

This drastic reduction in the number of specimens in the same time period was also noted in several animal species, such as the chimpanzee of East Africa, the orangutans of Borneo, the macaques of India, cheetahs, and tigers. Regardless of what degree of civilization it had reached, after this "genetic bottleneck," Homo Sapiens had to basically "start from scratch." No one is able to know how many Sapiens died, because we do not know how many Sapiens were alive at that time, whether there were thousands, or millions, or even many more. But if only forty survived, in any case it was a huge slaughter.

A possible external cause

What extinction-like event nearly wiped Homo Sapiens off the face of the Earth about 75,000 years ago? The clearest and most honest answer is that we do not know for sure. The paper we are reviewing states, among other things, "One possible cause of the ´genetic bottleneck´ that occurred in the human population may lie in a 6-year ´volcanic winter´ and a subsequent period of about 1,000 years of extreme cold. That glacial period could be the result of the catastrophic super-eruption of the Toba volcano in Sumatra about 71,000 years ago."

What is meant by a "volcanic winter"? A volcanic winter is virtually identical to a "nuclear winter," which would occur in an eventual World War III fought with thermonuclear bombardment throughout the Earth. Atomic explosions of several megatons across the continents would raise vast amounts of dust in the upper atmosphere. This suspended dust would prevent sunlight from reaching the Earth and thus cause the temperature to plummet within hours. In such a scenario, even if we were in the middle of summer with extremely hot temperatures, winter would return within hours and the temperature would plummet below zero. In addition, there would be a "continuous night," and daylight would no longer be visible. No longer being able to carry out chlorophyll photosynthesis due to the lack of light, all plants would die within a few weeks. No longer able to feed on plants, herbivores that survived the cold would starve to death within a couple of months. In turn, the carnivores, no longer being able to feed on the herbivores, would die within a year at most. If such a "nuclear winter" extended to the whole Earth, within a year much of the animal and plant life would be extinct, including humans. A "volcanic winter" also adds to this scenario the toxic gases exhaled by volcanic explosions. Truly an "end of the world" scenario.

What is meant by "Toba volcano super-eruption"? It must be said that this is still not a very in-depth event, and so there are different opinions about what actually happened. Let us try to understand it. First of all, there is still no definitive formulation as to when this phenomenon occurred, but the dating ranges between 69,000 and 77,000 years ago. It seems that at that time the volcano located below Lake Toba on the island of Sumatra erupted, causing the most powerful eruption in twenty-five million years.

As we mentioned earlier, at that time Neanderthals lived in Eurasia, Denisova in Asia, and Sapiens in Africa. How is it, some ask, that it was only the Sapiens who suffered "near extinction"? Some say that because they lived in a relatively "warm" climate in Africa, while the rest of the world was "nearly frozen," Sapiens felt the effects of climate change more than others. But, at present, no one can confirm or deny this fact.

Memories of an earlier time

A period of 75,000 years ago seems, to some, too distant to leave a "historical record" in human memory. Yet the evidence at our disposal seems to tell us otherwise. Sapiens, in fact, retain a memory that fits very well with what happened 75,000 years ago: the Flood. Perhaps many will wonder what relation the Flood might have to this event. Let us try to understand it together.

Interestingly, the spread of Flood legends around the world follows the path that Homo Sapiens probably took when they spread out from North Africa across the Earth. That is, they headed to the Middle East, Europe, and Asia. From there two routes: one south, which took them about 65,000 years ago to Australia. One northward, which took them to Siberia, and then by use of boats, about 30,000 years ago to Central America. The Flood legends, almost all of which are the same, are found in the same geographical path. This evidence makes one fundamental aspect clear. If the story of the Flood practically followed Homo Sapiens in all stages of its migration "out of Africa," then the event that then generated the memory of the Flood legend must have occurred at the beginning of this migration.

At that time, the Sapiens were just a group of people living in a fairly circumscribed geographical area, so that they all had a fairly similar memory of that event. Those who were saved from that extinction-like cataclysm, whatever it was, carried with them a common memory, which in time became the myth of the Flood, declined differently in distinct cultures. The "place" must therefore have been North Africa. The "time" must have been compatible with the beginning of the migration of Homo Sapiens from Africa, around 70,000 to 80,000 years ago. Conversely, it would not be possible for very ancient and distant populations to all retain the same memory.

Obviously, the story of the Flood cannot have occurred in the terms used in the Bible. The "Elohim version" of the Flood narrative says that a great flood killed almost all humans. The "Yahweh version" of the account, however, specifies that these waters were so abundant that the sea level exceeded the height of the highest mountains at that time. Genesis 7:19 says, "The waters increased to the point that all the highest mountains under the entire sky were covered." If the Flood was global, then these mountains that were covered by the waters must necessarily include the Himalayas, the Alps, the Rocky Mountains, and the Andes Range. The Himalayan Range has ten peaks exceeding 7,000 meters in height, while the highest peak is close to 9,000 meters.

This means that in order for the "Yahweh version" of the Flood to be credible, this planetary flood must have generated a tide that, in order to overtop the highest mountains on Earth, had to exceed the present sea level by about 9,000 meters. That is to say, a man who ideally stood on the present surface of the Earth would have looked up and, instead of the present atmosphere, would have seen only water in every direction, everywhere on Earth. The "surface" of these waters would have been at the same height where modern jumbo jets fly (8,500 meters high). This is about twelve times the height of the world's tallest skyscraper, the Burj Khalifa, which is "only" 829 meters high. The Earth would be transformed into a water planet.

To get an idea of what an enormous mass of water is needed to achieve such a result, we should multiply the total surface area of the Earth, or 510,100,000 km², by the height reached by the water, about 9 km, giving a total of 4,590,900,000 cubic kilometres of water. To the total obtained must then be added the mass of water that includes all the oceans, which being already below the waterline of the continents, were not touched at all by the Flood. The total volume of water from all the oceans is about 1,300,000,000 cubic kilometres, which when added to the waters that must have been above sea level up to about 9,000 meters above sea level, makes the stratospheric figure of 5,890,900,000 cubic kilometres of water.

But today all the water on Earth, including glaciers and underground sources, is only 1,400,000,000 cubic kilometres of water. The amount of water in the atmosphere in the form of water vapor amounts to only 135,000 cubic kilometres. Where are the other approximately 4,400,000,000 cubic kilometres of water needed to cover the highest mountain peaks? They are simply not there. We do not find them in the sea, we do not find them underground, we do not find them in the atmosphere. The volume of water needed to cover the highest mountains on Earth simply does not exist.

So the Flood could not have happened as it is told in Genesis. The waters of the seas could not have covered the highest mountains on Earth. Some say that when the Flood occurred the mountains were lower, and therefore less water would have been needed to cover the Earth. This is ridiculous, since all geologists around the world agree that the Alps, Rocky Mountains, Andes, Himalayas, and all other mountain ranges on Earth have been in that position for at least several hundred thousand years, since before Homo Sapiens made their appearance. But then since all ancient mythologies speak of a disaster that nearly extinguished humanity, what really happened?

4 - The first 'reload'

A tale between myth and reality

In contrast to Genesis, an equally ancient account exposes to us a more realistic view of what may have happened. This book is the Zoroastrian tale of Jamshid (in the language of the Avestā it is called Yima). This tale is set in what the Zoroastrians call "the age of Jamshid," an era of perfection at the beginning of human history, shortly after the creation of man. As is said for Noah's ancestors, these men of the Jamshid era are also said to have lived for an awfully long time, for several centuries. In this respect, too, the two accounts are overlapping.

Instead of the biblical Noah, the central character in this story is Jamshid/Yima, whom for brevity we will now call Yima. As in the legends of the Flood told in the Mesopotamian region, this account also says that humans "grew in numbers" on Earth exponentially, and this overpopulation caused problems. According to Yima's account, at one point Ahura Mazda, the monotheistic god worshipped in the cult of Zoroaster, warned him that the Earth would be hit by a true ice age, a succession of three extremely harsh winters that would exterminate much of humanity, the plant world, and the animal world. They are called the "three winters of Malkush," which would each have lasted an entire year. Rivers would freeze, vegetation all over the Earth would equally freeze. As the months passed, an increasing number of people would die of frostbite or starvation, leading to a probable extermination of the human race.

Ahura Mazda intervenes so that at least some specimens of humankind, animals, and plants can be saved. Yima is then given the task of creating an underground shelter, a kind of hypogeum called the "Vara," which would be a kind of "Underground Ark." When completed, this "Vara" is a kind of small underground city, situated on several levels, and square in shape, with each side about 3 kilometres long. An underground waterway, dwellings, roads, and an artificial lighting system are created. About 2,000 people, chosen from the best of the human species, as well as two specimens of each animal species and the seeds of many plants are housed in this "Vara." Ahura Mazda explained to Yima that after this "ice age" the snows would melt, and life would resume.

Yima's account and Noah's account are too similar to be a coincidence. As in the case of Noah, Yima is also given the precise plan on how to build the means of salvation. This character is told precisely which animal species to put inside, just as in the case of Noah. In addition, he is told to make a hatch for light (as in Noah's Ark), and the 'raven' that would be sent to check the new livability of the Earth also appears.

The remarkable realism of Yima's story is striking. Rather than talking about waters covering mountains all over the world (which never happened) this tale tells of the preparations made in an attempt to escape from an ice age that was about to befall humanity. So in Yima's story we are not talking about a planetary flood, but about a brief and intense global "ice age." And this aspect has little that is fanciful or legendary. Comparing this story and what is thought to have happened 75,000 years ago with the glacial period caused by the Toba supervolcano has some very remarkable aspects. Some see in the three "Malkush winters" a parallel with the approximately "six years" of glaciation hypothesized by the "genetic bottleneck" theory.

4 - The first 'reload'

Yima's account also addresses the thorny issue of how the survivors saved themselves. Someone warned them to make a kind of "underground bunker," fill it with supplies and possible survivors, both animal and human, and wait for the great cold to pass. Even this aspect of the tale, taken in its essentials, is of remarkable realism.

By the way, the term "Ark" included in the Bible does not mean "ship" either. The term used for "Ark" in Genesis 6:14 is תֵּבָה (tebah) which literally means "wooden box." This term cannot mean a "ship," because in Hebrew there was another term for ships, and it is אֳנִיָּה(oniyyah), and it is used later in the same book, in Genesis 49:13.

Conversely, the term used to refer to "the Ark," namely תֵּבָה (tebah), is also used in Exodus 2:3 to describe a "box" or a "closed basket of papyrus" in which a new-born child named Moses was hidden. Comparing Genesis 6:14 with Genesis 49:13 makes it clear that whoever wrote this account did not mean that the Ark was a ship at all, but a gigantic wooden crate-like structure. A shelter, in fact.

Native American Legends.

Cristóbal de Molina "el cuzqueño," who was born in Baeza in 1529 and died in Peru in 1585, was a Spanish cleric and chronicler who lived much of his life among the Incas of Peru. In his writings he told us that the inhabitants of that part of the Earth also had beliefs similar to those in Yima's account about humans escaping underground.

According to his retelling of an Incan legend, at first the Earth was inhabited by a race of giants. Then came over the whole

4 - The first 'reload'

Earth a global Flood, which covered everything but the tops of the highest mountains. Only one couple, a man, and a woman, survived the Flood. The creator god "Viracocha" arranged for their descendants to be "as if planted" underground, in caves and other hiding places, waiting for the time to bring them back to the surface. One day Viracocha's messengers would go around the Earth to resurface the humans hidden underground.

The legends of several Native North Americans also describe a primordial time when humans were underground. These legends are referred to as "emergence myths." For example, in the legends of the Jicarilla Apache of New Mexico, they tell of an early time period when the Earth was completely covered by water, and all living things, including humans, lived underground. Spying through an opening from underground, the humans saw at one point that the Sun was shining again on the surface, and with earnest efforts they managed to resurface.

The Inuit in one of their legends tell of a time when darkness reigned supreme because humans dwelt underground, where the Sun never shone. One of them, called Ganawagahha, discovered an opening in the rock and managed to emerge from the Earth. The Lenape Indians (also known as Delawares) also have similar myths and claim that at first humanity spent its life underground, from which it emerged at a later time.

The Zuni Indians believe that humans once lived underground, in a kind of multi-level underworld, where they resided on the fourth, lowest level. Two heroes managed to bring them out by making them climb up vine shoots to the surface. It is

4 - The first 'reload'

interesting to note the detail in this legend that the first days when the humans re-emerged from underground were not at all pleasant but were a real trauma for everyone. In fact, the humans looked like cave creatures, their skin covered with scales and dark. Any light, even the faint night light, was enough to cause discomfort to their eyes. It was only when they were able to get used to sunlight again that they were gradually able to assume the common appearance of present-day humans. A truly realistic description of a people coming out of caves.

4 - The first 'reload'

The Hopi Indians, Navajo and other Indian groups all have the same myth, of humans who ascended in many ways from underground to live on the surface of the earth. And all of these legends bring back the concept known as the "Four Suns," a term for a cycle of four worlds that existed before present-day humans.

In every legend told by Native Americans, humans have always been helped to emerge from the underground by nonhuman beings, called as appropriate "Elder People," "Brothers of Light," "Sacred People," or in other similar ways. Invariably these beings are described as similar to humans but preceding us on a similar path. Precisely because of this "human-likeness" on the part of the "Brothers of Light," many myths emphasize the ambiguous character of these beings. They would be capable of both helping humans survive cataclysms or resurrecting them from underground, but also of harming or exploiting them should they need it. In this they closely resemble the "Vigilant Angels" of the book of Enoch, who on the one hand teach men various arts, and on the other hand tyrannize them and indirectly cause the Flood that destroys them all.

Wanting to summarize, we can say that mainly in the Caucasian area and North America there are legends that mention not a Flood of water, but a "Great Cold" that came upon humankind. To escape, many of them were forced to take refuge underground for a considerable period of time. When the climate finally allowed, when the Sun shone again, humans returned to the surface, and rebuilt their world. Broadly speaking, this seems to be a description of what Homo Sapiens had to endure some 75,000 years ago in North Africa at the time of the "Great Cold" generated by the explosion of the Toba supervolcano. Of all the recollections of the Flood, this seems to be the closest to demonstrable reality.

How is it then that in many other legends found on various continents, not the glaciation, but a giant flood is remembered? Most likely, while some preferred to remember the beginning of the disaster, that is, when the Earth became "cold," others remembered the time when the snows melted, and the floods affected the survivors, decimating them. One story, therefore, does not exclude the other, but rather complements it.

In all the stories, none excluded, it is said that without "outside help," be it the "Brothers of Light" or "the gods," the Sapiens would all be dead. This aspect will also be taken up later.

PART 3

Dating:

75,000 years ago to 40,000 years ago

Topic:

The 'return' of Homo Sapiens

The second "reload"

Involved populations:

Homo sapiens

Neanderthals

5 - The Story of Sulawesi

We saw earlier that about 75,000 years ago, the Sapiens suffered a "near extinction," but later, around 50,000 years ago, they recovered. How could we describe this group of survivors? The land area near the equator was never totally subjected to glaciation while the Sapiens were alive. So it is only natural that that strip of land should be the site of the greatest evidence of their existence. Often, in many documentaries, humans who lived about 50,000 years ago are presented to us basically as cavemen, unable to write, unable to build complex tools, little more than hairless apes. But is this really the case?

Among ancient expressions of human creativity, some found works leave scholars puzzled. For example, in 2017, archaeologists Maxim Aubert and Adam Brumm, from Griffith University in Brisbane, Australia, made a sensational discovery on the island of Sulawesi, Indonesia. The find consists of a wall about 4.5 meters wide inside a cave, depicting a hunting scene.

Six animals are seen running away in this scene. Two animals appear to be representations of two babirusa, a species of wild boar that lives only on the island of Sulawesi. The other four animals are shaped to resemble Anoa, a species of buffalo that also lives on the island of Sulawesi. These six animals are hunted by eight partly human and partly animalistic beings armed with spears and perhaps ropes. The hunters are extremely insignificant compared to their prey.

Several archaeologists agree that this is not just a painting, but the first known attempt to create a story told in scenes. If so, it would be the first depiction of a drawn narrative in human history. Certainly, at least for now, the first therianthropic scene in human history is depicted in that wall. In fact, there is a direct reference to theriomorphism in the painting, in that the human beings depicted have some features that are clearly traceable to some animals. One hunter has a human body and the head of a bird, and another appears to have a tail.

By analysing with the radioactive decay system the organic elements used to paint the scene, researchers determined that that "drawn history" is about 44,000 years old. The hunters depicted in the Sulawesi Island cave are reminiscent of ancient Egyptian deities, who were described as part human and part animal (in particular, it was almost always the head that had nonhuman features). The same description of beings with "animal" body parts, clearly referred to as "heavenly beings," is also found in some parts of the Bible. In fact, in Ezekiel's famous vision (considered by many to be the account of a past Jew's encounter with alien visitors) he describes these "angels" or "visitors" as having a human body and the head and feet of a bull. In addition, the writer says they had wings. (You can read the first chapter of the book of Ezekiel to realize this).

Archaeologists dismiss the idea that the hunters depicted in that scene wore masks or other adornments that made them look like animals for hunting. According to them, dressing up as small animals would not have helped the hunters. According to archaeologists, these figures represent hybrids between animals and humans, and thus depict "mythological" beings.

This would not be the first time archaeologists have come across something similar. For example, in Germany, in the Hohlenstein-Stadel cave , a small ivory figurine, about thirty-one centimetres high, was discovered in 1939. The figurine dates as far back as 40,000 B.C. and is probably one of the oldest sculptures in the world. The statuette is called "the lion man," due to the fact that a human being with a lion's head is depicted. Another very ancient therianthropic image.

A painted wall dating back at least 17,000 years, if not more, has also been found in the "Grotte de Lascaux" in France. Among the various animal scenes, one has left archaeologists truly perplexed. We can clearly see a bird-headed, ityphallic human being falling to the ground disembowelled, next to a buffalo. At its side is a strange object, like a long rod with a bird on top. A kind of barbed wire fence demarcates the scene. Another therianthropic image. We thus notice a common way of depicting "from outside" or "mythological" beings, ranging from the territories of France to Indonesia, from 17,000 up to at least 44,000 years ago. How to explain such "homogeneity" in space and time?

Theriomorphism became among the Egyptians the customary way in which to represent deities. For example, the god Horus is depicted with the head of a falcon, Thot has the head of an ibis, Anubis has the head of a jackal, Tefntu has the head of a lioness, and so on. What is the point of these therianthropic figures, these drawings of humans depicted with animal heads, found drawn in caves and dating back 44,000 years? Are they really evidence that humans 44,000 years ago had already worked out their own deities, and thought that these deities lived with them, participating in their hunting parties, for example?

If the answer to this question were a "Yes," this would be the first documented case in human history in which human beings depict on rock a "concept," that is, something "unreal" or "intangible" transported into real life. (In fact, if those entities had not existed, they would have represented an "abstract concept" implemented in a real-life context, a hunting scene.) But this conclusion that homo Sapiens of 44,000 years ago not only had abstract concepts but were able to represent them artistically would revolutionize Stone Age history. It would make those ancient humans extremely modern, very much like us. In fact, those paintings would not be quite different from the "Sistine Chapel," where Michelangelo drew several scenes that encapsulated a concept, the "Christian religion."

Or were those mythological figures just an attempt to rationally represent something that ancient homo Sapiens could not understand? Is it possible that those mythological beings were merely depictions of human-looking beings who appeared to ancient homo Sapiens to be gods, and therefore they drew them differently, appealing to their imagination? If so, were those drawings simply depicting the everydayness of life at that time, and describing a time when "non-human" beings had visited the homo Sapiens of that era? Were they the same ones who had helped them survive during the "Great Cold" 75,000 years ago?

After all, the "deification" of what is not fully understood is a phenomenon well known to sociologists. Especially during World War II, some populations that had lived in almost total isolation came into contact with modern civilization. Some of these populations found themselves, not by their own choice, near the military bases of the warring factions. In an effort to resupply the military bases located in these territories, which could not be reached by land or sea, cargo planes distributed food, basic necessities and other equipment by making parachute jumps from the planes.

Inevitably, for distinct reasons, some of these supplies ended up in the hands of the natives, who literally saw food and other useful things raining down from the sky, in the form of sacks or various canned goods thrown from planes. This was a situation that greatly pleased the natives, who received food and various equipment for free. What happened when, when the war was over, the launches ended, and the freighters no longer arrived in those areas?

In several cases real forms of worship were developed to propitiate the return of the freighters through various rituals. Simulacra in the shape of airplanes were created. Some Indigenous people who had been guiding the soldiers and had seen the landing runways of the planes, 'imitated' the manoeuvres that the ground personnel performed to direct the planes to land. Others lit signal fires, and so on. In short, these gestures became rituals that were mixed with other ancient beliefs held by the natives, effectively creating a new religion, namely the "Religion of the Cargo." It took truly little to turn mere human beings, even airplanes, into deities. All in a truly short span of time, just a few years.

Simple humans flying airplanes were considered gods just for throwing a few boxes of food and little else at a more technologically backward population. Could this also have been repeated for human-like beings but who came "from outside"?

One thing is certain: whether the Sapiens of 44,000 years ago already had their own imaginary 'gods', or whether these 'gods' were the representation of anthropomorphic beings not belonging to that place or era, their presence in those ancient paintings profoundly changes our conception of our prehistoric ancestors. At a time immediately following the "genetic bottleneck" that ended 50,000 years ago, their thoughts were already turned to "nonhuman" beings, whether they were the object of their imagination or their welcome guests.

6 - The second 'reload' of humans

Time continued to pass inexorably. Until, sometime between 30,000 and 40,000 years ago, suddenly, and quickly, an entire "human family" became extinct. Let us take a closer look at this "second reload." About 200,000 years ago Neanderthals (Homo neanderthalensis) appeared on Earth. (Some specimens appeared perhaps 400,000 years ago, but it appears that they were only a handful.) Neanderthals were humans generally of white skin and light eyes and appear to have reddish hair. They were quite robust, with a fairly pronounced chin. They were distinguished by their stocky frame and heavy eyebrows and were strikingly similar to us. We share 99.5 percent of the same DNA as them. This is because when Homo Sapiens arrived in Europe from Africa, they interbred several times with Neanderthals. Even, it is estimated that there are thousands of people still alive today who have up to 20 percent Neanderthal DNA in their genetic makeup.

Genetic evidence suggests that Neanderthals lived in small groups, like villages. They populated all of Eurasia, all the way to Britain (which at that time was not an Island but was attached to the European continent by a huge plain, now submerged). For much of the time, the regions inhabited by Neanderthals were very cold, sometimes covered by ice. This explains why they had "depigmented," that is, white, skin. This helped them survive in cold areas.

They were good hunters of birds, even birds of prey such as golden eagles or vultures. But unlike what you might think,

The second 'reload' of humans

they did not hunt birds just to feed on them. They used their feathers as ornamentation. So they already had a distinct aesthetic taste. From the remains found, it seems that they favoured black feathers to adorn their clothing, somewhat like some Native American tribes did tens of thousands of years later.

The group led by Stephen Wroe, of the University of New England, explains that their computer model of the structure of Neanderthals indicates that they were able to speak just like us. The scholar says, "Many argue that our ability to speak and language is among the fundamental characteristics that make us human. If Neanderthals also had language, then they would have been truly human." If they were able to speak, as it seems, then they could efficiently transmit information to each other. They therefore had the basis for creating a "culture."

Neanderthals and music

Like Homo Sapiens, Neanderthals had also developed music, as they were able to make flutes using some long bones to which they applied holes. One specimen of these "Neanderthal flutes" has been found, which is called the "Divje Babe flute," named after the archaeological site where it was found. It consists of the femur of a cave bear, to which a number of extremely precisely drilled holes have been applied. This bone is about 55,000 years old, and the instrument made from it should be about the same age (not everyone agrees that it is a flute, but that is currently its official designation: Neanderthal flute).

The finding of this flute should not be underestimated, nor should it be regarded as "just another" archaeological find. To create a complex wind instrument, such as a flute provided with holes, means that the person who made it must have had some kind of musical notion, and at the very least had the concept of musical notes. In fact, only if you have the concept of musical notes can you create an instrument that, through holes, can reproduce them. And if there are musical notes, it is certain that there was some kind of music to reproduce, after humming it for some time.

But this is not enough. The oldest wind musical instruments usually make only one sound. A classic example is the Australian Aboriginal Didgeridoo, a kind of large hollow reed without holes, capable of emitting only one kind of sound. The second step is usually the construction of the "pan flute." This is a set of reeds without holes, each capable of making only one sound, each cut differently so that each reed produces a sound of a different pitch. Side by side, the various reeds of the "Pan Flute" allow various notes to be played.

The construction of a flute with holes, in which various sounds can be modulated with a single reed by alternately closing the holes, represents a huge musical evolution from the Didgeridoo and the "Pan Flute." It is for all intents and purposes a modern instrument, requiring considerable musical development behind it over a considerable period of time. Without having some musical knowledge behind it, such an instrument could not even be conceived. Lastly, making a flute from bone is no joke for anyone, even a modern luthier. Neanderthals of 55,000 years ago had the musical knowledge and technical ability to make a flute with holes made from a bone. It is almost like seeing a plane fly while there were dinosaurs.

But this is not the end of the story. As all music historians know, in every culture the first instruments to appear are always percussion instruments, since they are the most intuitive and the easiest to make. If Neanderthals had come to make flutes with holes, then those flutes were accompanied by several other musical instruments, starting with percussion. At this point it would be a mistake to consider Neanderthals as mere "cavemen." Music in humankind is always inextricably linked to some kind of culture.

Neanderthals also excelled in other art forms. In Spain they have found rock paintings belonging to Neanderthals, dating back at least 64,000 years, or 20,000 years before the oldest paintings attributed to Homo Sapiens. Groups of animals, dots, geometric figures, and handprints, painted in ochre and black, make up paintings of rare beauty. Neanderthals, therefore, knew how to express themselves using paint with great skill.

They were able to make sharp, handle-less flint knives for cutting meat. They had made 'denticulates', the forerunners of modern 'tooth' saws. They were able to make flint axes. Recent findings on the use of 'red ochre' by Neanderthals would seem to indicate that they practised rituals and therefore may have believed in some sort of deity.

The second "reload"

Yet despite their unquestionable capabilities and merits, Neanderthals were the first "definitely humans" to leave the Earth's scene. Between 30,000 and 40,000 years ago, they became extinct. This leaves researchers very puzzled, because at that same time, "black" Sapiens from Africa arrived in the Europe inhabited by "white" Neanderthals. How come the Neanderthals became extinct, and the Sapiens did not? Since both Neanderthals and Sapiens were in effect human beings like us, this is the first example of "selective extinction" of humankind. Of the Neanderthals, not a single one remained alive. Conversely, there is no record of Sapiens facing extinction at that time.

Scholars propose various hypotheses about this extinction. Some have tried to explain this "selective" extinction by placing the blame for it squarely on Homo Sapiens. According to this theory, when Sapiens and Neanderthals came into contact by crossing DNA, the Neanderthals were infected with diseases for which they had no defence. But others wonder why the opposite did not also happen. Others bring up "the Laschamp event," or the reversal of the Earth's magnetic field that occurred about 41,000 years ago.

At that time, in addition to changing polarity, the Earth's magnetic field also decreased in intensity, decreasing over the course of about 440 years to 75 percent, then 25 percent, and then 5 percent, before returning to normal. As the Earth's magnetic field shield failed, ultraviolet radiation directly hit the Earth, killing many animal species. According to some researchers, among the "species" affected was Neanderthal man, due to a genetic predisposition that made him particularly sensitive to ultraviolet radiation. But even this explanation has provoked opposing voices.

Others propose that there was some kind of "World War" between Neanderthals and Sapiens, and the latter won. Others suggest the idea of a climate change, a natural disaster, or a virus that affected only the Neanderthals and not the Sapiens. There are still other theories, but the truth is that to date no one can explain with certainty why this species suddenly disappeared from the face of the Earth.

This is, for all intents and purposes, the second "reload" that has affected an entire human family, without exception. Unfortunately, it will not be the only one. Did the same viruses sent to "modify the DNA" and make them evolve, later "turn off" these past humans? Let us continue our quest to find out.

PART 4

Dating

From 40,000 years ago to about 15,000 years ago

Topic:

Earth's geography during the Ice Age.

Involved populations:

Pre-Greek civilization

People of Sundaland

People of Sahuland

Ancestors of the Nazca

Ancestors of the Maya

Ancestors of the Aztecs

7 - Ice Age

What world did the Neanderthals live in when they became extinct? It was a distinctly different world from ours. Let us try to describe it. Ice sheets covered much of northern North America, northern Europe, and Asia, and profoundly affected Earth's climate by causing drought, desertification, and a sharp drop in sea level.

Most of the water had collected in glaciers, which were enormously larger than today's glaciers. Because so much of the water in the seas was "frozen" in glaciers, the sea level was lower than it is today. It is estimated that the sea level was about 125 meters lower than it is today. As a result, the geography of planet Earth was also different.

The "English Channel" that divides England from France today did not exist. In its place, from Normandy to Denmark stretched a huge plain, encompassing England and Ireland, and much of the surrounding sea. From Paris, therefore, we could walk to both London and Dublin. Much of the Adriatic Sea also did not exist. Instead, there was a huge plain that joined Italy and Croatia in half.

The Mediterranean during the Ice Age

Plato's account contained in the dialogues "Critias" and "Timaeus" tells us something that very few people highlight. Without mincing words, we are told that some 11,500 years ago there was a "Greece" that no longer exists today. In fact, to be more precise, it tells us that there was a "Mediterranean" that no longer exists today.

In the dialogue "Critias" in fact, it is said: "Concerning the geography of our land [Greece] ... the [southern] borders reached as far as the Isthmus. In the direction of the Continent the borders extended as far as the heights of Cithaeron and Parnetes. The boundary line then descended having on the right the Oropia and on the left the sea, excluding the Asopus ... The whole of Greece today is just a long promontory stretching far out into the sea, away from the rest of the Continent, while the surrounding sea is deep everywhere, even a few meters from the beaches.

During the 9,000 years since then, many great cataclysms have occurred. Yes, 9,000 years, for that is the number of years that have elapsed since the time I am telling you about. And during all this time, because of the many cataclysms that have occurred, the mass of earth that has come off the heights has not created downstream accumulations of earth sediments of a certain size, as has happened in other places. But the earth that fell from the heights sank all around, out of sight, all the way into the sea. The consequence of all this is that compared to what was then, there remain what can be described as the bones of the worn-out body of a corpse. As in the case of the small islands, all the richest and fattest masses of soil ended up in the sea, and there remained the mere skeleton of what that land was.

But at that time, however, when the country was intact, its mountains were high, and there were hills covered with fat soil, the plains of Felleo, and there was an abundance of forests on the mountains. Traces of these still remain today, for although some of the mountains now only allow for the sustenance of bees, not so long ago you could still see roofs of timber cut from the trees that grew there, which were of a sufficient size to make imposing buildings. Many other kinds of tall trees also grew there, but also many pastures that brought plenty of food for livestock.

In addition, the land was able to use the water from the autumn rains. Not as it is now, as if flowing water is lost from the bare earth into the sea. But there was a fine clay soil that received abundant rainfall in all places. The waters flowed into the hollows of the streams that descended from the heights, providing abundant springs and rivers everywhere." - End quote.

As we read, this account tells us that Greece was affected by enormous climatic changes that radically altered its geological and morphological structure. It is said that in comparison to what it had been in 9,600 B.C., Greece of 600 B.C. could be compared to the bones of a corpse compared to a living body. For millennia, these phrases were understood as fables, or Plato's imaginings. No one, or hardly anyone, gave them any weight. But modern discoveries in the field of geology and the study of climate change completely re-evaluate these words of Plato. Or rather, they re-evaluate "the source" of his information, which by his own admission were once again the Egyptian priests of Sais. Let us now examine what the scientists of our time have discovered on this subject.

Ice Age Greece

Again, at least in the general view, the words reported by Plato turn out to be dramatically true, and we wonder how Egyptian priests could have known this. From the reconstructions made by geologists, we understand that present-day Greece is quite different from that of 9,000 years before Plato. In fact, the current coastline of Greece that we all know dates "only" to about 4,000 BCE.

Before that, during the Pleistocene (the Ice Age period), many of today's islands were either joined together (such as the Cyclades) or belonged to modern mainland Greece (such as the Sporades, or the islands of the eastern Aegean). The sea level was up to two hundred meters lower than it is today. Because of the low sea level, there were large, well-irrigated coastal plains in what is now the North Aegean Sea. Greece had a large number of plains that faced in the direction of the Adriatic Sea, and these are completely submerged today. The whole area between the island of Salamis and the Dardanelles Strait was one large plain, and so the Black Sea at that time was an enclosed sea. At that time, most of mainland Greece was covered by thick forests.

According to a study by Tjeerd H. van Andel and Judith C. Shackleton, titled "Late Palaeolithic and Mesolithic Coastlines of Greece and the Aegean," reconstructions of the paleogeography of Greece and the Aegean show that about 18,000 years ago the northern Aegean and the northern Adriatic formed large coastal plains crossed by many rivers. There were also extensive plains off the coast of Ilia and the present-day Gulf of Corinth, and along the Anatolian coast.

Many of what are now islands could be reached on foot at that time. So the priests of Sais had told Plato the truth. The Mediterranean Sea was much shallower, and its geography was different from what it is today.

A civilization before Athens

According to scholars, the well-watered northern coastal plains of Ice Age Greece may have provided subsistence for a population that lived quite independently of the resources of the northern mountainous regions and provided easy access to the Greek peninsula. In this regard, according to an article in the 23 August 2011 online version of Phys.org, it is said that Peloponnesian sailors may have travelled to the Aegean Sea even before the end of the last ice age. In fact, before the Bronze Age the island of Melos was already known for its obsidian deposits. This is a natural glass of volcanic origin that is created when lava cools very quickly. It was much sought after in prehistoric times for making sharp tools, such as knives. It is still used today to make scalpel blades. This activity may have taken place on Melos Island from 15,000 years ago, or even at an earlier time.

Evidence that people were coming and going from the island of Melos even before the end of the last ice age is found in Franchthi cave on the Peloponnesian peninsula in southern mainland Greece. This cave is quite far from the island of Melos. Yet Professor Nicolaos Laskaris, who with his colleagues published an article about it in the September 2011 issue of the Journal of Archaeological Science, says the following: "Until now, the obsidian remains that had been found in Franchthi Cave dated to around 8,500 BCE." But a modern obsidian dating technique turns back the hands of time to before 15,000 years ago. Moreover, the distance of the finds from Melos Island implies that people were able to reach the islands in a very ancient period. Evidently, they were using some type of boat that is still unknown. Thus, there was a seafaring population in Greece engaged in trade and crafts at the height of the Ice Age, before 15,000 years ago. But it was not only Greece that was profoundly different from what we all know. The rest of the world also presented enormous surprises.

Sundaland and its sisters

The name Sundaland was first proposed by Reinout Willem van Bemmelen, a world-renowned geologist and volcanologist, a particular scholar of Indonesia's geological formations. He wrote about it in his "Geography of Indonesia" in 1949, based on his research during the war. The name Sundaland is used to describe what is for all intents and purposes a small "Sunken Continent," which during the glacial period was located roughly between the China Sea and southern Indonesia. Technically, the name "Sundaland" refers to the submerged continental shelf located there, and which during the Ice Age (before 15,000 years ago) was above sea level. The extent of Sundaland is calculated to be about 1,800,000 square kilometres. Before Reinout Willem van Bemmelen, other scholars had already put forward the hypothesis that a large, submerged expanse was hidden in that area. But it was only in recent times that satellite images of the seabed have fully confirmed these theories.

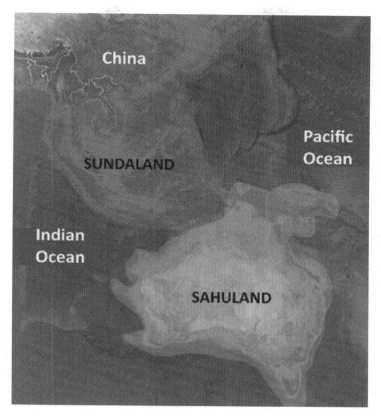

But other submerged areas also exist. When the sea level was much lower than it is today, that is, before the Deglaciation that occurred 14,500 years ago, the continental shelf around Australia, which is now submerged, was dry land. That submerged land, along with the rest of Australia, is called "Sahuland." So Sahuland was considerably larger than present-day Australia and had much more fertile coastal land than today. Regarding this land, its existence was suggested in 1845 by George Windsor Earl. But it was only around 1970 that biogeographers coined the terms "Sahul" and "Sahuland."

7 - Ice Age

In this day and age, although they may seem strange to the uninitiated, the names "Sundaland" and "Sahuland" are quite common among Geology scholars. Looking at satellite maps of the Earth available in recent years, the boundaries of Sundaland and Sahuland appear truly clear, submerged by about a hundred meters of water. In fact, all we have to do is turn on our mobile phone, open Google Earth or Google Maps, or equivalent programs, and point to Indonesia. At this point, simply turn on the zoom so that you can see Indonesia from the highest possible vantage point. Do not focus on the mainland, but on the sea around Indonesia. As the view widens, you will notice how for hundreds and hundreds of kilometres, the sea level around that area is extremely low. Then suddenly the waters become deep, oceanic.

This phenomenon is due to the fact that underneath the water of the Pacific Ocean is a completely inundated continental block, enormously larger than the islands that sprout from the sea at that point. That is Sundaland, once only theorized, while today, thanks to modern satellites, it is visible to the naked eye for anyone who wants to admire it. In contrast, the submerged area around Australia, also visible using satellite, is Sahuland.

Lush vegetation

What was the weather like in Sundaland when it was a landmass? Although most of the planet was in the grip of the Ice Age, the equator line passed through Sundaland. So, despite the fact that on and off for the past 110,000 years the Ice Age raged over the entire Earth, it was "relatively warm" in Sundaland. This is not to say that there were no glaciers. On the contrary, they were present, and they were also quite extensive. But unlike much of the Earth, Sundaland had not only ice, but also forests. In fact, being a volcanic territory and probably subject to some sort of tropical monsoon, it was an extremely favourable terrain for the growth of forests and plants. As a result, several researchers claim that forest persisted in certain parts of Sundaland throughout the last glacial period.

Others have observed that the submerged riverbeds of Sundaland's continental shelf have clear evidence that their banks were covered with trees. So if forests existed even during the very cold Last Ice Age, in the early periods of the Deglaciation, before water inundated much of its coastline, Sundaland was a kind of earthly paradise.

What evidence do we have that Sundaland and Sahuland were inhabited at the time of the Deglaciation? The earliest traces of Homo Sapiens in Australia (i.e. Sahuland) date back at least 65,000 years, and there are suspicions that they may still be earlier. Are there also traces of homo sapiens in Sundaland? Most archaeologists and anthropologists are convinced that, from the West, Homo Sapiens arrived in Taiwan, and from there spread throughout Southeast Asia, all the way to Australia. But not everyone agrees with this view.

Some famous scholars, including William Meacham, Stephen Oppenheimer, and Wilhelm Solheim, claim that in their migration, Homo Sapiens stopped first in Sundaland, and then later in Taiwan. According to these scholars, from Sundaland, homo Sapiens colonized virtually all of Oceania and South Asia. So Sundaland would be a kind of "Mother Earth" for all those populations. According to Stephen Oppenheimer, this is the reason because we can be assumed that the first area of Asia to be densely inhabited was Sundaland. The other parts of that stretch of sea were colonized by Sundalanders fleeing their land that was gradually being inundated.

The first known pyramid

The hands of time keep moving until we reach about 28,000 years ago. We are still in Indonesia, which was once the middle area of Sundaland. Gunung Padang is a megalithic archaeological site located in the village of Karyamuktia, about 150 km south of Jakarta. It was discovered in 1914. Researchers from Indonesia's National Centre for Archaeological Research visited the site in 1979, and extensive research has been conducted since then. Some assert that Gunung Padang is the first pyramid in the ancient world. The oldest part of this pyramid would date back as far as 28,000 years.

According to the online science journal livescience.com, in a Dec. 17, 2018, article, researchers once thought that the Gunung Padang site was actually a hill of natural origin, on which a series of terraces and stairways had been built. So although it might have appeared to have a shape reminiscent of a truncated pyramid, in reality it would have had nothing to do with actual pyramids. It was therefore only a mound 'modelled' in the shape of a pyramid.

Conversely, according to a statement by researcher Danny Hilman Natawidjaj to livescience.com newspaper, the Gunung Padang pyramid would not be completely natural in origin. At least part of it would be a man-made construction. In that case, if the team of researchers led by Danny Hilman Natawidjaj is telling the truth, then Gunung Padang is indeed the oldest pyramid we know of. These findings are fiercely contested by some geologists, who insist that the oldest part of Gunung Padang is of natural origin, and not man-made.

According to the article published in the prestigious nationalgeographic.grid.id on December 19, 2018 "Gunung Padang is not simply the hill that it appears to be, but it is a series of ancient structures with foundations dating back about ten thousand years (or even older). The study shows that the structure not only covers the upper layer, but also envelops a slope of about fifteen hectares. In other words, its structure is not only superficial, but is rooted deeper. Using a combination of different surveying methods, including georadar (GPR), seismic tomography and archaeological excavations, the research team [of Prof. Danny Hilman Natawidjaj] affirmed that Gunang Padang is not a completely artificial structure, but was built in later prehistoric periods. The upper part consists of stone columns, walls, roads, and open spaces. In contrast, the second layer is located about 1-3 meters below the surface. According to researchers, this second layer was previously mistaken for natural rock formations. In reality, these are columnar basalt blocks arranged in a matrix structure. Below it, there is a third layer that consists of grouped rocks and a large basement that extends to a depth of fifteen meters. The fourth layer consists of basaltic rock that was somehow modified or sculpted by human hands."

According to Danny Hilman Natawidjaj, a geologist at the Indonesian Centre for Geological Research, the various areas of the site were subjected to C14 radiocarbon examination and yielded surprising results. The C14 carbon examination would reveal that the ruins of the surface area have been dated between 3,000 and 3,500 years ago. We are about 1,000 B.C., before Rome became an empire. But things do not end there. According to researchers, below the surface, at a depth of about three meters, there is a second layer consisting of columnar basalt blocks. The Indonesian researchers, using the C14 radiocarbon dating system, tell us that this second layer was built between 7,500 and 8,300 years ago. We would be in about 6,000 B.C., when the first Sumerians made their appearance.

Also according to the researchers, there would be a third layer, extending up to fifteen meters below the surface. According to C14 radiocarbon investigations, this layer dates to about 9,000 years ago. We are therefore in 7,000 BCE. According to traditional archaeology at that time there was no writing, no cities, and man was in complete ignorance. But it did not end there.

According to the researchers, below this layer would be a fourth layer, the remains of which, according to C14 radiocarbon surveys, could be dated as far back as 28,000 years ago. What does this mean in practical terms? It means that, when the Deglaciation began 14,500 years ago, the oldest part of this "pyramid" had already existed for at least 14,000 years. If, as it seems, the Gunung Padang structure was a kind of artificially constructed ceremonial "pyramid," this would prove the existence of a civilization that predated the last Deglaciation by 14,000 years. A civilization that existed at least 28,000 years ago. A real archaeological "atomic bomb" in short.

But, as we said, not everyone seems to agree. In the 2014 Indonesian journal "sains.kompas.com," archaeologist Harry Truman Simanjuntak suggests that the site may have been built much more recently, perhaps between the second and sixth centuries AD. It would mean that this site would be between 1,400 and 1,800 years old. The time distance between the two dates is too great, almost 26,000 years difference, to be a simple "error." It is clear that completely different assessments are being made. The article proposed by Harry Truman Simanjuntak does not mention whether counter-analyses were carried out using C14 radiocarbon, and whether these gave different results, or whether it was just his "sixth sense" as an archaeologist that suggested this different dating. New dating techniques are increasingly disproving the "hunches" of archaeologists, and so it would not be the first time that such different opinions about the dating of a site have been created.

The value of this megalithic site is not so much about its technological aspect. (Of construction technology, in truth, there is truly little). Rather, if Prof. Danny Hilman Natawidjaj, and the Indonesian Centre for Geological Research, are right (and no one so far has produced any factual evidence to the contrary), this would be proof that an organized civilization existed in Sundaland as many as 28,000 years ago, at the height of the Ice Age. Indeed, to build stairways and altars, and to carve a hill, means that society was sufficiently developed to produce deities, perhaps a priestly order, and certainly a large group of worshippers. Probably, the builders of Gunung Padang were the same descendants of the artists who painted the Sulawesi "mural" some 44,000 years ago.

8 - Before the Maya

As we saw in the previous chapter, there is evidence that from at least 44,000 up to 28,000 years ago a human group thrived in Sundaland, ranging from paintings on walls to modifying a hillside to create a kind of pyramid. Incredible to say, it seems that very ancient populations in Central America had been aware of the partially submerged continents of Sundaland and Sahuland for centuries. Charles Étienne Brasseur de Bourbourg (1814 - 1874) was a 19th-century Flemish abbot. In addition to his clerical profession, the French abbot is universally known for his significant contributions to the knowledge of Mesoamerican peoples. In fact, Charles Étienne Brasseur was also a famous writer, ethnographer and archaeologist who specialized particularly in the study of the Maya and Aztec civilizations.

According to the scholar, the Maya remembered their homeland as a "continent located in the Pacific," and which had later sunk. They called this continent by the term "Land of Mu." How did the Maya know about the "sunken continent" in the Pacific Ocean? Was it just an incredible coincidence? Or were their ancestors really from Sundaland?

Again, if we would only listen to science, and not to our prejudices, the Mayans would be absolutely right. Their ancestors came from Sundaland. How do we know for sure? According to Kenneth M. Olsen, PhD, a biologist specializing in plant evolution at Washington University in St. Louis, we have irrefutable evidence that navigators from the Sundaland

and Sahuland area managed to get as far as Panama, Central America, in pre-Columbian times.

The "living proof" of these shifts are coconuts, the fruit of the Cocos nucifera palm. This researcher has found that all coconut plants, wherever in the world they are found, originate either from India or from the area that used to be Sundaland. Moreover, the professor explains that, at least as far as great distances are concerned, the coconut plant does not migrate naturally, as seeds of other plants do. In its case, it has to be taken by human beings to other distant areas in order to take root there as well. If the coconut plant arrived in Central America in pre-Columbian times, it means that sailors from the Sundaland area arrived in America before Columbus and planted it. There is little to argue with that. This is amply confirmed by the study of the genome of coconut plants, much to the chagrin of those who thought something like this was "impossible." But there is further "overwhelming" evidence.

On September 3, 2015, the article "Genetic Evidence for Two Founding Populations of the Americas" was published in the prestigious journal "Nature," featuring as authors geneticists from several prestigious universities, including Ponto Skoglund, Swapan Mallick, Maria Cátira Bortolini, Niru Chennagiri, Tábita Hünemeier, Maria Luiza Petzl-Erler, Francisco Salzano, Nick Patterson, and David Reich. Subsequently, also in "Nature," the article "A Genetic View of America's Populations" by Ponto Skoglund and David Reich was published on August 6, 2016.

These articles, among other things, consider the results of DNA tests conducted on the Karitiana or Caritiana people, an

8 - Before the Maya

Indigenous people of Brazil, who live isolated in a reserve located in the Western Amazon. Today this population, which has almost completely disappeared, has only 320 members. They live by farming, fishing, and hunting, and have almost no contact with the outside world.

DNA testing has shown that the Karitiana, along with the Surui and Xavante, other Indigenous peoples of Central and South America, all originate from Sundaland. They come from the landmasses of the Andaman Islands, Papua New Guinea, and Australia. But it is virtually certain that their ancestors inhabited the whole of Sundaland when it was not yet submerged. In fact, scholars think that the ancestors of the Karitiana came from an unknown "Y population," from which in turn the present-day natives of the Andaman Islands, Papua New Guinea and Australia were derived and lived in that same geographical area. Most likely they were the original inhabitants of Sundaland. Scholars are unable to say exactly when this migration took place. They only know that it occurred in the distant past, around the time of the Last Deglaciation.

If the Maya really wrote in their documents that their ancestors came from the Pacific, they were not mistaken. At this point, after all these confirmations, we can say that it is highly likely that Charles Étienne Brasseur really read in some Maya treatise that they came from a people located in the Pacific Ocean, whose land ended up underwater. The French abbot's ideas are receiving surprising confirmation. If "two clues make a proof," then it is entirely possible that the ancestors of the Maya really came from Sundaland in a distant time.

8 - Before the Maya

Refugees from Siberia

The Native peoples of Central and South America do not have only one ancestor, but they have two. As it were, they have a "mother people," who are identified as the "Y people," and who are the original inhabitants of Sundaland from the distant past, around the time of the Deglaciation. But they also have a "father people," who are the Iñupiat, from Siberia. In fact, recent DNA studies of Central American peoples tell us that the ancestors of the present inhabitants migrated from none other than Siberia, by boat, more than 30,000 years ago. Just a few years ago such a statement would have made many laugh, but today the overwhelming evidence brought by DNA analysis leaves many speechless.

For most of the 20th century, archaeologists thought that the American continent had been colonized in a massive way from North America about 13,000 years ago. At that time, in fact, due to climate change, a corridor had opened across the Bering Strait. They were therefore convinced that the "first Americans" were Sapiens from Siberia. According to this hypothesis, these humans had moved from Siberia to North America. Later, a little at a time they moved to Central America, and then to South America.

But around 2020, some researchers published the results of the discovery of human remains in Chiquihuite Cave, Mexico. Excavations were started in 2012. More extensive excavations were carried out in 2016 and 2017. The work was published in the journal Nature. What was found in the cave completely revolutionized the opinion of archaeologists. The study, presented by Ciprian Ardelean, an archaeologist at the

8 - Before the Maya

Autonomous University of Zacatecas (Mexico), and his colleagues, suggests that people lived in central Mexico at least 26,500 years ago. The professor says, "It takes centuries, or millennia, for people to cross Beringia and arrive in the middle of Mexico." Later, he adds, "It takes many years of previous presence for them to get there if they came by sea or land." This means that humans were likely in Central America long before 30,000 years ago.

Most of the material in Chiquihuite Cave comes from deposits dating between 13,000 and 16,600 years ago. This leads scientists to speculate that humans may have used the cave for more than 10,000 years. This is an incredibly long time for humankind. This would mean that humans not only arrived in the Americas earlier than is commonly believed, but that they somehow circumvented the huge ice caps of the time. Now many archaeologists are convinced that the colonization of the Americas did not start in the North and go as far south as they did. In fact, before 15,000 years ago North America was almost completely covered with ice. So it was not "colonizable." The first North American culture, the Clovis, only inhabited that area from about 15,000 years ago.

But if there are traces of humans in Mexico dating back 30,000 years, this means that humans colonized "first" the warm areas of America that were located in Central and South America. The North American culture, the Clovis, therefore, came only 15,000 years "after" the first humans migrated from Siberia by sea to Mexico. In this new reconstruction, the ancestors of the Maya, Incas and Aztecs are the original people of the Americas. Probably some ruins of the ancestors of these civilizations could be backdated by 10,000 or 20,000 years, or more. This is another "atom bomb" for archaeology.

Geoglyphics of the Sea People

In Peru, in the Atacama Desert (or Nazca Desert), the remains of something grand exist. In this desert, in 1547 A.D., a Spanish chronicler, Pedro Cieza de León, noticed the existence of mysterious lines drawn on the ground, but it was not clear what they were. Pedro Cieza de León mentioned them briefly in one of his books, but over time that finding was completely forgotten. It was only during the last century, when airplanes began to fly over Peru, that their existence again became known and brought to the attention of the general public, and it was realized what they actually were.

Today we know that hundreds of "geoglyphs" (not to be confused with "hieroglyphs") have been drawn on the ground in the Atacama Desert, ranging in size from a few meters to the size of several modern soccer fields. Some extend for miles. These geoglyphs are mainly of three types. Some are perfectly straight lines, even kilometres long, drawn on the ground, as if indicating trajectories. Others are geometric in nature, forming huge triangles drawn on the ground (in a few cases rectangles are also drawn). Still others are truly giant pictographs, depicting, for example, a spider, orca, heron, vulture, whale, hummingbird, and many other figures drawn from everyday life.

These lines are actually not real "drawings" on the ground. The entire Atacama Desert is covered by a thin layer formed by small dark volcanic rocks. The ground below, on the other hand, is much lighter in colour. The "designers" simply moved the dark stones to the two edges of a kind of small path. In this way, the dark edges where the stones accumulate, in contrast to the light background of the ground, seen from above look like lines drawn on the ground. The combined paths of these "paths," when viewed from considerable height, form patterns.

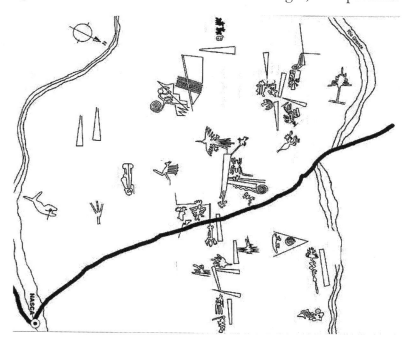

This detail raises an initial "puzzlement." The so-called "pencil effect" that results from shifting the pebbles at the two edges of a path can only be noticed when observed from a certain height. At ground level, on the other hand, it is not possible to understand this phenomenon, let alone imagine its effect on a large scale. How did the "designers" understand that by moving the pebbles on that particular ground in a certain way, they could draw figures visible from above?

Also, it should be mentioned that the dark pebbles moved to the edges of the "paths" are small and light. The fact that they have remained in their position for millennia, in an earth battered in some seasons by intense winds, raises many questions. In fact, these pebbles are not held together by any glue. How come meteorological events did not erase these designs, as would have happened in any other desert area of the world? It is a real mystery.

The only explanation currently available to understand this "anomaly" is a climatic one. Indeed, it has not rained in the Atacama Desert for about 2,000 years, which is why rain would not have moved the small pebbles, "erasing" the patterns on the ground. In addition, according to several physicists, the strong heating of the soil by the scorching desert sun creates a kind of "warm air blanket," about a meter high from the ground, which acts as a thermal "barrier" against the wind. This kind of "thermal blanket" would have prevented the wind from moving the pebbles. At present, there do not seem to be any alternative theories that could otherwise explain this very strange phenomenon of "motionless pebbles" for millennia.

The impossible point of observation

The designs drawn on the ground are quite elaborate, and very well done, perfectly proportioned. How is it possible that the inhabitants of the Atacama Desert made such large drawings, some larger than several soccer fields, without the possibility of viewing them from above? One possibility is that they initially made the drawings on a small scale and subdivided them using a grid. Then they should have reproduced a similar but enormously larger grid on the ground, perhaps using ropes and stakes driven into the ground. If the grid were accurate, at this point it would have been enough to focus on the portion of the design contained in each individual square of the grid, reproducing in that space only the bit of "design" contained within. Eventually, square by square, the final drawing on the ground would look identical to the original but enlarged hundreds of times.

Of course, this is only a plausible hypothesis. There is no direct evidence that this was the case. Such a solution would have required considerable artistic and mathematical skills on the part of the makers of the drawings, as well as a good deal of inventiveness. Did the direct descendants of the peoples who landed in Mexico from Siberia some 30,000 years ago already possess this knowledge? Recall that, in our days, such work is done in art high schools, and only on simple drawing sheets less than a meter on a side.

But there seems to be no alternative to this theory. Conversely, we would have to admit that somehow the "designers" knew how to fly. Only in this case would they have been able to make drawings of such enormous proportions. It must be said that even if they had resorted to the "grid" method, in many cases the "draughtsmen" did not have the opportunity to check directly whether the drawings had been made accurately or not.

In fact, only some designs are partly visible from the hills. Others are not the least bit perceptible at ground level, but it would take a plane flying at high altitude to observe them in their entirety. Yet, to date, not even the slightest error in the making of these "geoglyphs" has been revealed. The question, then, is for whom were they made? If the local population could not admire them, who were the observers who would look at these masterpieces?

There are many theories about these giant drawings, but no certainties. Some think that the whole area where the drawings were made is a kind of immense open-air "astronomical observatory," and that the drawings themselves formed a kind of "astronomical calendar." Others think that the traces of the drawings, or the straight lines, indicate water-related routes. Still others think that the various drawings indicated areas where the various clans, each corresponding to a symbol, positioned themselves during certain religious festivals. Still others have speculated that they are landing strips for alien spaceships. The truth is that, at present, these are merely unprovable conjectures.

The authors of the geoglyphics

Who created those giant drawings? Several of the themes used to trace some of the large drawings of the Atacama Desert (but not all of them) have also been found reproduced in the everyday objects of the Nazca people. It is clear, therefore, that the first "suspects" are indeed the Nazca. However, it is unclear, and cannot be proven, whether the Nazca provided the 'models' to the designers of the gigantographs, or whether the Nazca simply 'copied' the models of the gigantographs in their daily lives. One cannot know for sure "who" copied "whom."

The Nazca are a population that, according to the most recent studies, migrated from Siberia at the time of the last ice age. In fact, some DNA samples from some Nazca mummies that have been found make it clear that this population came from Siberia. They are therefore not descendants of the Native Americans of North America, as was once thought. It is therefore extremely likely that they are related to the people who migrated from Siberia about 30,000 years ago to Mexico. If this is the case, at least some geoglyphs in the Atacama Desert may be as much as 30,000 years old, or more.

How did the Nazca arrive in South America from Siberia? Since North America at that time was completely frozen, it is realistic to assume that the ancestors of the Nazca, after crossing the Bering Strait, descended the Atlantic Coast of North America in boats, sailing under the coast until they reached the warm region of South America. That they were a people from the sea (and not from the land, as was once believed) is also evident from the nature of certain geoglyphics, such as that of the whale or orca. These oceanic animals would have been absolutely unknown to a people who came from inland.

A stunning ancient people

In recent years researchers have made astounding discoveries about the Nazca people. They were anything but "cavemen." They were able to build boats sturdy enough to travel from the North to the South Americas, although probably under the coast. They were capable of building an amazing network of underground aqueducts, which are fully functional even today. They were capable of building huge underground silos, where they could safely store the fruits of their harvest. Even, they were able to perform drills to the human skull without causing the death of the patient. (Even today it is not known what these drills, mostly completely circular, were used for.) In this their medical knowledge probably rivalled that of the Egyptians, who were once believed to be the only ones able to operate on the skull without causing the death of the patient.

Evidence done with radiocarbon also confirms that the Nazca were a very ancient civilization that did not descend from the ancestors of the Native North Americans (i.e., the Clovis culture) as once thought. In fact, some arrowhead remains of the Nazca that have been found are about 1,000 years older than the oldest find attributable to the Clovis culture of North America. So the Nazca predated them on the American continent. Nazca villages and cemeteries have been found dating back to at least 4,000 B.C., telling us that their civilization existed long before that. By analysing in detail the terrain occupied by the Nazca at more than 3,000 meters above sea level, the shells of some snails dating back 4,000 years were discovered. This means that the Atacama Desert, as well as the Sahara Desert, was once a wetland covered by vegetation. It was therefore a very hospitable place to settle. This wet condition probably lasted until 2,000 years ago. Then climatic conditions changed rapidly, and the whole area became desert, leading to the inevitable end of the Nazca people.

When they were plotted

When were the geoglyphs of the Atacama Desert drawn? It is not possible to date these drawings with radiocarbon, since they are only stones forming small "paths" traced on the earth.

There is no organic form to refer to and use radiocarbon dating on. Any proposed date is therefore only conjecture derived from indirect clues. As we have already mentioned, the similarity of these large drawings to those engraved in the Nazca pottery suggests that they made them. To be fair, as we noted in the previous paragraphs, it could also be the other way around. It is also possible that the Nazca "copied" on their pottery the large geoglyphs drawn by others, bringing them back into their art. There is no way to determine what was done before and what was done after. It is commonly believed that these drawings on the ground were traced between 800 B.C. and 200 A.D.

But not everyone agrees with this dating. As we have said, some lines on the ground draw ocean animals, such as the whale and the orca. There is nothing strange about a seafaring population drawing aquatic animals. But the question is, how long did the Nazca remain a "people of the sea"? The remnants of their civilization seem to indicate that for most of their time the Nazca became a peasant civilization, devoted to agriculture and trade. So their "seafaring period" belongs to the early part of their history. Although the Nazca continued to be fishers even after their settlement, their fishing activity was based on the use of nets towed from the shore, and not with deep-sea boats. There is no evidence of Nazca boats being used for fishing. So the possibility that they spotted whales and orcas from the shore on a daily basis, or even caught them in order to get a good look at their bodies and thus draw them, is rather remote, although it does exist.

This would indicate that at least the "marine geoglyphics," such as orca and whale, may belong to their distant past, which began perhaps as long as 30,000 years ago. To draw orcas and whales, these had to be animals belonging to their everyday life. But only a people of the sea would have dealt with orcas and whales on a daily basis.

But the whale and the orca are not the only geoglyphics that have attracted scholarly attention. The spider geoglyph, for example, raises many questions. In fact, according to many, this geoglyph would describe a tiny spider belonging to the Ricinulei family, a species found only in the Amazon rainforest (1,500 km further north). Moreover, this spider has the peculiarity of having its reproductive organ placed on its leg, exactly as it seems to be depicted in the Nazca spider. Since this organ is only a few millimetres in size, it really remains a mystery how the Nazca knew about it. (According to others, however, it is not a spider but an ant. Similar depictions have also been found in the pottery of the Nazca that seem to indicate ants.)

Also depicted are geoglyphs such as the monkey or the hummingbird, animals that did not live in the area of the Nazca (According to some, the monkey geoglyph is just the accidental union of two geoglyphs, that of a feline and a spiral). All of these geoglyphs whose original patterns come from a quite different environment from that in which the Nazca lived seem to support the idea that the ancestors of the Nazca reproduced on the ground the animals they found during their migration from Siberia to South America. If so, those drawings would be thousands of years older than what is believed today. They could be as much as 30,000 years old or more.

8 - Before the Maya

What do they represent

The results of various research have shown that the Nazca lines do not appear to be an astronomical calendar, as some have thought in the past. Nor are they tracks indicating underground water conduits, as others have thought. Nor are they landing strips for spaceships, as the more imaginative have thought. What are they then?

The question to ask is whether all the geoglyphs were made at the same time, or whether they accumulated over time. The fact that they are all grouped in the same place makes us think that they all belong to a particular group of geoglyphs, created for a specific purpose. Given the enormous size of the drawings on the ground, visible in their entirety only from above, the message encapsulated in them is directed primarily to any observers who were "up above," real or presumed. The entire area containing the Nazca lines is thus a kind of message addressed to "deities" or "outside observers." What message did the Nazca want to address to these "celestial beings"?

According to some, the various animals depicted by the Nazca lines were symbols of belonging to certain clans, and during various religious rituals they served the distinct groups to position themselves during celebrations. But this theory has several inconsistencies. For example, only some of the Nazca lines represent animals. Most of the drawings, however, are straight lines, sometimes miles long. Thus, it is not possible that they represent only "clans." Moreover, as we mentioned earlier, these drawings are very fragile. It would be enough for a crowd to walk on them to ruin them. It is really unlikely that they were created to be walked on.

It is therefore highly likely that the area of the desert used by the Nazca to "paint" on the ground their gigantographs is a narrative of something that was close to their hearts. The fact that the work is primarily addressed to those who could look down on it from above, and thus "their deities," seems to indicate that it is a kind of memorial, a reminder of something that had happened in the past.

Although later generations may have added some "details" that did not exist in the "first version" of the depiction, it is likely that the "main subject" of the story remained the same. What did the Nazca want to talk about with their gigantographs?

Humans have always seen in the firmament, in the sky, the shapes of animals, objects and characters from their everyday lives. Even the various geoglyphs drawn on the ground by the Nazca most likely represent groups of stars, which they identified with certain subjects or animals they had come into contact within their daily lives. But one cannot speak of a true astronomical calendar, or an astronomical observatory, as if those constellations drawn on the ground corresponded exactly to something verifiable from a scientific point of view.

We cannot know how the Nazca joined, by means of imaginary lines, the various stars to "mind-draw" images or characters in the sky. There is nothing astronomically relevant in those geoglyphics. Looking at the stars, anyone can imagine giving groups of stars any shape that crosses his mind. It is therefore completely useless, as well as impossible, to try to figure out which stars the people of Nazca were referring to with their geoglyphs. We can say that they painted the sky as they imagined it, without intending to represent astronomically valid constellations. Rather they have an "astrological" sense, as if according to the makers of those drawings there was some kind of connection between the Earth and the sky.

But if the distinct designs created on the ground by the Nazca represented groups of stars or constellations, this fact raises a fundamental question. If one looks at the Nazca lines as a whole, one can see how all the various animal drawings, and thus the "constellations," are located toward the "North." At the Northeast end, a whale was drawn on the ground (even today in the southern area a group of stars is called the "whale constellation," but there is no evidence that this is the same constellation drawn by the Nazca. It is just a probability).

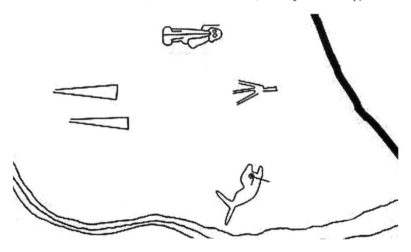

In the immediate vicinity of the "whale" was drawn a group of "triangles" that appear to be coming from that direction. And immediately afterwards, in the immediate vicinity, the only "humanoid" figure in the whole area was drawn on the ground. This figure was named "the Astronaut," because both its head and body vaguely resemble the shape of a man in some sort of suit and helmet. Few other triangles are drawn in other places in that "firmament."

What do these "flying triangles" that seem to "furrow" the sky represent? The whole complex of geoglyphics traced by the Nazca seems to tell us that, in the same context that allowed their imagination to see among the stars the shapes of various animals, they sprouted objects that they traced back to triangular shapes. Since, although highly stylized, almost all the images traced in the Atacama Desert correspond to something real, there is no reason to think that those triangles on the ground are meant to indicate anything other than "triangular objects that flew in the sky." (Moreover, there are also objects that, in two dimensions look like rectangles, but in three dimensions would be " cigar-shaped.")

But the questions do not end there. If indeed all the Nazca lines are some kind of giant painting, what might the awfully long straight lines that in some cases measure kilometres depict? These, too, seem to cross the "sky" composed of the various animal-shaped constellations. Rather than representing "landing strips for spaceships," as some claim, these kilometre-long lines represent exactly what they appear to be: luminous beams that cut across the sky. And the only "bright beams" crossing the sky visible to an observer on the ground are "shooting stars," or meteorites, or comet fragments.

The Nazca made a depiction in symbols of an event that their ancestors had witnessed first-hand, and which was passed down from generation to generation. A period of time when, among the various constellations, beams of light representing meteor showers or comet fragments cut across the sky, falling to Earth. And at that same time mysterious triangular objects appeared in the sky. The human geoglyph, with a raised hand, could tell us that someone similar to a human made contact with them.

We note that this is a recurring theme over time. Peoples who passed down the memory of the "Great Cold" that happened 75,000 years ago tell us about the "Brothers of Light" who came to their rescue. In Sulawesi, a 44,000-year-old painting depicts strange beings with human bodies and animal heads. Now, in a population that migrated 30,000 years ago from Siberia, a giant painting is drawn where, among the various constellations, mysterious triangles are seen in the sky. And as we shall see later, it did not end there.

Geopolymers in the Andes

Is there any evidence that, at some time in the past, pre-Columbian peoples came into contact with "visitors"? In their studies, several archaeologists have noted that, in several cases, when examining the ruins of past Mesoamerican peoples, the question arises as to the weight and shape of some of the rock blocks used in the construction of the various temples of those peoples. Some blocks weigh dozens of tons and have a shape that was difficult for past peoples to reproduce. In recent years, this "anomaly" has been the subject of study by some research centres.

In early 2018, the Universitad Catolica San Pablo del Peru, and the Geoplymer Institute (led by Prof. Joseph Davidovits) made public some studies done on the archaeological sites of Tiwanaku and Puma Punku. Without going into too much technical detail, we can say that the researchers tried to give an explanation based on science, and not just archaeology, of how it was possible for the builders of Tiwanaku and Puma Punku to transport boulders of rock that weighed up to 180 tons up mountains nearly 4,000 meters high (Yes, you read that right, one hundred and eighty tons of rock moved 4,000 meters high!). Such a challenge would be bordering on the impossible even for us 21st century humans, let alone an ancient people. Recall that at the time when the Puma Punku and Tiwanaku megalithic complexes are thought to have been built, the local people did not possess iron, did not use pack animals to carry loads (they only had llamas at those heights), and most likely did not use the wheel either.

In addition, they did not have large tree trunks on which to slide rocks, since the trees in the area are little more than shrubs. The ropes to be used for hauling could not have been overly strong, because they were made basically of biological material of plant or animal origin. The fact that those peoples, with such primitive technology, were able to move those heavy blocks is therefore a real mystery. Project researchers led by Prof. Joseph Davidovits have tried to give a scientific answer free from preconceptions. According to their studies, these people managed to accomplish this genuine "miracle" by creating geopolymers, that is, synthetically created artificial rocks. Let us see how and why they came to this conclusion.

Part of the study considered four distinct red sandstone blocks found at Puma Punku, weighing between 150 and 180 tons each. Traditionally, those rocks were thought to have come from some rather nearby quarries located in the Kausani, Amarillani and Kalla-Marka areas. However, by conducting a petrographic analysis of the rocks in question, researchers say the results indicate something different. The minerals found in the four megalithic rocks appear to have come from the Kalla-Marka quarry, except for one detail. The rock samples have a high concentration of Natron (chemical formula Na_2Co_3). This substance appears to have come from a small lake called Laguna Cachi, located hundreds of kilometres further south from Puma Punku. How is it possible for the same rock to appear to come from two distinct parts of the country? In nature this should not happen.

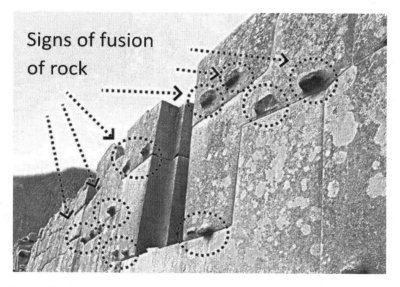

According to the research team, these rocks would not have been transported from the quarries as individual blocks of stone weighing several tons. Rather, they would be geopolymers, that is, synthetic or artificial rocks. This would mean that the Tiwanaku people would have pulverized the rock blocks at the various quarries of origin, and then in the form of small debris would have transported them to the place where they were to be used. Transporting simple bags of debris was infinitely easier than transporting very heavy slabs of rock.

Once on site, after gathering all the necessary materials and preparing the "shapes" of the rocks, using Natron from Laguna Cachi Lake, the Tiwanaku would be able to initiate a kind of rock "solidification" process, thus obtaining a geopolymer, i.e., a synthetic rock. So the four megaliths of Puma Punku would not be natural stone blocks, but stone blocks fabricated on site by the Tiwanaku.

If indeed the ancient Tiwanaku were able to pulverize and then reassemble certain types of rocks, this would solve many mysteries. For example, it would solve the mystery of how they were able to transport 180-ton blocks around the Andes. If Professor Joseph Davidovits were right, the Tiwanaku would never have transported such large rocks. They would simply have loaded onto the backs of the llamas only the "ingredients" to build those stones. Once they had calmly unloaded all the necessary materials, like modern chemists they would have created what they needed.

Professor Joseph Davidovits also considered the hardest rocks found at Puma Punku; the H-shaped blocks made from volcanic andesite (considered diorite by some). Volcanic andesite has a hardness similar to quartz, ranging between 6 and 7 on the Mosh scale. The hardness of this rock makes it really difficult to understand how it was possible for the Tiwanaku to drill small holes, perfectly round, and about thirty centimetres deep, into some of the blocks. They look like they were made with a modern drill. On other blocks, perfectly orthogonal cuts and incisions were made, even within the rocks themselves. Especially the joints where 90-degree internal angles are created seem impossible to make on a rock like andesite using simple primitive hammers or chisels. It is too hard a rock to work accurately using these tools. To make such carvings would require drills and circular saws equipped with diamond tips, or even lasers. Until recently it seemed an unsolvable mystery.

Petrographic analysis of samples of volcanic andesite blocks taken from those rocks shows the presence of air bubbles, even the size of 0.5 millimetres, both in the surface and inside the material. In addition, along with the other elements, an organic-type substance is present within the rock. Again these are features that cannot be found in nature. According to Professor Joseph Davidovits these are all features that highlight that the volcanic andesite blocks of Puma Punku are actually also geopolymers, that is, synthetic or artificial rocks. Again, then, the builders would have taken material with a sand-like consistency and through a chemical process created blocks of andesite that we might call "synthetic."

In the case of the andesite blocks, this would explain the incredible precision achieved in making them, despite not having the proper equipment. According to the professor, the Tiwanaku (or whoever made them) would have basically constructed large mud bricks from an andesite-based dough. Before this mixture hardened, they would have worked the blocks. Acting on a soft amalgam, even quite simple but sharp hernias were able to produce a high-precision result. Once hardened, these blocks would display the extraordinary carvings and exceptional appearance they have today. In one word: "brilliant.

But to give any value to this hypothesis, we need to identify the chemical used by the Tiwanaku to accomplish this process. To dissolve a rock like volcanic andesite, according to the professor, some kind of acid is needed. The acids that can be obtained from plants available in South America are different, such as carboxylic acid, oxalic acid, acetic acid and the like. According to the researchers, these acids are perfectly capable of dissolving the red sandstone rocks found at Puma Punku and other megalithic sites in the area. However, according to the professor, these types of acids do not work on the established volcanic andesite rocks. It follows that in order to initiate this type of process, the builders must have used unconsolidated volcanic andesite.

The necessary acid could be obtained by subjecting certain vegetables commonly used in that area, such as fruits, potatoes, corn and the like, to certain processes. Those who think this is too simplistic should remember that the first fabricated ballistic missiles, the famous German V2s, had a fuel composed largely of ethyl alcohol, obtained by fermenting potatoes. Being able to derive chemicals from natural elements is synonymous with great intelligence.

Hints of this exist in local cultures. The Huanka, an ancient civilization located in present-day Peru, asserted that they had an extract made from a plant that was capable of "softening" stones, a kind of "acid." The Spanish conquerors had found in the stories of the Tiwanaku a "legend" that their sages knew of a plant capable of melting stones. From a chemical and physical point of view this is perfectly possible, and for us 21st century humans it is also quite simple, but it was not so for an ancient people. Until the present day this has been considered by all to be pure legend. But Professor Joseph Davidovits, as the study progressed, had to at least partially recant.

However, melting the rock is only 50% of the work required to build something. In order to get the job done, one must be able to solidify the material again. As we saw earlier, according to Professor Joseph Davidovits, to re-solidify red sandstone the builders of Puma Punku would have used Natron. To solidify the andesite again, "Guano," a kind of local fertilizer made from animal excrement, would have been used. The remains of "Guano" should therefore be the organic remains found in the volcanic andesite samples analysed. To prove that this process is really feasible, and not just a theory, Professor Joseph Davidovits prepared and showed to the press some samples of materials made in his laboratory with the same process used according to him by the ancient Puma Punku builders.

At this point the question is: Who gave the ancestors of the Mesoamerican peoples this knowledge of chemistry about making geopolymers? How long have they possessed them? How did they pass them on? More and more evidence tell us that part of the history of Central and South America should be completely revised.

PART 5

Dating:

From about 15,000 to 13,000 years ago

Topic:

Earth's geography during the Deglaciation

Involved populations:

Pre-Greek civilization

People of Sundaland

People of Sahuland

Nan Madol Civilization

People of Mount Atlas

9 - The End of the Ice Age

Between 17,000 and 15,000 years ago, gradually, the huge glaciers that covered almost all of North America and almost all of Europe began to melt. According to scholars, two factors must have played a key role in this melting. The first was a change in solar irradiance. In fact, much of the climate changes that occur on Earth are caused by 'solar activity. The second trigger was probably the activity of some huge volcanoes that emitted greenhouse gas, which contributed to the warming of the air.

The Earth changed enormously because of the Deglaciation. Waters rose all over the world by at least 120 meters. The vast plain that joined Italy and Croatia became in time what we call the Adriatic Sea. The 'huge plain that connected France, Germany, the Netherlands, and Denmark to England became in time the stretch of sea we all know as the "English Channel." Much of the coasts of China and the Americas were gradually swallowed up by the waters. As the glaciers of North America and Europe receded, the earth's geography changed.

Greece after the Deglaciation

The Aegean sea level also rose an average of 125 meters, submerging a large number of plains and human settlements. This sea rise occurred very slowly. But despite this, the loss of coastal plain has drastically changed the resource base in many areas. According to some studies, sea level rise has resulted in a loss of lowland for the Aegean archipelago of about 70 percent. Each island has lost between 20 percent and 90 percent useful flatland space. The geography of Greece has indeed been transformed. On the whole it is understood how many probably very fertile plains ended up in the sea, returning a much more mountainous Greece than it had been before.

According to researchers, particularly the period between 14,310 ± 200 and 13,960 ± 260 years ago, "record floods" hit Greece. For example, some speculate that while the Deglaciation was in progress, due to a climatic phenomenon, the Black Sea and the Caspian Sea reduced their total water volume. At some point after several centuries, the Mediterranean Sea violently overflowed beyond the Bosporus. This created a huge and sudden flood that flooded forever the plain that stretched from the Aegean Sea to the Bosporus, and the northern Black Sea.

This gigantic flash flood would be dated to around 14,000 B.C. According to some researchers, the melting of the glaciers that then covered Scandinavia produced a huge amount of water that poured into the Caspian Sea. This huge amount of water would quickly fill the Caspian Sea basin, in turn creating a violent overflow of this sea, which flooded an area at least three times its original extent. But it did not end there. The amount of water from melting glaciers was such that the waters of the Caspian Sea flowed in two different directions. In the east the waters flowed into Lake Sarygamysh. The mass of water received by Lake Sarygamysh was such that the lake in turn overflowed, and a second lake much larger than Sarygamysh itself was created to the north of this lake.

The waters of the Caspian Sea also overflowed to the east and flowed into a large depression in the earth's surface (the Kuma-Manych Depression), eventually flowing into the waters of the present-day Sea of Azov. But the Sea of Azov at that time was joined to the present Black Sea. A chain reaction was triggered, and in turn the level of the Black Sea grew extremely fast, reaching the point of creating a large overflow around its original reservoir. At some point the Black Sea overflow found its outlet through the Bosporus and the Dardanelles Strait. As a final act, the overflow reached the Mediterranean Sea, creating a true "chain tsunami" along the coasts of that sea.

The Bosporus and the Dardanelles Strait lie just across from the Aegean Sea, the sea that washes the Peloponnese. As we have said, there were many fertile plains at that time, and there were already a seafaring people who traded in obsidian. A gigantic tsunami from the Black Sea must have hit them full force, sweeping them away. Much of the waters of the "new" Caspian Sea never receded. So whatever human settlement there may have been around its shores lies buried under water.

What cultural level could the people of that time have reached? As we mentioned earlier, as early as 15,000 years ago they were a seafaring people, who were probably based on the island of Melos. They were also craftsmen, and they were able both to build the boats needed for the crossing (the workmanship of which is unknown) and to make sharp objects by working obsidian. But it is likely that these civilizations submerged by ancient tsunamis were much more than that.

North Africa after the Deglaciation

It was not only Europe that was heavily affected by melting glaciers. The latest research regarding the transformation of the Earth during the Deglaciation tells us that this phenomenon had a direct and extremely profound impact in North Africa. The latest research using satellites whose radio waves are capable of "looking under the sand" testify that huge lakes, some as large as Switzerland or Austria, were created in North Africa after the Deglaciation.

These giant lakes were formed in the North (Lake Fezzan, Libya); in the South (Lake Chad, between Chad, Niger, and Nigeria); in the West (Lake Chotts, Algeria); and in the East (Lake Turkana, in Kenya). There were also a large number of large lakes scattered throughout the territory, but smaller than those we have listed. Based on their stratigraphic data, we understand that these must have been permanent open-basin lakes. This would mean that during their presence there was an high level of moisture throughout Africa. South of Mount Atlas, nothing resembled today's Sahara Desert.

The giant Tamanrasett River

An article in the Nov. 10th, 2015, issue of "Nature," titled "African humid periods triggered the reactivation of a large river system in Western Sahara," describes a giant river that cut cleanly through part of North Africa. According to this study, along the coast of Mauritania are the remains of huge sediment deposits from one or more rivers. These deposits are indeed huge. But in our days in that part of Africa there are no rivers of a size that could create a phenomenon of that magnitude. Some have suspected, therefore, that immediately after the Deglaciation a giant river was created that flowed through Northwest Africa from the Atlas mountain range to present-day Mauritania. Subsequently this giant river would dry up.

Driven by this suspicion, the researchers tried to see if they were right. To get their answers, they used Japan's PALSAR satellite, which is capable of conducting geological surveys beneath the Saharan sands. In the area where the remains of ancient river sediments were found, the satellite discovered off the sea in front of Mauritania a underwater canyon, called Cap Timiris, a full four hundred kilometres wide! (The article reporting the discovery is titled "Cap Timiris Canyon: A Newly Discovered Channel System offshore of Mauritania," first authored by Sebastian Krastel).

A canyon consists of deep fissures in the rock, caused by water or winds. (A striking example is the Grand Canyon in the USA). Unlike "normal" canyons, submarine canyons are found underwater. They form at the meeting of two faults, or near ancient river courses. How did a 400-kilometre-wide underwater canyon form in front of Mauritania? That underwater canyon is not located near a fault. So this hypothesis is ruled out. The only explanation presupposes the simultaneous occurrence of two conditions. (1) Over the past 15,000 years, the sea has gradually penetrated inside the coast of Mauritania. (2) The spot where the canyon is located today must have been the mouth of a giant river with a water flow capacity equal to that of today's largest rivers in the world.

The article in the journal "Nature," dated Nov. 10, 2015, titled "African humid periods triggered the reactivation of a large river system in Western Sahara," first authored by C. Skonieczny, talks about "a large river system in Western Sahara, which draws its sources from the Hoggar Plateaus and the South Atlas Mountains in Algeria. This so-called

9 - The End of the Ice Age

Tamanrasett River Valley has been described as a possible vast and ancient river system."

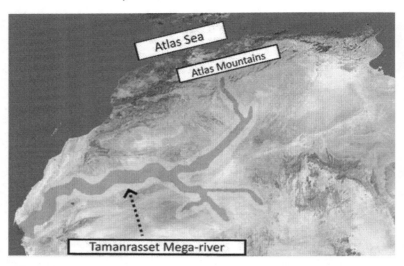

As is mentioned in the article, using PALSAR the researchers peeked under the desert sand, starting from the underwater canyon in front of Mauritania, and going inland. The researchers found that that underwater canyon was really the mouth of a huge river, now dried up entirely . Although the satellite was only able to "see" the last 520 km or so of its path, scholars think the original river was much longer.

In fact, the "Nature" article adds, "Full reconstruction of the river's path was not possible using the PALSAR satellite due to the presence of thick sand dunes, which severely limits radar detection of underlying sedimentary structures. However, the branch of the river network identified in this study represents one-fifth of the total length of the Tamanrasett Fossil River highlighted by the Topographic Simulation System [used previously]." This means that the Tamanrasett River could have been as much as five times larger, since part of it was generated from the Atlas Mountains located in Algeria, which are about 2,000 km away.

The researchers, therefore, think that the Tamanrasett River in its entirety may have been comparable in size to the Ganges River, which is about 2,500 km long. Moreover, the riverbed reached a width of 90 km. This river was so large that, at ground level, it could resemble a real sea in many of its places. From the point of view of an observer on the ground, and especially from the point of view of a Greek storyteller, the Tamanrasett River created a real "island" in North Africa, which then disappeared. Why can we say that?

A "big island" in the Sahara

The term by which the central part of Greece is referred to is Peloponnese. This word comes from the Greek Πέλοπος νῆσος (Pelopos Nesos), meaning "Island of Pelops." The Peninsula's name is derived from the legendary figure of Pelops. According to Greek mythology, Pelops was the son of King Tantalus from whom the Mycenaean civilization of the 11th-15th centuries descended.

Although that area of Greece is known by the name "Peloponnese Island," the Peloponnese is not actually an island. It is a peninsula connected to the rest of the Continent by a small strip of land at the point where the city of Corinth is located today. In our modern parlance we should call that area the "peninsula of Pelops," and not "the island of Pelops." But despite this realization, the very great Greek playwright

Sophocles (496 B.C.-406 B.C.E.) calls it in his works the "golden island of Pelops."

These historical and geographical evidence lead some scholars to believe that, in ancient times, the Greek term "nisos," or island, might have taken on a somewhat broader meaning in some cases than the modern one. Our current definition of an island is: "A portion of land completely surrounded by a sea, river or lake." An island is usually understood to mean something much smaller than a Continent. For example, Australia is technically an island, being completely surrounded by sea. But it is so large that no one would call it an island. It is a Continent surrounded by sea.

Conversely, it is possible that in ancient times, in at least some circumstances, the Greeks could call a "quasi-island," that is, a land almost completely surrounded by water, by the term "island," as in the case of the Peloponnese. So if a Greek writer had described the geographical conformation of North Africa after the Deglaciation, he would have said that south of Mount Atlas (the mountain range of Morocco) was a large "island." This was surrounded to the north by a "Great Sea" (the Mediterranean), and to the south by a "Little Sea," the giant Tamanrasett River. This is exactly what Plato did in describing "the island" he called the "Land of Mount Atlas," or "Atlantis." This may surprise many, but at least geographically, after the Deglaciation, in North Africa, this land really existed.

The "smaller islands" of Atlantis

From the account of the "Timaeus" it is understood that "in the empire of Atlantis," about 11,500 years ago, there was a group of smaller islands, rather close together, which starting from the "Great Island of Atlantis" allowed to reach the "Continent." These were located near the Pillars of Hercules, that is, in the vicinity of the "Strait of Gibraltar." In the dialogue "Timaeus" the following is said: "There was an island located opposite the Strait that you call ´the Pillars of Hercules´. The island was larger than Libya and Asia combined, and it was the way to other islands. From these islands you could go to the mainland across from it, which was surrounded by a true open sea. For the sea that lies on this side of the strait I mentioned earlier is like a harbour, with a narrow entrance. But that other is a real sea, and the surrounding land can truly be called a 'Continent.' Now in this island of Atlantis there was a great and wonderful empire that ruled over all that island, but also over other islands and parts of the Continent." Can we also identify these smaller islands that were located near the "Big Island" created by the Tamanrasett River?

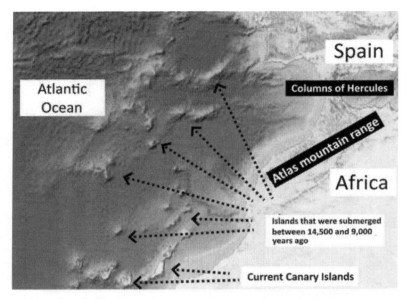

Probable "minor islands" of Atlantis

Looking at the area with the help of satellite (which also allows us to see the mountain ranges that lie beneath the sea), we notice something interesting. Between the present-day Canary Islands and the area opposite Cadiz, Spain, before the waters of the Deglaciation caused the sea level to rise, there must have been an almost uninterrupted series of small islands or islets. From the border between present-day Mauritania and Morocco, these led all the way to southern Spain and Portugal. (Note: We say "present-day Mauritania" because in the time of the Greeks and Romans Mauritania had different borders than it does today. In ancient times Mauritania included roughly the territory of the coastal areas of present-day Morocco, Algeria and Tunisia.)

In the area between southern Spain and Mauritania there really existed islands and islets that no longer exist today. This is a strong additional clue that confirms how the tale of Atlantis was not the "flour of the sack" of Plato, or even Solon. By the time these characters were alive, the sea had risen about 125 meters, and the islets mentioned by Plato in his account no longer existed. Even the archipelago near Cadiz was no longer observable.

How did Plato, or Solon, speak of islands and islets that neither they nor any sailors of that time were any longer able to observe? Only someone who had lived thousands of years before them, and who had already sailed "beyond the Pillars of Hercules" of that time, could have known of their existence. Solon's account, reported by Plato, is evidence that there were a people of "oceanic navigators" who sailed there 15,000 years ago.

The "Continent" of Atlantis

In the dialogue "Timaeus" the following is said: "From these islands one could **pass to the mainland opposite**, which was surrounded by a true open sea. For the sea that lies on this side of the strait of which I spoke before is like a harbour, with a narrow entrance. But that other is a real sea, and **the surrounding land can truly be called a continent.** Now in this island of Atlantis there was a great and wonderful empire that ruled over all that island, but also over other islands and **over parts of the Continent.**" From this part of Plato's dialogue we understand that part of the Empire of Atlantis was on a large island, part on smaller islands, and part on a

Continent. Which Continent is Plato referring to? We understand this by analysing the next dialogue, the " Critias".

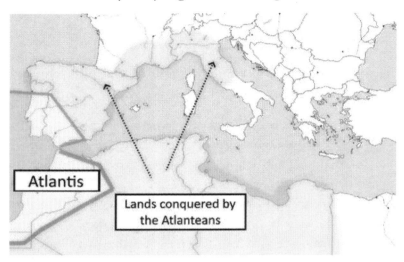

Atlantis

Lands conquered by the Atlanteans

In the description of Atlantis that is given in the dialogue "Critias," the name of one of the territories of which this empire was composed is mentioned. It is said, "The twin brother born after [King Atlas] was called Gadiro. In Greek, his name was Eumelo, while in the local language it was Gadiro. He had received as his lot the end of the island toward the Pillars of Hercules, opposite the region now called Gadirica." According to the philosopher, "opposite" the Gadiric region was the "island" of Atlantis.

According to the Greeks of the time, in which part of the world was 'Gadira' or the 'Gadiric region'? In the mythological account of the Twelve Labours of Hercules, it is said: 'The island of Erizia is located near the stream of Ôkeanos (the river Ocean), and its current name is Gadira'. According to this account, Gadira was located near the river that, according to the Greeks, surrounded the flat Earth. So it was located near the Strait of Gibraltar, near Spain or Morocco.

But we have another clue about Gadira. The name "Gadir," meaning "fortress," is the original name of the Spanish city of Cadiz. In ancient Greece, it was known as Gadeira, and at the time of the Roman Empire as Gades, hence the present-day gentilisation of 'gaditan'.

All this makes us realize that the "Continent" over which, according to Plato, "Atlantis" ruled, was none other than Spain, with its city of Cadiz. As we said, the "smaller islands" of Atlantis were the present-day Canary Islands. The "Big Island of Atlantis," on the other hand, was a piece of North Africa that had become a "quasi-island" when the waters of the Deglaciation created the giant Tamanrasett River that cut that area of the Earth cleanly through. According to Plato, over 11,500 years ago, and thus after the Deglaciation, a thriving civilization had developed in that area of the Earth, which he called "Atlantis." For centuries we thought this was an invention of the philosopher. Now, however, science tells us that, at least geographically, Atlantis really existed.

10 - The End of Sundaland

Many of the great civilizations flourished near the sea, lakes, or rivers. This was the case for Egypt, for Greece, for Rome, for Babylon, for the Phoenicians, and for many others. There was always an effort to build the great cities near waterways that could be used both as sources of water to sustain life and as riverways on which to move and trade. But what was an obvious advantage in "normal" times became a major disadvantage in the time of the Last Deglaciation. Many of the waterways swelled, submerging nearby settlements. Eventually, the Deglaciation that occurred in the past millennia sent a territory nearly twice the size of the U.S. underwater, and those territories are still underwater.

Thus, there is a possibility that, of all the settlements of past humans, the most advanced ones were located along the very plains that were submerged by the Last Deglaciation and are now more than 125 meters deep. Consequently, it is not wrong to think that in some areas, particularly those near the areas inundated by the waters of the Last Deglaciation, archaeologists today are finding only the remains of the "poor relatives" of Homo Sapiens. They are finding the remains of those who lived inland, whose cultural level may not totally coincide with the technological level of the peoples who lived by the sea.

In our own times we are witnessing exactly the same phenomenon: today many forest-dwelling tribes seem to live like stone men, while other "homo sapiens" plan to colonize the planet Mars. It is likely that at the time of the Last Deglaciation the most advanced peoples were located along the shores of the seas. And it was probably the peoples of Sundaland who suffered some of the most devastating effects of the events associated with the Deglaciation.

Of course, it did not happen overnight. It took centuries. But despite this, some civilizations were inexorably swept away by the seas, giving rise to the first "environmental refugees" in history. It is believed that in the vicinity of Sundaland there were three major waves, three giant tsunamis, in which the sea covered much of Sundaland and Sahuland, and then receded, at least in part.

These tsunamis were not due to the waters of the Deglaciation, but to the sudden subsidence of part of the Antarctic ice shelf due to rising temperatures. When untold numbers of tons of ice suddenly sank into the sea, gigantic waves were created. These three mega-waves hit Sundaland and Sahuland presumably about 14,500 years ago, 11,500 years ago, and 7,500 years ago. On those three occasions, probably a great many people were swept away by the power of the waters. Much of Sundaland, over time, disappeared underwater, leaving what we now call Indonesia and the neighbouring islands. Sahuland, too, as the glaciers melted, was submerged, leaving what we now call Australia and Papua New Guinea. Perhaps, the most famous and mysterious "victim" of this cataclysm in Oceania was the incredible city of Nan Madol. What are we talking about?

The end of the "Venice of the Pacific"

"A Venice that existed before Venice itself existed," is how one can define the city of Nan Madol. Like the famous Venice, and perhaps more than Venice, Nan Madol is a city built "in the water and on the water." The expression "Nan Madol" literally means "between spaces," and it is the name by which we know that ancient city today. It was originally supposed to be called Sou Nan-leng or Sau Nalan, which means "Cliff of Paradise."

This town is located on Temwen Island, a small islet with a maximum width of about two kilometres. In turn, this small islet is almost attached to the island of Pohnpei, located in the Caroline Islands, a vast archipelago in Micronesia. Pohnpei has a total area of 347 km² and is more than 1,000 km from the nearest mainland, Papua New Guinea, and more than 2,000 km from Australia.

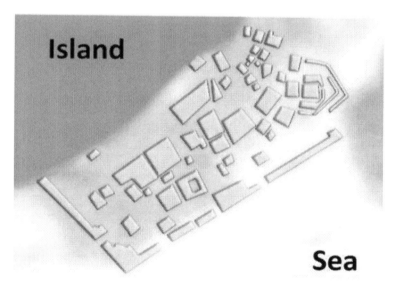

Ruins emerged of Nan Madol

The city, located in the Pacific Ocean "in the middle of nowhere," is built in a lagoon, and encloses an area of about 1.5 km long by 0.5 km wide. There are strong suspicions that this mysterious city is the sole survivor of the Sundaland people. But the city is almost 2,000 km east of what would have been the eastern border of Sundaland, and about 1,000 km northeast of ancient Sahuland. Why did they build it so far away? Judgment about this city remains hanging in the balance to this day. Nan Madol is in fact probably the most mysterious archaeological site on Earth, and the attempt to decipher it is driving archaeologists and anthropologists crazy.

Built before the Last Deglaciation

The most extraordinary aspect of this city lies in the fact that it was artificially built on the sea. Nan Madol consists of about ninety-eight artificial islets, many of them squared off as if they were rectangles or trapezoids. These islets are connected by a network of canals and underground passages, with walls as high as twenty-five meters and as thick as seventeen meters. It is the only city in the world to have been built, at least partially, on a coral reef.

Regarding this there is one aspect that usually few people highlight. Nan Madol was not simply built on the reef at the points where it emerged from the sea. For example, looking at what appears to be the "boundary wall" around the town, one can see that its foundation starts from about 1.33 meters underwater. In fact, at that point the reef is significantly lower than the current sea level, but the builders still built on top of it. At other points, the reef is even shallower, and so the walls begin at an even lower level than the sea.

For example, divers have found blocks that appear to be made of columnar basalt, i.e., the material used in the construction of Nan Madol, even at a depth of 24 meters, and far away from the emerged ruins. At present no one can say how many and which of those columns are really made of basalt (and thus are part of the city ruins), and how many are made of coral, and thus are natural constructions. To know this they would have to be drilled with a small drill bit, one by one, to assay their strength, but no one has ever done that. However, their presence suggests to us that it is possible that on that side of the island, the original city of Nan Madol was much larger than the present one and began at a considerably greater depth. But careful research is needed to confirm this.

Artistic representation of Nan Madol

In addition, there are points where the walls of Nan Madol start directly from the seabed. As for the city´s "boundary wall," the precision with which the stones of the walls were arranged underwater is the same as with which they were arranged out of the water. There does not seem to be any difference. The blocks used for construction were arranged with great care from the seabed upward. This "detail" upsets the whole picture one normally has of Nan Madol. Why? Let us ask: How was it possible to start the construction of the walls of Nan Madol from below sea level?

10 - The End of Sundaland

Let us examine various hypotheses. Let´s start with hypothesis (1). The walls of Nan Madol were built underwater and then raised until they came out of the water. Is this possible? No. Basalt blocks as heavy as fifty tons were used in the construction of the walls of Nan Madol. We, men of the 21st century, could not do it without resorting to specialized ships, heavy cranes, and teams of divers. It is therefore excluded that men who lived thousands of years ago could do it.

Hypothesis (2). Nan Madol was built above the water level in relatively recent times, and then the islets gradually sank below sea level. Because of the sinking of the island, over time the water submerged everything. Is it possible for this to have happened? No, negative answer. Geologists have evaluated this hypothesis. According to their studies, Nan Madol never sank in the past, and it is not sinking in the present. This hypothesis, therefore, is also to be ruled out.

Hypothesis (3). Nan Madol was built on land, and then the sea rose up and covered the portion of the wall that we see today under the sea. This hypothesis is scientifically acceptable. Researchers tell us that the Pacific Ocean rose about 125 meters because of the Deglaciation that occurred about 15,000 years ago. This hypothesis is therefore both logical and based on science. At present, therefore, in the absence of alternatives, it seems to be the only really acceptable hypothesis. But the only reasonable answer, which can explain the construction of Nan Madol without resorting to "aliens," catapults the construction of this mysterious city into the very distant past. We are talking about the period before the Deglaciation, before Sundaland and Sahuland were submerged, before 15,000 years ago. Nan Madol, then, may be the oldest city in the world, at least until now.

A "bunker" pile dwelling

The islets of Nan Madol were made almost entirely of columnar basalt blocks, with some coral as filler. This type of columnar basalt is of volcanic origin and has the peculiarity of being formed from rocks that resemble small logs with a hexagonal base. This particular shape of columnar basalt is entirely natural and is caused by the cooling process of lava. In addition, this rock contains traces of magnetite, which gives it slight magnetic properties.

Nan Madol is not the only site where locals used columnar basalt as a building element. A similar system was also adopted on the nearby island of Leluh. But it seems that Nan Madol is older. The builders of Nan Madol used these "hexagonal logs" of columnar basalt as if they were logs of wood, carefully stacking them on top of each other to erect the various islets. Each layer of basalt logs is rotated 90 degrees relative to the one below and the next. The logs in the various layers vary widely in size. They range from small basalt "logs" with a base of about 20 x 20 cm, and about 1.5 meters long, to huge "logs" 8 meters long or more. The weight also varies greatly among the logs used in the various layers. It starts from about one quintal for the smallest "logs," up to fifty tons (and according to others to close to one hundred tons) for the largest basalt "logs."

This stacking begins in some cases from the seabed, in other cases from the reef, and continues to the surface, creating artificial islets. Why did they use such an original construction system? It is to be ruled out that when it was designed, Nan Madol was located on the seashore. The city has no pier-like structure, or harbour, nor any structure used for boat use. Moreover, the "boundary wall" that looks out to sea today tells us that the city was located inland. (The only surrounding walls built on the beach of cities in general were built to protect against invasion. But a city located in the middle of the Ocean had no enemies from the sea to protect itself against.)

So why did they build their houses on pedestals that, after the ocean level rose, became islets? Rather than a Venice by the sea, Nan Madol's original image of itself was that of a "fortified and indestructible pile-dwelling," complete with walls. It was a true "pile-dwelling bunker."

This should not surprise us. Wikipedia says: "According to archaeological evidence, pile dwellings were a norm of architecture in the Caroline Islands and Micronesia, and are still found in Oceania today... The pile dwelling is built on a structural wooden platform supported by piles always made of wood driven especially into the bottom or bank of rivers, lagoons, swamps, or sometimes even on dry ground, supporting one or more huts made of thatch, wood, reeds, or other material... The materials used in the construction of these dwellings were mainly: wood, thatch (for huts) or bamboo reeds. Piles had a great development and became widespread in the Neolithic period." - End quote.

The function of a pile dwelling is basically to raise above the ground the floor where humans live on a daily basis. The reasons why this way of building one's dwellings had some success is because of the level of protection it provides. By living on a "higher floor" than the ground, one is at least partly protected from the aggression of some animals, especially at night. In addition, if one is near a waterway, this type of construction at least partially protects the inhabitants from flash floods.

Why, in the case of Nan Madol, was very heavy columnar basalt used as the building material instead of the more practical and lighter wood? By using slightly magnetic columnar basalt logs arranged in a lattice pattern, the builders achieved a structure that could easily reach the desired height. At the same time, it is so durable that it can remain standing even against tsunamis over the centuries. The existence of Nan Madol is the most striking testimony to the fact that the engineers who built it knew exactly what they were doing. When you think that construction can be as much as 14,500 years old, we shudder to imagine what kind of civilization lived in those latitudes during that time.

However, the main reason for the "fortification" of Nan Madol probably lay in the fear of "being wiped out" by some unspecified external threat. Perhaps the wooden piles had already been built and then destroyed. So the builders wanted to build something stable and that would be able to withstand it. And from the results it must be said that they succeeded fully in their purpose.

11 - The Hidden Metropolis

On September 16, 2019, a consortium of universities, among which one can mention Johns Hopkins University in Baltimore and Stanford University, broke the news that Nan Madol underwent an "X-ray" with airborne "Lidar"-type instrumentation. This means that the island was flown over by planes and drones mounting an advanced detection system. These systems have the ability to penetrate under the green cover of forests, showing details that are not normally visible by satellites or the naked eye.

The results of this "radiography" were published in the study titled "Airborne LiDAR Reveals a Vast Archaeological Landscape at the Nan Madol World Heritage Site," first authored by Prof. Douglas C. Comer. The Lidar survey showed that a rich and complicated network of roads and canals is visible beneath the trees on Temwen Island, on whose coast Nan Madol is located. Among other things, the study says, "The system [of roads and canals on Temwen] is comparable to the islets and structures on Nan Madol in terms of the complexity and magnitude of effort that would be required to build and maintain it. The investment in labour, for example, and the level of social organization required to build and maintain the Temwen system would seem to be similar to what would have been required to build and maintain Nan Madol." In short, the "Lidar" analysis tells us that Nan Madol was not 1.5 by 0.5 kilometres in size, as was thought until recently. In fact, the "city system" occupied the entire islet of Temwen. The whole thing was therefore at least five times larger, and what we now call Nan Madol was just the "elevated quarter," the seat of the local aristocracy.

The canal system allowed them to retain rainwater and then release it later, either to use as drinking water or to irrigate the land. This would explain one of the island's biggest questions: how could they live there if there were no water sources on Temwen Island? The recent discovery tells us that the builders of Nan Madol were able to obtain the water they needed to live, and to cultivate the land intensively. Further investigation may verify whether this system once extended to the entire island of Pohnpei. This would have made Nan Madol probably self-sufficient in both water and food.

The mystery of the construction

To understand the great misgivings about the construction of Nan Madol, one aspect cannot be ignored. Temwen Island and Nan Madol are located practically attached to Pohnpei Island. This small island has a maximum diameter of about 30 km. All around the island is just the Pacific Ocean, for at least 1,000 km (except for small islands and atolls located here and there). What workforce could a small island only 30 km wide offer? Considering that much of the island was used for agriculture, and most of the men were engaged in fishing, the number of employable workers hardly exceeded 1,000. Let us keep this well in mind as we examine the construction of Nan Madol.

One of the most unexplained mysteries of Nan Madol, is where the columnar basalt blocks it was built with came from, and how they were transported. Being of volcanic origin, Pohnpei Island may provide the type of basalt used in the construction. But some chemical tests on the basalt used seem to indicate something strange about its origin. In fact, according to a study conducted in 2016 by Professor Mark McCoyu, using "X-ray fluorescence" technology, it appears that 40 percent of the basalt used in construction definitely came from the opposite side of the island, called Sokehs, about 25 kilometres away skirting the beach. It is currently not possible to indicate precisely where the rest of the basalt used came from. But if the whole island is there, and there is only sea around it for about 1,000 kilometres, where could the "unknown" basalt have come from? The only sensible answer is that it comes from the bottom of the sea. This means that when the construction of the city was started, the sea must have been much shallower, to the extent that other quarries emerged, which are now submerged. Conversely, it is not clear how to explain this unexplained aspect. But if the sea must have been much lower when the city was built, this confirms that it was built before the Deglaciation, before 15,000 years ago.

Another strange thing is that no trace is seen of the quarry on the opposite side of the island, from which 40 percent of the material would have been taken. So, according to the latest studies, if basalt from a particular quarry on the island was used, it would have been used "to the last drop," until the entire quarry was exhausted. This is the only way to explain the current absence of quarry remains. If this were not the case, then all the basalt in Nan Madol would come from off-island, from a deposit with identical characteristics to that of Sokehs. The problem is that the nearest mainland is 1,000 km away. Or, the quarry would have to be located underwater, submerged by the waters of the Deglaciation, which again would move the making of the city into the distant past.

But even willing to concede that the columnar basalt came from the same island, it is unclear how the builders of Nan Madol would have transported it through the lush vegetation and steep gradients of a volcanic island. No trace has been found of any path that had been made to transport the very heavy blocks, which, let us remember, weighed fifty tons in some cases.

Since they could not be dragged through the local jungle due to the highly uneven terrain and dense vegetation, the basalt blocks would be transported "on the shoulder." But experiments from the real thing showed that blocks weighing more than 750 kilograms at a time could not be transported by this method. This, therefore, seems to be an impossible solution. Moreover, it must be remembered that although they are almost attached to each other, Pohnpei Island, and the small island of Temwen are currently separated by the sea, albeit a shallow one. This would further complicate the transportation of material from one island to the other.

Given the impossibility of transporting the basalt blocks across the island, some researchers have speculated that the building material was transported by sea. But even in this second hypothesis, things do not get much better. Some researchers built boats similar to what the builders would have used and placed a 50-ton block of basalt on top of it. The boat immediately sank. Even trying to carry much lighter blocks of only one ton, the rafts or boats capsized after a while.

But even if the builders had ships capable of carrying 50-ton loads, this probably would not have been sufficient. As any cargo ship captain can easily illustrate, moving a 50-ton load from a medium-small boat by simply pushing it "arm" out of the boat would cause the boat to immediately tip over as soon as the load was moved from inside the boat to the outside. The displacement of the centre of gravity would be too great for the boat to remain stable. To move such a load from a small boat to the yard on land, without the boat tipping over, requires at least one crane placed on land, lifting the load in a vertical direction relative to the boat. But could a people who did not know the wheel have cranes that lifted fifty tons or more? More importantly, did they have boats large enough to carry that load?

It might have been better if the builders had used large two-hulled catamarans, with a transport platform in the middle, which could be pulled directly to shore with their cargo. With two hulls available, it was more difficult for the boat to capsize. The very people of Oceania are the inventors of the "catamaran," so it is possible that they used them. But if you put a 50-ton boulder on bamboo rods, they would break. You needed really big, strong catamarans to be able to carry those weights.

Catamarans had to be pulled ashore for both loading and unloading. The Egyptians transported by river from the Asswan mines "only" 8,000 tons of granite to build the interior of the Great Pyramid. According to some calculations, the people of Nan Madol had to transport at least 750,000 tons of columnar basalt. We are talking about one hundred times more weight than was transported by sea to build the "granite heart" of the Great Pyramid. But if creating the fleet that was used to transport the granite for the pyramids took the power of the largest empire of that time, what was behind the "fleet" that transported a weight almost one hundred times as much?

And where did this large fleet come from, if Nan Madol was located on a small island 30 km in diameter, perhaps with only 1,000 workers on hand, and the mainland was at least 1,000 km away? These considerations lead us to think that Nan Madol was built during a period of time when Sundaland was still emerged, the people of Sundaland were still alive and powerful, and thus contributed decisively to the construction of this mysterious city. Conversely, one cannot explain where the labour force needed to build this masterpiece on the sea came from.

Transported via beach before the Deglaciation?

Local legend has it that the columnar basalt blocks of which Nan Madol is composed "floated" through the air until they were deposited in the established places, guided by the "magic" of two shamans and something that flew, and was similar to a "dragon." But let us talk about a legend. The actual construction of Nan Madol took place when the Pacific Ocean had a much lower water level than it does today (we speak of a difference of as much as 125 meters in depth). As can be seen from the satellite images, beneath the shallow waters around Nan Madol lies a beach about five hundred meters wide. This wide beach, or plain, surrounded the entire island before the Deglaciation.

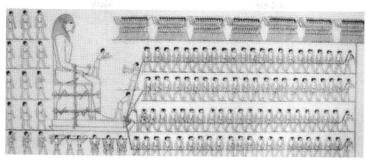

Reconstruction of the Djehutihotep wall painting

In many ways, this large strip of sand is reminiscent of the environment in which Egyptians moved loads of up to fifty tons. In fact, in the tomb of Djehutihotep, a powerful Egyptian ruler who lived around 1900 B.C.E. and ruled under Pharaohs Amenemhat II, Senusret and Senusret II, a fantastic painting has been found that tells us a lot about the technology of the Middle Kingdom Egyptians. In the painting we can see a statue of a human being sitting on a throne, approximately seven meters high, and weighing an estimated 50 to 60 tons. The whole scene in the painting is about the transportation of this colossus. It is clear from the painting that until 1900 B.C., the Egyptians did not yet know the use of the wheel for transporting people or objects. This large statue is painted firmly tied to a huge sled, perhaps made of alabaster. The sled was dragged at full force, with its very heavy load. A man, at the front of the sled, is painted pouring liquid onto the ground. Presumably, he was lubricating the ground to reduce friction, perhaps by means of water mixing with sand, or perhaps using some kind of oil.

So the Egyptians had found a documented way to transport loads of 50 to 60 tons on the sand, even though they did not know the use of the wheel for transportation. Is it possible, then, that the people of Nan Madol did something similar using the beach in front of them, which was about five hundred meters wide, before the level of the Pacific Ocean rose? If this conclusion were true, it would mean that the "technological capability" of that people was also at a level equal to that of the Middle Kingdom Egyptians. There are many "official" archaeologists who compare the construction of Nan Madol to that of the pyramids, especially in relation to the population employed to build it. But if this is the case, then it was an empire whose traces have been lost that built Nan Madol.

But the situation is even more complicated than that. The Egyptians transported limestone boulders of that size by dragging them on sleds only a few hundred meters, since the main quarries were always located close to the constructions. Nan Madol's basalt quarries, on the other hand, were at best twenty-five kilometres from the construction site. It seems impossible that the workers at Nan Madol could have borne the weight of transporting the basalt blocks on sleds along the beach, a distance of 25 km. And this every day, every week, every month, every year, for a period estimated to be between 400 and 800 years, as we will see later. Besides all, assuming a "relay" of five hundred meters for each group employed in the transport, theoretically for each boulder transported it would have taken as many as fifty times as many men as those employed by the Egyptians in building the pyramids, for a boulder of the same size. But where did all that enormous workforce come from? A powerful nation was needed, certainly not a group of islanders.

Ultimately, these rock blocks were not simply transported and "abandoned" on the beach. Some basalt "logs" weighing fifty tons were raised up to a height of twenty meters above the present sea level, and carefully placed on top of other blocks. It is physically impossible to raise a basalt "log" weighing fifty tons by hand, and it seems that the people of Nan Madol did not have our modern mechanical "cranes." At the very least, therefore, ramps had to be built to drag the blocks up to the wall where they were to be placed. These ramps could not be too steep, otherwise the basalt blocks ran the risk of going back instead of up. So the ramps had to be quite long. If 50-ton basalt blocks were carried to a height of twenty meters, the ramp on which they were carried could be as long as one hundred meters. But could ramps have been built over the sea? We would definitely say no. So this is further confirmation that Nan Madol was built when the whole area around the city was dry before the Deglaciation 15,000 years ago. And it is also proof that there must have been an "imperial" type of organization behind this construction, and certainly not a 30-kilometre islet in the middle of the sea.

Moreover, given the particular type of construction, in which very heavy blocks alternate with much lighter blocks, it is likely that some type of winch equipped with a counterweight system had to be used for the heavier blocks. But this presupposes a knowledge of elements of physics, techniques, and materials that one would think men of that time must not have possessed. Whichever way you look at it, Nan Madol was a huge project to manage, too big for a single island. For those times, a city of that size was equivalent to a modern metropolis.

Nan Madol bears the invisible signature of a great vanished empire.

The construction times

Talking about construction time with regard to Nan Madol is by no means a detail. It is not known exactly how much the total weight of columnar basalt transported to build the islets amounts to. Conservative estimates speak of a total of 750,000 tons. These numbers are enough to make us realize that the construction of Nan Madol easily rivals the mythical construction of the Great Pyramid of Giza.

Most of these blocks were arranged with manic precision. Even, in some places there is a distinct "artistic cut," in which the corners of the buildings rise upward, as in traditional Chinese buildings. But doing these things takes a long time. Let´s make a comparison. In the first century, the Romans built the "Colosseum," or Flavian Amphitheatre. Its construction was started by Vespasian in 72 AD and was inaugurated by Titus in 80 AD. It later underwent further modifications made during the empire of Domitian around 90 AD. When the Romans built the Colosseum, they had an incomparably greater availability of labour (thanks to slaves) and economic resources than the builders of Nan Madol. Moreover, the Romans were known throughout the world for their exceptional skill in construction. The Roman roads, their bridges, and the aqueducts they created, just to name a few, not only still exist today, but in a great many cases are still fully functional.

The Romans knew the use of the wheel in transportation, used wagons drawn by strong oxen (which reduced labourers' fatigue), knew the iron with which to cut and smooth stone blocks, knew about cranes, pulleys, and a host of other technical and architectural systems. As far as we know, none of these "ancient technologies" were available to the builders of Nan Madol. The Romans also had an ace up their sleeve: they knew the use of the arch in architecture, which allowed them to raise multi-story buildings with some ease, saving time, material, and workforce. Roman engineers had an advantage over Nan Madol builders in every respect.

The Colosseum is an elliptical-shaped structure, with a maximum width of 189 meters and a minimum width of 156 meters. The arena, also elliptical, is eighty-seven meters long and fifty-five meters wide. In view of the fifty-five meters maximum height, the total volume of the Colosseum is about 1,320,000 cubic meters. But, being an amphitheatre, the Colosseum is largely empty inside. So the volume of the built-up part alone is much smaller than the total volume, on the order of 0.1 million cubic meters. Its built-up area was constructed using about 100,000 cubic meters of travertine, with a total weight of about 275,000 tons.

Nan Madol weighs at least "3 times" as much as the Colosseum, weighing "at least" 750,000 tons (but some say it weighs three hundred times more). It is enormously larger than the Colosseum, measuring 1.5 x 0.5 kilometres. While the Colosseum stands on land, Nan Madol stands on water. The Colosseum, in its present form, was built by the highly advanced Romans, with all their economic and technological power, in a period of time between 8 and 18 years (depending on your point of view). Making this comparison, the powerful Roman Empire, to build Nan Madol, would have taken between 24 and 54 years at the very least. How long would it have taken the inhabitants of a 30-kilometre-diameter island, who possessed none of the technologies that the Romans possessed? Between 240 and 540 years? Or ten times longer? Or one hundred times longer?

Taking into account that at least some of the columnar basalt used for construction came from 25 kilometres away, or from other islands located hundreds of kilometres away, many people wonder: but could the locals really build something like Nan Madol? According to several scholars, the total population of the island at the time Nan Madol is thought to have been built could not have exceeded 25,000. Subtracting from this number the nobles, women, children, and the elderly, there would hardly have been more than 2,500 available workers, young and strong. Considering those employed in other activities (such as fishing, farming, or the army), it is thought that about 1,000 workers were used exclusively for the construction of the islets. Would these workers have been enough?

To think that a single island only 30 km wide, with a total population of 25,000 (at best), could have provided the useful workforce for this huge construction is just a pleasant joke. It is simply obvious that Nan Madol is the offspring of a civilization with a population similar to that of Old Kingdom or Middle Kingdom Egypt, and with a level of technology similar to theirs. Where did they end up? Probably under the waters of the Deglaciation, which swept Sundaland and its civilization away. Of course, if all this were not to be true, then those who hand down the island's legends would be right. According to them, the basalt blocks were transported by "non-human" entities, causing them to levitate in the air, and on their own they positioned themselves where we find them today. Everyone chooses his own explanation.

PART 6

Period:

About 13,000 years ago

Topic:

The Asian "reload"

Involved populations:

The Denisovians

12 - The great Asian "reload"

As we read in previous chapters, rising waters across the Earth had disrupted the geography of the planet. Any population near the sea or waterways, or in the valleys, was potentially at risk of being decimated by the floods. This "global cataclysm" claimed some excellent victims. We are quite sure that a civilization centred on the island of Melos in the Mediterranean Sea was wiped out. The inhabitants of Sundaland were also hit hard. The fantastic city of Nan Madol in time was abandoned because it was ending up inexorably under the waters. But it is highly probable that the destructive events of the Deglaciation did not wipe out only a few existing civilizations. Things were much worse than that. Because of the ripple effect triggered by the Deglaciation, an entire "human family" suffered a "reload," being totally wiped off the face of the Earth. After the "reload" of the Neanderthals, which took place about 40,000 years ago, we then witness the "reload" of another "human family," the Denisova. Who are they?

Probably at the same time that Neanderthals were appearing in Eurasia, and while Sapiens were appearing in Africa, another human "family" was making its appearance: in Asia and Oceania the Denisova were appearing. The Denisova is known from few found physical remains, and consequently most of what is known about them comes from DNA evidence. According to scholars, the Denisova appeared perhaps 300,000 years ago, and appear to have lived in Asia up to 11,500 years ago. Incredible to say, this is precisely the date, according to Plato, of the disappearance of Atlantis. If this were true, it would not be "just" "prehistoric" man. At least in Asia, it is extremely likely that his "history" overlapped with that of the various Sapiens civilizations. Let us also analyse this "reload."

I Denisova

A few years ago, a group of researchers speculated that further variation of humans had existed in the past. An article entitled "Excavating Neandertal and Denisovan DNA from the genomes of Melanesian individuals" appeared on science.sciencemag.org on April 8, 2016. According to this study, "scientists analysed DNA from 1,523 people from around the world, including 35 inhabitants of the Bismarck Archipelago, a group of islands off Papua New Guinea."

Analyses have shown that the inhabitants of Malaysia are the only ones to have inherited a not insignificant percentage (1.9 to 3.4 percent) of the genes of an "unknown variation" of human being, now extinct: the Denisova. (Some genes of this "variation" are present in virtually all Sapiens everywhere, but in very small amounts.) Moreover, this genetic heritage has also been found in Spain, and precisely in some bone remains in the cave of "Sima de los Huesos." The work, again conducted by the Max Planck Institute for Evolutionary Anthropology in Leipzig, caused quite a stir, because no one, not even they, expected to find this "unknown variation" in Europe.

A few years earlier, in 1989 (but the research was not revealed until 2012), a group of Australian and Chinese researchers made a discovery of human remains at the Maludong Caves in China. In the opinion of the researchers, as can be read in a March 14, 2012 "Plos One" article, these remains do not appear to be from Homo Sapiens, or any other known variations. Moreover, these remains are very recent, dating to a period close to 11,500 years ago. Several have suggested that these remains also belong to the same "unknown variation" found in Spain and in the Malay population. This variation is called "Denisova homo," named after the Denisova cave in Siberia where the first remains were identified.

According to Focus magazine, "[one of the] hypotheses suggests that these fossils may belong to the species of humans that paleoanthropologists call Denisova, from the [Denisova] cave in Siberia where they were found [for the first time]; only tiny bone fragments have been found of them, but DNA analysis has established that some of their genetic makeup is present in Southeast Asian human populations." DNA evidence suggests that the Denisova were dark-skinned, with dark eyes and hair. Other aspects of the body, however, were similar to Neanderthals, who were instead light-skinned and generally had red hair.

In just 10 years, the discovery of an ancient variation of the genus "Homo" found mainly in Asia, the "Denisova," has shaken many of the theories about Homo Sapiens that seemed to be "certainties" by then. A 2011 study found that Denisovian DNA is prevalent in Australian Aboriginal peoples, nearby Oceanians, Polynesians, Fijians, East Indonesians and Mamanwans (from the Philippines). But this is not found in East Asians, West Indonesians, Jahai (from Malaysia) or Onge (from the Andaman Islands). The presence of Denisovian DNA in areas of the sea, and its absence in the mainland, would indicate that the Denisova arrived by sea. But given that we are talking about a period hundreds of thousands of years ago, this "possible" ability of the Denisova to navigate the open sea is puzzling to say the least.

They were probably Denisova people who painted the Sulawesi mural about 44,000 years ago. Perhaps the builders of the Gunang Padang pyramid were Denisova people. It is possible that they were Denisova, or their descendants related to Sapiens, the builders of the mysterious Nan Madol

Herodotus and the Denisova

The ancient Greek historian Herodotus (born about 484 B.C.) was certainly not a palaeontologist, and he knew absolutely nothing about the various "human families." But a detail in one of his writings suggests that he may have unwittingly given us some information about the "last Denisova" who existed. Let us see why. In Book IV of his "Histories," in verses 184 and 185, Herodotus gives a very strange description of the population of the Atlanteans. The writer says, "[The] Atlanteans claim not to feed on any animals and not to dream." Before explaining this sentence, let us ask a question. Herodotus was born about 50 years before Plato. How did Herodotus know of the existence of the "Atlantean people" decades before Plato? From the information available to us, this people no longer existed in North Africa during the time of his lifetime.

In his writings, Herodotus says he had a prolonged stay in Egypt. So the most likely source of this story is the same as Plato's: the Egyptian priests. So Herodotus' account was completely independent of Plato's. It also predated Plato's. All this indicates that Herodotus' "source," namely the Egyptian priests, was "genuine." Herodotus wrote this detail according to an account he had received from the priests of Sais.

A vegetarian people

In fact, Herodotus defines the Atlanteans as a completely vegetarian people. But from what we know, the earliest known "vegetarian movements" are all religious in origin. They date back to Zoroastrian, Hindu, and Buddhist practices, where respect for life translated in many cases into a refusal to eat meat. But we are talking about "Eastern" practices, from Iran to India, which remained unknown in the West for many centuries. And then, in religious movements, to be vegetarian or not was something that concerned individuals. How was it possible for an entire nation to be vegetarian, even millennia before the birth of the great religions that sponsored this lifestyle? And why did they not eat meat?

But the implications of this description are much deeper. When Herodotus wrote his account, the Sahara had already been a dry land for centuries. It is practically impossible for a large people of several million people to eat only vegetables in the middle of the desert. In order to be "entirely vegetarian," it is obvious that this people had to be able to draw food from considerable agri-food resources. This could certainly not be said of the peoples living in the Sahara at the time of Herodotus. There is no mention of vegetarian peoples in North Africa and, given the level of aridity in that area, it was probably not even possible for them to be vegetarian.

On the contrary, it is a fact that, until Sundaland was submerged by the waters of the Deglaciation, even during the Ice Age this area was an oasis rich in plant food. Was Herodotus confusing something? It is strange that a Greek historian would conceive of such an anomalous way of life, and one with no match in the civilization of his time. It is difficult for Herodotus to have written something like this if someone had not given him this information. This "someone" was surely the Egyptian priests of Sais, who were visited by Herodotus. But the people described by the Egyptians could not have been the Mediterranean people of their time. They were probably referring to another place, and another time. But there is another puzzling detail.

Humans without dreams

Herodotus describes the Atlanteans as "people who did not dream." This is an even more surprising statement than the first. Scientifically speaking, dreaming is the neurological process that is particularly (but not only) activated when, during sleep, our brains enter the REM phase. This phase of sleep is characterized by rapid eye movements. It is not known exactly why we dream. All we know is that all homo sapiens dream. Whether we remember dreams when we wake up or not, this makes no difference.

Professor Patrick McNamara Ph.D., a psychologist and professor of behavioural neuroscience at Boston University, who specialises in the study of dreams, states in one of his articles: 'The ancient Greek historian Herodotus relates in Book IV of his Histories that many thousands of years ago, in North Africa, near the mountain called Atlas, there was once a particular group of people. ´The natives called this mountain ´´The Pillar of Heaven´´ and they named themselves after it, calling themselves Atlanteans or Atlanteans. They are said to eat no living things and never have dreams´.

These few lines from the "Histories" have prompted many speculative scholars to link the Atlanteans to the "supposedly mythical" island of Atlantis [...] The Atlanteans had supposedly achieved great levels of spirituality, scientific, artistic, and technical success, but then faced catastrophes through wars and natural disasters. Refugees from Atlantis fled to North Africa, Persia and elsewhere. In Persia, the Atlanteans joined the Magi and Zoroaster to start that great religious tradition. In North Africa, the Atlanteans settled near Mount Atlas and then interacted with the initial stages of ancient Egypt and helped start that great religious tradition, and so on. The Atlanteans described by Herodotus, according to speculative scholars, may have been the "refugees" from Atlantis. It is unclear why beings of such an advanced civilization mentioned not dreaming. But whatever the cause, I have been unable to find other mentions of a culture that did not dream." - End quote.

As Professor Patrick McNamara Ph.D. says, with the exception of this reference by Herodotus, there is no people in all of human history who were said not to dream. In fact, especially in ancient peoples, dreaming was a state of consciousness related to the "supernatural." In dreams "spirits" communicated with shamans or other members of the community. In dreams ancestors spoke with their descendants. Prophecies and omens were received in dreams. To say that a people, as a whole, were unable to dream would destroy all this religious scaffolding that has always been part of homo sapiens' lives. Did Herodotus make this up? Of course it is possible, but it is unlikely. It is clear that Herodotus, at least 40 years "before" Plato, by saying that these people did not eat meat and did not dream, meant to tell us that there was a group of humans profoundly different from us.

If the Atlanteans, as a people, did not have this brain characteristic, namely the need to dream, then they had a genetic variation at the "population" level that directly affected their brains. Add this to the fact that "as a people," and not as individuals, they did not eat meat, and all this makes the Atlantean people distinctly different from the rest of the "Homo Sapiens" family.

Probably what Herodotus calls "Atlanteans" were humans who descended from another branch of the Homo family, which interbred with Sapiens: the Denisova. The possibility that the brains of the Denisova were at least in small part different from ours, and that is why "perhaps" they did not dream, is contemplated in the findings of the Max Plank Institute. In the August 30th, 2012, article, titled "Ancient genome reveals its secrets," it says verbatim, "The researchers also generated a list of about 100,000 recent changes in the human genome that occurred after the Denisova split. Some of these changes affect genes associated with brain function and nervous system development." Could it be that, among the changes induced by genes that acted on brain function, some influenced "dream" function? We will probably never know, but it is a possibility.

Denisova's "reload"

In any case, whether Herodotus told the truth or not, after 11,500 years ago there are no other traces of the Denisova. They disappeared completely from the face of the earth. Only a few genes remain of them in the DNAs of some populations, especially in Oceania. Their disappearance coincides with the catastrophe caused by the Deglaciation, and it is therefore likely that this was the cause that exterminated them. With them disappears not only a "human family," but probably the oldest known human civilization. A civilization that was based in the Sundaland area but had carried their "seeds" around the world.

At this point we note that there have been at least three "major reloads" in the "human family." About 75,000 years ago, Homo Sapiens suffered a "near extinction." About 40,000 years ago,

12 - The great Asian "reload"

Neanderthals were wiped off the face of the earth. At the latest 11,500 years ago, the same fate befell the Denisova. Of these three human families, only one, the Sapiens, somehow managed not to become completely extinct. How they managed to do so is unclear. But the challenges did not end at that time.

.

PART 7

Period:

About 12,800 years ago

Occurrence:

The impact of comet fragments on Earth

The "Younger Dryas"

Involved populations:

Göbekli Tepe Civilization

Clovis Culture

Other cultures unknown

13 - The "Younger Dryas"

The period of 'deglaciation' continued for thousands of years. The warm climate had made Earth a much more comfortable place. Although the Neanderthals had become extinct, and the last Denisova specimens were going the same way, the Sapiens seemed on their way to populating all of Earth without major problems. Unfortunately, things did not turn out that way. The mild and pleasant climate that was taking hold over much of the Earth was interrupted by two sudden and brief ice ages, called the Older Dryas (Older Dryas) and the Recent Dryas (Younger Dryas). These events happened approximately between 12,900 and 11,650 years ago. But the effects continued to be felt for quite some time.

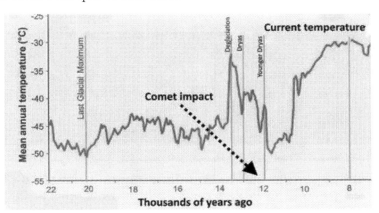

Obviously, the immense glaciers that occupied all of North America and much of Europe before the Deglaciation did not reform. And the waters did not recede, as they did during the Ice Age. Despite this, the global temperature, in most of the Earth, fell by several degrees, creating a "perennial winter" for some years. For example, the average annual temperature in Britain is estimated to have dropped to -5°C. It seems that of the two "Dryas," the first had a limited effect. Conversely, the second, namely the "Younger Dryas," had an almost global effect, and was brief but very intense.

According to the latest studies, it was none other than a bombardment of celestial bodies that temporarily halted global temperature warming and brought back, albeit briefly, a small "ice age." In fact, it seems that a vast number of bolides, asteroids, or comet fragments struck the entire surface of the Earth, causing enormous amounts of dust to rise. These "artificial clouds" would have blocked sunlight for some time, leading to a huge drop in temperatures. Let us now see in more detail what happened.

The danger from the sky

It is now a certainty in the scientific community that a comet or comets of considerable size collided with Earth around 10,794 B.C., about 12,800 years ago. Near Earth's atmosphere, the cometary swarm exploded, causing a huge trail of fragments of varied sizes. These hit the earth's soil on at least four continents. The impact had a double effect. In the areas where the large meteorites fell, there was a destructive effect typical of a hydrogen bomb of several megatons. Whatever had been in the vicinity of the various areas affected by this type of impact was blown away, pulverized.

There was also a second side effect. From the areas where the most devastating impacts had occurred, a cloud of dust arose such that it obscured sunlight for some time, at least in part. Suddenly it became night almost everywhere. The temperature dropped suddenly. Although the full details are not known, it is assumed that some plant species died, and in turn some species of herbivores that fed on those plants died. Probably some species of carnivores that fed on the herbivores also followed their fate, in an inexorable chain effect.

The death of herbivores contributed in turn to the decline in the production of biological methane. Methane is a greenhouse gas less present than carbon dioxide, but with as much as twenty-one times the capacity to make the atmosphere warmer (some say as much as eighty times). A sharp decrease in biological methane in the atmosphere may have contributed to a further decrease in temperature. A vicious circle was created that fuelled the cold. These phenomena then created a small but intense ice age in large areas of the Earth.

The comet impact theory had been put forward several decades ago by several scholars, but the doubts of the scientific community were greater than the certainties. Surprisingly, however, in recent times some researchers have uncovered a series of evidence showing that comet impacts on the Earth really happened. The journal "Nature," on March 6, 2020, published on its website an article titled *"Evidence of Cosmic Impact at Abu Hureyra, Syria at the Younger Dryas Onset (~12.8 ka): High-temperature melting at >2200 °C,"* which outlines scientific evidence that speaks in favour of the tremendous impact of a celestial object in the Abu Hureyra, Syria, area about 12,800 years ago.

At the end of the introduction, or "abstract" of the study, it is stated verbatim, "The wide range of evidence supports the hypothesis that a cosmic event occurred at Abu Hureyra about

13 - The "Younger Dryas"

12,800 years ago, simultaneously with other impacts that deposited high-temperature molten glass, molten microspheres and/or platinum on four continents at other sites involved with the Younger Dryas."

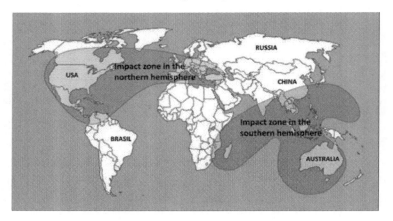

An ancient meteoric bombardment

Let us reconstruct it from the beginning. Abu Hureyra is one of the most important archaeological sites in the world. Located in northern Syria, it is the archaeological site where the oldest traces of agricultural activity by humans are found. Archaeologists have found there the remains of several types of grains, including rye. From the remains found, it is noted that about 1,300 years after it was inhabited, suddenly the population of Abu Hureyra was gone, or for some reason, much of it no longer existed.

Until recently, it was unclear what could have caused this. Analysing Abu Hureyra's remains recently, researchers found microspheres of molten glass present on virtually everything, whether in biological remains, masonry remains, or soil. They

13 - The "Younger Dryas"

also found nanodiamonds and traces of suessite, a rare mineral on Earth but common in meteorites. Traces of minerals rich in chromium, iron, nickel, sulphides, titanium, iron, platinum, and iridium were found, minerals that typically make up asteroids.

To produce the glass microspheres containing those materials, temperatures above 2200 °C are required. For comparisons, we can recall that steel melts between 1,300 °C and 1,500 °C. Titanium melts at about 1,700 °C. To understand at what temperatures these microspheres form, James Kennett, professor emeritus of geology at the University of California, Santa Barbara, said, "Such a high temperature would completely melt a car in less than a minute." No "natural" reaction, chemical or otherwise, that could develop on Earth spontaneously would reach those temperatures. According to scholars, the only event that could generate something like that on Earth is a "cosmic impact." A celestial object must have struck the vicinity of Abu Hureyra, disintegrating whatever it found in its path. It probably did not create a crater because the comet, or its debris, disintegrated in the atmosphere.

According to scholars, the most obvious traces of comet bombardment globally consist precisely in the finding of vast numbers of these glass microspheres, combined with an amount of platinum far beyond the norm. This concentration of platinum is typical of comets. In the past years, several scholars have asserted that they have found these glass microspheres at a number of sites, which are, among others: Abu Hureyra, Arlington Cyn, Barber Creek, Big Eddy, Blackville, Blackwater, Chobot, Cuitzeo, Gainey, Kimbel Bay, Lingen, Lommel, Melrose, Murray Springs, Ommen, Sheriden Cave, Talega, Tropper.

13 - The "Younger Dryas"

The majority of these sites are concentrated in the US. Others are found in Canada, Mexico, Venezuela, Germany, Syria, and Turkey. It is entirely likely that these glass spheres are found in many other areas of the Earth, but no one has ever looked for them. According to the researchers, the amount of molten material produced in the form of microspheres could not have been formed by the impact of a single large comet alone. It took thousands of impacts on four continents to produce all that material. Simply put, the Earth was literally bombarded by a swarm of thousands of cometary debris about 12,800 years ago.

According to the journal Nature, these impacts probably resulted from a series of comets that struck Earth over a short period of time. These comets, which are basically composed of ice and rock, when they get too close to the Sun, and thus in the vicinity of Earth, are prone to break up into thousands of fragments between 10 and 1,000 meters in diameter. Because of the enormous speed at which they travel, each of these fragments is capable of producing catastrophic explosions. Thus it was these comet fragments that struck the Earth, and caused as a side effect the Younger Dryas, a brief but intense "extra" ice age.

The journal says verbatim, "The largest clusters of cometary debris are believed to be capable of causing thousands of airbursts within minutes in an entire Terrestrial Hemisphere. An [Earth] collision with such a million-kilometre-wide debris cluster would be thousands of times more likely than a collision with a 100-kilometre-wide comet or a 10-kilometre-wide asteroid." According to the journal Science, the impact at Abu Hureyra was just one of an exceptionally considerable number of impacts that occurred in a brief period of time, within a radius of more than 14,000 km in the Earth's northern and southern hemispheres.

The "fire from heaven" of the Bible

This impact probably even left a trace in one of the most famous books ever, the Bible. We are talking about the tale of "Sodom and Gomorrah," narrated in chapters 18 and 19 of the book of Genesis. In the following excerpt we quote the most significant passages from the tale.

Quote beginning - "Afterwards, about noon Yahweh appeared to Abraham among the great trees of Mamre, as he was sitting at the entrance to his tent. Abraham looked up and saw three men standing at some distance from him. As soon as he saw them, from the entrance of the tent he ran to them and bowed with his face to the ground and said, "Yahweh, please, if I have your approval, do not leave. Stop by your servant! Please allow me to wash your feet. Then rest under that tree. Since you have come here to your servant, allow me to bring you a piece of bread to refresh you, and then you can set out again." Then they said, "All right. Do what you said."

[...]

The three men got up to leave and looked down in the direction of Sodom. As they went in that direction, Abraham accompanied them for a stretch of road. And Yahweh said, "I will not hide from Abraham what I am about to do."

[...]

13 - The "Younger Dryas"

After that Yahweh said, "The charges against Sodom and Gomorrah are really serious, and their sin is very serious. I will go down to see if they really act according to the charges that have come down to me, and, if not, I will know." Then two of the three men left there, and went on their way to Sodom; Yahweh, however, stayed with Abraham. So Abraham approached him and said, "Are you really going to wipe out the righteous along with the wicked? (For his nephew Lot was living in Sodom with his family). [...] Finally, Abraham said, "Yahweh, please don't be angry, let me speak one last time! Suppose there are only ten of them." Yahweh replied, "To protect the 10 I will not destroy it." When he had finished talking to Abraham, Yahweh left, and Abraham returned to his tent.

The two angels arrived in Sodom toward evening. Lot was sitting at the entrance to the city wall. When he saw them, he immediately went to meet them. He then knelt down with his face to the ground and said, "My lords, please come to your servant's house. Spend the night with me and have your feet washed. Then you will rise at dawn and resume your journey." They said, "No, we will spend the night in the town square." But he was so insistent that the two agreed to his hospitality. So Lot prepared a banquet in his house, and he baked loaves without yeast, and his two guests ate.

They had not yet gone to sleep, that all the men of Sodom, from the youngest to the oldest, surrounded the house, forming a crowd. And they called Lot and said to him, "Where are the two men who came to you tonight? Bring them out to us, for we want to have sex with them!"

Lot then went out, stopping at the threshold of his house, and closed the door behind him. He said, "My brothers, please do not do this evil thing. Please, I have two daughters who have never had sexual relations with a man. They are virgins. Please let me bring them out to you so that you can do whatever you want to them. But don't do anything to these men, because they are my guests, and they are under my protection." The men said, "Back off!" And they added, "This foreigner has come to live here, and now he even dares to judge us! Now we will do worse to you than to them!" So they crowded around Lot and made to break down the door. Then the two men inside the house stretched out their arms, pulled Lot inside and closed the door. At the same time they struck blind the men who were in front of the house, from the smallest to the largest, and they could no longer find the entrance to Lot's house.

So the two men said to Lot, "Do you have any people you care about in this city? Get everyone you love out of this place! We are about to destroy everything, because the accusation against the inhabitants of this city has really become too great before Yahweh, so much so that Yahweh has sent us to be destroyed!" So Lot went out and went to speak to his sons-in-law, who were to marry his daughters. He said to them, "Move! Get out of here, for Yahweh is about to destroy the city!" But his sons-in-law thought he was joking, and they did not listen to him.

When it was almost dawn, the angels insisted to Lot, saying, "Move! Take your wife and your two daughters who are here with you if you do not want to be wiped out for the sins of the city!" But Lot could not make up his mind, so the men, because of Yahweh's compassion for him, took him, his wife and his two daughters by the hand and forcibly led them out of the city. As soon as they were outside, one of them said, "Get to safety! Do not look back and stop anywhere on the plain! Flee to the mountains if you do not want to be killed too!"

[...]

Lot arrived at the city of Zòar when the sun had already risen. Then from the heavens, from Yahweh, on Sodom and Gomorrah rained fire and brimstone. So Yahweh destroyed these cities and the whole plain, including all the inhabitants and vegetation. Lot's wife, however, looked back and became a pillar of salt.

In the morning Abraham got up early and went to the place where Yahweh had appeared to him. When he looked down toward Sodom and Gomorrah and the whole plain, he saw something spectacular! Thick smoke was rising from the earth to the sky, straight up like the thick smoke of a furnace! " - *End quote.*

An objective examination

Wanting to remove from the narrative all the religious elements typical of Judaism and the "worship of Yahweh," what does this story tell us? The narrative tells us that in the area near the present-day town of Al Kalil (Hebron), about thirty kilometres south of Jerusalem, three "heavenly" beings with human likenesses warned a Sumerian nomad, named Abraham, from the city of Ur, of what was to take place a couple of days later. They told him that an entire area of the Middle East, where numerous cities stood, would be wiped out.

Shortly thereafter, several cities located in an area near the southern shore of the Dead Sea were destroyed by something that appeared to be "fire that fell from the sky." Most strange is the detail that is mentioned later. The Sumerian nomad had his camp at a distance of more than fifty kilometres from the place of destruction, on a hilly area. But in spite of this great distance, looking in that direction toward the plain, he had managed to see "a dense smoke rising straight up from the earth like the thick smoke of a furnace" reaching the sky.

Let us consider these three aspects. (1) The distance of the observer from the object of his observation. (2) The detailed description of a column of smoke rising straight up to the sky (at a time before the explosion of the first atomic bomb by millennia). (3) The effect there was on the cities in the area, which were completely pulverized.

Considering these three aspects, what could the Sumerian nomad, referred to in the Hebrew Scriptures as Abraham, have seen? The only kind of explosion the observer could have seen more than 50 km away, which caused a cloud of smoke rising straight up to the sky, and which had disintegrated the cities of an entire province, were the effects of a thermonuclear-type explosion. But since there were no nuclear weapons at that time, the only thing that could have generated such an explosion is the impact of a meteorite or comet in the area.

This idea is far from far-fetched; it is totally supported by science. In fact, we previously mentioned the article in the journal "Nature" dated March 6, 2020, entitled "Evidence of Cosmic Impact at Abu Hureyra." This article points out that in the Middle East, in an area not too far from the Dead Sea, there was an impact with a celestial object. The article makes it clear that it is highly likely that other impacts occurred, a short distance away. Although the impact crater has not yet been found, glass/platinum microspheres, which can only form at elevated temperatures, have been found. So, according to the scholars, there was an explosion that generated so much heat that it could melt a car in less than a minute. The explosion was therefore nuclear level.

Whoever wrote the account of the destruction of Sodom and Gomorrah (in its original version, without the religious embellishments) could not have invented something that man had never seen. The tale describes something that "like fire" comes down from the sky, hits an area the size of a province, disintegrating it, generating a column of smoke that rises straight up to the sky. Not to mention the detail that from a hilly area that scene could be observed from over fifty kilometres away. All of this closely resembles a "nuclear mushroom," which can be visible even from a very great distance. That the observer was at a great distance is also confirmed by the fact that the shock wave generated by the explosion did not sweep him away.

Having failed to give themselves any rational explanation of that catastrophic event, considering the poor scientific knowledge of their time, the surviving eyewitnesses embroidered around it the story of "God's judgment" on Sodom and Gomorrah. The description is so realistic that it cannot be ruled out that the destruction of Sodom and Gomorrah is a recollection of the destruction of some town or village near Abu Hureyra, obviously fictionalized and included in the Bible. Incidentally, this would explain why the remains of those cities have never been found. With temperatures generated by the impact exceeding 2200 °C, not even a memory remained of those cities, probably made of mud bricks.

Some deductions

Combining the scientific evidence of comet impacts in that area of the Middle East with the account of Sodom and Gomorrah, we gain some insights. (1) We know when the original episode that "kicked off" the legend of Sodom and Gomorrah happened: we are around 10,800 B.C. (2) The biblical Abraham, the one who recounts the destruction of Sodom, is actually the voice of one of the survivors. (3) The account clearly mentions a number of cities that existed in that area. In addition to the city of Sodom, the city of Gomorrah, the city of Zòar and other unnamed "cities of the District" are mentioned.

This aspect makes it clear that if cities existed (regardless of their size), then some form of civilization existed in that area 12,800 years ago. Confirming this, in recent years the village of Jerf el-Ahmar, and the megalithic site of Göbekli Tepe, both located near Syria, and both dating to about 12,000 years ago, have been found. (We will examine them in detail later). The account is not wrong when it says that there were several inhabited villages or towns in that area.

Has anyone visited us?

There is another aspect that we should not underestimate. The account speaks of a rescue "attempt" by celestial beings toward humans who were in the area that was about to be hit.

13 - The "Younger Dryas"

According to the tale, celestial beings referred to as "angels" warned some inhabitants to leave that area immediately, because within a few hours it would be destroyed by "fire from heaven." But to many these words seemed to be "a joke." (See Genesis 19:14).

What is interesting is that although the narrative refers to these three people as "Yahweh," the name of the Hebrew god, three beings in every way similar to humans are actually described. From the account it appears that one was a kind of "coordinator," while two others were the material executors. These ate, drank, walked, exactly like any human being. Their mission also had little that was "transcendental." They simply invited people to leave town, as if they knew what was about to happen. Rather than real deities, they had the appearance of beings "informed" of events. Of course, one cannot speculate too much, because we do not know how many and which details are "ancient," and which were instead added by the Jewish priests to make the story "supernatural."

The "rescue" turned out to be a half-hearted failure. Except for three human beings, all the others died. Of course, this part of the story may be just a legend, or the distorted version of events. However, the book of Genesis is not the only one that tells of the presence of "heavenly" beings in connection with the comet bombardment. Other documents, much older than the Bible and extremely "secular," also narrate their involvement. For example, in some Göbekli Tepe stelae this is a fairly common theme. We discuss this in the next chapter.

14 - A tale in a stone

As we have said, the Bible is not the only ancient book to tell us about the comet bombardment, and the "celestial beings" who came to the rescue. A very ancient site tells of the same events. We are talking about Göbekli Tepe, a site that is at least 12,000 years old.

The discovery of Göbekli Tepe has forced even the most reluctant of historians to have to reconsider our prehistory. In a March 5, 2009, Mail Online article, Ian Hodder, a researcher in Stanford University's archaeology program, said, "A lot of people think [the discovery of Göbekli Tepe] can change everything. It completely changes the game. All our theories were wrong." What made a famous archaeologist from a prestigious university, and many of his colleagues, say that science must admit that its archaeological theories about man's past are largely wrong, and everything must be revised?

Until before the discovery of Göbekli Tepe (a Turkish term meaning "the pot-bellied hill"), the earliest human civilizations were thought to be the Sumerian (and generally Mesopotamian) civilization, the Minoan civilization (destroyed by the Santorini volcano explosion) and the Olmec civilization in South America. Moreover, it was thought that it was the gradual invention of agriculture that prompted "primitive" humans, basically hunter-gatherers, to unite in communities, and in time to initiate civilization and religion. The discovery of Göbekli Tepe, however, seems to shatter all these certainties.

14 - A tale in a stone

Among the most striking aspects of the discovery of Göbekli Tepe we certainly find its dating. According to radiocarbon analysis, the oldest buildings currently found are dated at a minimum between 9,500 and 10,500 B.C., which is a period between 11,500 and 12,500 years ago. This means they are about 6,500 years older than Stonehenge. The remains of Göbekli Tepe are more than 5,000 years older than the Sumerian civilization.

Central monoliths

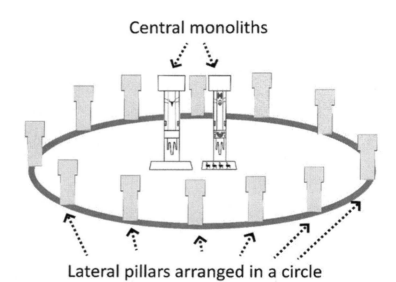

Lateral pillars arranged in a circle

We are thus talking about a culture that was most likely contemporary with both part of the last Ice Age and the Deglaciation that occurred 15,000 years ago. Göbekli Tepe, therefore, is contemporary with the city of Nan Madol, and it preceded by a brief time the civilization that Plato called by the name of "Atlantis." Moreover, it was almost certainly one of the few cultures (or civilizations) we know of that may have experienced first-hand the effects of the rain of fragments from comets that impacted the Earth about 12,800 years ago. Most recently, he directly experienced the Younger Dryas on himself. We therefore understand why the study of this and other sites in the same area may change our awareness of our prehistory.

Until the discovery of Göbekli Tepe, it was believed that humans barely managed to survive during that time period, and therefore lacked the material time, knowledge, and resources to build stone houses. It was also believed that they had not yet had time to create their own deities or temples. But where archaeologists thought they would find only simple isolated huts, this time they have found a remarkable number of megalithic structures made entirely of stone, made so well that they remain standing after at least 12,000 years. This is why archaeology is now divided into "before" and "after" the discovery of Göbekli Tepe.

The settlement

But let us go in order. First of all, what is Göbekli Tepe? Since 1995, for archaeological scholars, this has been the name of an excavation site, discovered by pure chance by a local shepherd, Savak Yildiz, when he noticed that some strange, worked rocks were sticking out of the ground. After contacting those in charge of a nearby museum, excavations were carried out in that area, directed for many years by renowned German archaeologist Klaus Smith, until his death in 2014. The site was only opened to the public in 2019. Göbekli Tepe is located only a few kilometres away from the city of Şanlıurfa in Turkey. (Incidentally, according to ancient Kurdish legends, Şanlıurfa is said to be the city of "Ur" mentioned in the book of Genesis, from which Abraham is said to have come.)

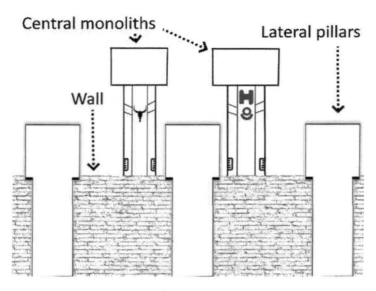

Think of the astonishment, the utter disbelief of the archaeologists, when they unearthed several large circular structures, vaguely resembling those at Stonehenge. Each circular structure, about 10 to 30 meters wide, consists of two large central T-shaped monoliths composed of limestone rock. These monoliths can reach up to twenty feet in height. The larger monoliths weigh about 10 to 15 tons, while others are lighter. They were hewn from the limestone rock, and thus are not simply "rectangular pieces of stone" found by accident and set up. They are blocks cut from the rock and shaped, just as modern stonemasons make blocks from marble quarries.

In each circular structure, or enclosure, around the two central monoliths, as if to form a closed circle around them, other similar pillars had been erected, also T-shaped, also made of limestone, but smaller, about three meters in height. Various animals were carved on these blocks with great skill. The few human figures carved are mainly headless, or faceless. Only a single carving of a woman seems to appear at the entire site. All other human figures are male.

A circular stone wall about two meters high filled the space between the various outer pillars, arranged in a circle around the two monoliths. The door of this wall, which was square, was carved from a single stone block. Each circular structure thus consisted of two central monoliths, many circular pillars lower than the central ones, also in the shape of a "T," with a surrounding wall and an entrance. The presence of a doorway and the shape of the pillars, with the top wider than the base, according to some suggests that the circular buildings were covered by some kind of roof, which rested on both the two central monoliths and the pillars arranged in a circle. The roof was probably made of wood, formed by several bundles that converged from the circumference toward the centre, about 3 meters higher. The whole formed a kind of "yurt," the typical Tatar tent, but made of stone and wood. It should be mentioned, however, that so far, no remains of any kind of roof covering have been found.

There is also a noteworthy detail. The pillars today are joined by a kind of circular dry stone wall. However, at least some of the pillars, such as the famous "Vulture Stele," contain designs that are partly covered by the drywall. This can only mean three things. The first is that the pillars were first accompanied by images and then placed inside the wall (but it is not clear what the point is of carving images that will later be hidden by the wall). Or it means that when the pillars were erected, the drywall was not contemplated in the original design. Therefore, it would be a later addition, which is why it would partially cover some sculptures. The third hypothesis, however, is that the Göbekli Tepe pillars did not belong to the structure we see today but were transported here from some other place. These pillars, then, were used as "building material" or "decorative" by the builders of the site, but their original use was different. This third hypothesis would make the pillars even older.

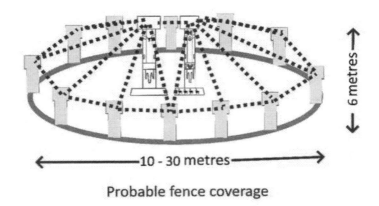

6 metres

←———————10 - 30 metres———————→

Probable fence coverage

The Göbekli Tepe site is about three hundred meters by three hundred meters in size. It has an older part (consisting of three circular structures) located in the centre of the settlement and a newer part (consisting of rectangular structures) surrounding it. The two areas are separated from each other by a time span of about 2,000 years. The structures built in the middle area, the older circular-shaped ones, are similar to each other, but not identical. Some closely resemble the megalithic structures of Stonehenge. Others are elliptical in shape. Only a few of these circular structures have been unearthed. Others lie buried still completely underground.

The outermost area consists of rectangular structures about twenty meters wide, and they appear to have been used for community purposes. Others are smaller, however, and appear to be studios, but it is not known what they were used for. In general, archaeologists tend to dismiss the idea that these were dwellings. They infer this from the fact that Göbekli Tepe was originally located on top of a hill. This was not an ideal place to build an encampment, within sight of everyone. In addition, it seems that it lacked an adequate water source to support a number of people compatible with a village. However, rainwater pools were also found, as well as areas used for flint working.

A mysterious end

Another still unexplained aspect of the site is its transformation over time. As the centuries passed, the first circular stone structures were buried. Later others were erected on top of them. But for some reason, each subsequent building complex was smaller than the one that had been buried, and not larger, as one would expect from an evolving civilization. Oddly enough, the builders' skills seem to have declined over time, and not improved, as is the case in our own day, for example. Göbekli Tepe society seems to deteriorate with each "cycle" of burial/reburial. No one can explain why this strange phenomenon occurs.

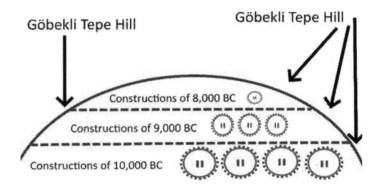

After several rounds of burial/reburial, the remains remained permanently underground, as if they had exhausted their function. But what exactly was that function? None of the buildings were burned or torn down, as if they were meant to be destroyed, or as if they had been attacked by an enemy people. The site was simply filled with earth, as if to bury it peacefully. Some scholars say that when the inhabitants of the area had to migrate, they made a kind of "burial" to buildings they considered sacred. While this may certainly be true, it would not explain why other, entirely similar but smaller buildings were built on the buried buildings.

Other structures, however, appear to have undergone a climatic event that somehow buried them. The period coincides fairly well with that of the Last Deglaciation. Therefore, it cannot be ruled out that, at least the oldest circles, were subject to a landslide of the original hill, perhaps due to heavy rains from the Deglaciation. The same fate seems to have befallen the other "twin settlements" near Göbekli Tepe.

For what purpose were they built?

Göbekli Tepe was initially thought to be a funerary structure. Archaeologists were convinced that as the excavations continued, in time the graves of the locals who had been buried would emerge. To the amazement of the researchers themselves, no human remains were found in any of the enclosures. This is especially strange, because to this day "sacred" structures are inextricably linked to burial. However, after years of excavation, researchers had to surrender to the evidence: Göbekli Tepe is not a necropolis or cemetery. The initial idea was therefore discarded. What else could it have been?

It seems that, in any case, this was a "community" structure, something that drew many people to that hill. In fact, another surprising discovery made at Göbekli Tepe concerns the large amount of biological remains found. These remains prove that a large amount of meat had been consumed there. Given the large amount of animal remains used as food that were found, it is thought that large banquets of animal meat were prepared at that site.

But the archaeologists, to their amazement, discovered that all the animal remains found at the site are composed of game, and not farm animals. Even the few wheat remains found are all of wild, and not cultivated, origin. This would mean that, essentially, even after the construction of Göbekli Tepe, the builders who made it had remained hunter-gatherers, and did not become farmer-farmers, which the inhabitants of the earliest known cities later did.

This evidence shatters another certainty of anthropologists. Previously, it was thought that city-building was only the "logical outcome" of agriculture and animal husbandry, which allowed many humans to have the food resources to live together in relatively small spaces. But Göbekli Tepe's discovery clearly indicates that the reason humans chose to build villages, or small towns, was other. In fact, they built a place that appears to be the first "nucleus" of a small town, while continuing to be hunter-gatherers.

Göbekli Tepe demonstrates that the fact that humans were hunter-gatherers did not prevent them from having the knowledge of engineering, logistics, organization of personnel and labour force, artistic stone working, and all that was needed to build that site. Göbekli Tepe is a site that, in terms of the difficulties of construction compared to the time it was erected, has nothing to envy the Pyramids. So whoever built those walls must have had a similar organizational structure: there was someone who planned, someone who commanded, and others who executed. But such a structure implies a society that would have existed at least 6,000 years before the Sumerian one. (Previously, the Sumerian civilization was thought to be the beginning of the earliest human societies.) For many, this evidence is unacceptable. Moreover, the concept of "society" is ill-suited to the idea that people had of hunter-gatherers, that is, that they were "free and independent," untethered to other communities. Göbekli Tepe shows that social structures are much older than once thought. They already existed, at a minimum, at the time of the Deglaciation, a full 15,000 years ago.

A mysterious belt

In the centre of the "stone circle" were two monoliths, which for convenience we will call Monolith A and Monolith B. These two monoliths are just under six meters high, about thirty centimetres thick and about 140 centimetres wide. Multiplying their volume by the weight of the stone from which they were made, we estimate that they must weigh about 15 to 20 tons. The head of the monolith is wider than the rest of the body, so it shows the typical "T" shape of the rest of the pillars found at Göbekli Tepe. The two monoliths in the centre of the stone circles are the only ones that have a base to fit on, so they can stand on their own, without having to lean against any wall.

Both monoliths depict highly stylized human features. But they are not human, as they are rectangular and headless. They may depict deities, or beings "from outside" that the inhabitants of Göbekli Tepe thought they had come into contact with. Both are depicted shirtless, covered only by a loincloth. They wear a kind of belt from which hangs the skin of a 4-legged animal equipped with a tail. This is probably the skin of a fox. The details are carved with great care. This casts doubt on the period and place where the monoliths were carved. To be shirtless, equipped only with a loincloth, these are beings that lived in a hot place. But, as we have said, up to this time Homo Sapiens had had to deal with cold, not hot weather. The only warm areas were near the equator. The two monoliths seem to be a "jarring" note in Göbekli Tepe, as if they belonged neither to that place nor to that time.

Monolith 'B'

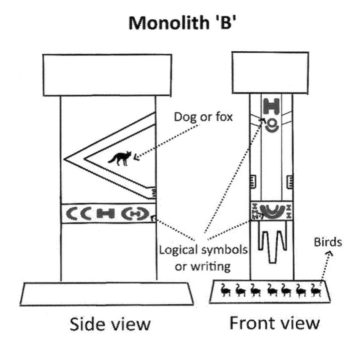

Dog or fox

Logical symbols or writing

Birds

Side view   Front view

The Monolith B belt is perhaps the most mysterious thing in all of Göbekli Tepe. In fact, along the belt buckle run a series of symbols that appear to be letters. On the front one can point to a kind of capital "I" with rather wide ends, followed by 2 similar "I "s rotated 90 degrees. In the centre of the belt, directly on the animal's skin, there appears to be a large "U," and a smaller one inside it. On the right are what appear to be 2 capital "I "s, placed one on top of the other.

Turning to look at the sides of the monolith, in the area where the belt runs, the message is even more complex. There are several "U "s rotated 90 degrees in both directions (they can also be described as capital "C "s). Something similar to this inscription appears: "C C H C H C (upside down)." The same symbols also appear in other places in Göbekli Tepe. Whatever they mean, they are not representations of any animals or tangible things. They are clearly abstract symbols, and thus can be considered ideograms, if not actually letters.

The late Prof. Klaus Smith, the excavation supervisor, while working at this site pointed out that the drawings on the pillars of Göbekli Tepe were not carved at random but have a very precise meaning. According to the professor, in addition to depicting real animals, the drawings also contain some abstract and other logical symbols. The presence of abstract and logical symbols among Göbekli Tepe's drawings elevates those carvings to a new level, to the point that they can be regarded as the "progenitors" of a form of writing. This comparison exploded like a real "atom bomb" in the ideas of anthropologists, because the first officially recognized human written form, cuneiform, appears only 6,000 to 7,000 years after Göbekli Tepe was built.

This is not to say that the Göbekli Tepe carvings are a true writing system possessed by that people. If this had been their way of writing, the site would probably be full of these symbols. But it is not. These symbols appear very rarely in Göbekli Tepe, although they are present. If they had a writing system, why does it not appear anywhere else? And why did it not develop later? There are no answers. This is why the symbols on the belt of monolith B are the real "jarring note" of the entire site. If the sculptors could have imagined in their imagination something similar to the two monoliths (whether they were real or imaginary visitors matters little), they certainly could not have imagined the concept of "writing." The "leap" would have been too great.

So what are ideograms on the belt of a sculpture predating 10,000 B.C. doing there? Seeing those ideograms on a 12,000-year-old sculpture is equivalent to seeing a dinosaur in New York City. But the mystery gets even more complicated. In the nearby village of Jerf el-Ahmar, built at least 11,500 years ago, "mnemonic symbols engraved 5,000 years before the appearance of writing" were found. Upon examining them, researchers found that they resemble small drawings, like those found in ancient caves. They are probably the "parents" or "grandparents" of hieroglyphs. But they are completely different from the symbols that appear on monolith B, which look eerily like "letters" instead.

The only way to explain the inscriptions on the belt of Monolith B is to assume that it is not "Göbekli Tepe's handiwork." That belt comes "from the outside." Those symbols bear too much resemblance to a writing system to be random, but they are used too infrequently at the site to suggest that they are a local product. It seems that no one from nearby villages has ever used them.

There can therefore be only two plausible hypotheses. (1) The entire monolith belongs to another place and time, as everything so far seems to indicate. (2) The sculptors who made monolith B simply tried to "copy" something they were not fully aware of, something that might as well have been "letters" or "symbols," and then made it part of their culture.

Could the marks on the belt of this monolith indicate that an ancestor of ours really saw something "strange" in the past?

Did it try to "copy" symbols it saw on a "visitor"? Or was it a writing system they saw "human visitors" using, and clumsily tried to copy? Regardless of the origin of those symbols, it seems that there is indeed "writing" on the belt of monolith B at Göbekli Tepe. But it seems that the writing was not theirs, and that it did not come from that place. And that makes that belt even more disturbing.

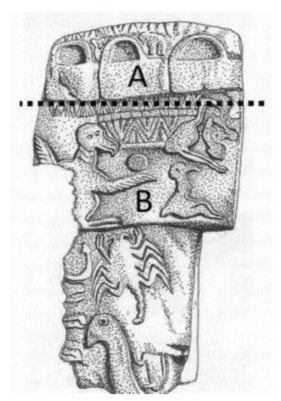

The two mysterious stelae

The only certainty about Göbekli Tepe is that a distressing memory was engraved on the walls in this settlement. This is contained in two of the oldest stelae in Göbekli Tepe, namely the "Vulture Stele" and the "Crane Stele." Wanting to greatly simplify, the Vulture Stele is a kind of "calendar," which attempts to place in time certain events that have occurred over the millennia. These events include both the Ice Age and the comet bombardment that occurred about 12,800 years ago. The Crane Stele, on the other hand, focuses particularly on the comet bombardment, and gives us a few more details.

The symbol of the snake

Several types of animals were engraved or carved on the stelae at the Göbekli Tepe site. But the depiction of one animal species exceeds all others by several orders of magnitude. In the entire Göbekli Tepe site, twenty-three groups of snakes have been depicted, totalling more than two hundred specimens. This site could therefore be called "the snake site." The number of snakes depicted exceeds the number of all other animals combined by many times. And these snakes have a very strange feature: with few exceptions, they all move from the top down. They seem, therefore, to fall from the sky. Certainly, an unusual movement for a snake, which slithers horizontally.

According to many scholars, the various animals carved in the various stelae, although not all of them, depict constellations. The Nazca in America thousands of years before them saw whales, orcas, spiders, monkeys, and the various animals they had encountered in their wanderings in the sky. Conversely, from what we see in their stelae, the people of Göbekli Tepe saw in the sky vultures, scorpions, frogs, bulls, giant geese (or

Genyornis), and other animals they had come into contact with. And so far, there is nothing strange.

In this context, what might the "snakes coming straight down from above" represent? Most likely they represent comets or asteroids. The typical tail of a comet is the result of the solar wind blowing on its "canopy" as it approaches the Sun. This means that when it is possible to observe a comet with the naked eye, it almost certainly must have already developed its "tail." As the comet gets closer to Earth, this extremely rarefied tail becomes increasingly visible.

A comet extremely close to Earth would show a very bright "head" and an awfully long "tail" in its wake. It could therefore have the appearance of a "snake of light." So the snake symbol does indeed represent a comet that came close to Earth. Often, comets that come too close to the Sun explode into a thousand pieces. If this had also happened to that comet, as it reached its perihelion relative to Earth, by the force of gravity its fragments would have plummeted to our planet, as seems to have actually happened about 12,800 years ago. From the point of view of an observer from the past, it would have seemed that from one "big snake of light" came many "little snakes of light," which is exactly what is seen in Göbekli Tepe's sculptures.

The symbol of the "visitors"

Another element of the Vulture Stele is two sticks arranged perpendicular to each other, with both ends enlarged. They look almost like a capital "I" and an "I" rotated 90 degrees. This is perhaps the most profound symbol among those depicted in the stele because it does not represent something real, such as an animal or a man. Conversely, it represents an idea or concept. It is therefore a true ideogram, a concept put in writing by men who lived at least 12,000 years ago.

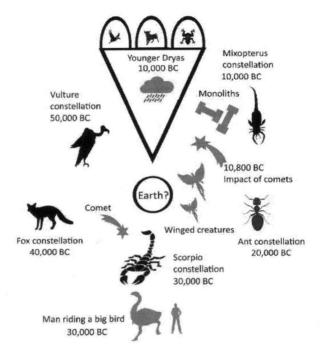

This is the same symbol that appears on the belt of one of the two monoliths placed in the centre of the circular building "D" at Göbekli Tepe. We can find it respectively on the right and left of the thong of that monolith. What is the relationship between the events described in the stele and that symbol? Does the artist want to tell us that the two monoliths performed some action at that point in the story? If the circle in the centre of everything were to represent the Earth, that would place the two monoliths, or what they represent, clearly "in space."

Extinct animals

We can note that at least three "apparently prehistoric" animals appear in the stele, which are thought to have already been extinct by the time Göbekli Tepe was made. (1) A giant bird of the family Dromornithidae (perhaps a Genyornis). (2) An extinct prehistoric scorpion species, perhaps a close relative of Mixopterus (3) An extinct giant ant, similar to "Titanomyrma lubei." Of course, some may think that these were artist's mistakes, or that he worked from imagination. And that may certainly be true. But the two "central monoliths" in the centre of each "stone circle" also have features that seem to move them far into the past. In fact, they wear loincloths and are clearly shirtless. This would indicate a time period when the climate was particularly hot. Or it tells us that the original sculptors lived elsewhere, in an area of Earth with a hot climate. Or both. But that would shift the narrative several tens of thousands of years in time. Thus, the information contained in the Vulture Stele may be among the oldest in human history.

The story

Wanting to summarize the narrative of the Vulture Stele, we can say that there are four key elements: (1) The central disk. (2) The inverted triangle. (3) The animals around the central disk. (4) Other symbols that tell events. The Vulture Stele depicts a number of animals arranged around the circle representing the Earth. Of these animals, those that are supposed to represent constellations, starting from the left, are:

the Vulture, the Fox/Dog, the Scorpion, the Ant and the Mixopterus.

It is clear that the way these constellations were engraved in no way aimed at "astronomical accuracy." The artist was not engraving a star chart. Those five constellations represented five different time periods. They were meant to represent a kind of "clock." Just as the hands of the clock indicate a different number from time to time, and in this way mark the passage of time, in the same way the observer could wheel through different events that had happened in the distant past of his people.

In this kind of "clock," or "circular calendar," one notices that the element that occupies the entire top, and literally divides the calendar in two, is a kind of inverted triangle. Looking even higher, the sculptor indicates what the inhabitants of Göbekli Tepe were doing at that time: they were inside shelters to shelter from the "zig-zag element," the brief ice age known as the Younger Dryas, which happened between 12,800 and 11,500 years ago.

According to archaeologists (and it is also confirmed by its contents), this stele was engraved around 10,000 BC. From the information obtained by anthropologists, it seems that the earliest remains of Homo Sapiens in the Göbekli Tepe area date back to around 60,000 BCE. So, in principle, the stele can recount events that occurred between 60,000 and 10,000 BCE. This means that, on average, each "constellation" could also indicate an approximate period of 10,000 years (Of course, we are not saying that this is necessarily the case, but it is just an indicative reasoning to understand what time frame we are talking about).

We do not know on the basis of what astronomical cycles the sculptor assigned each constellation to last for a certain period of time, and it is not our intention to guess. These details are simply unknown to us. Considering that it was not the sculptor's intention to provide precise dates, we can only speak of "approximate dates."

By analysing the stele, it is understood that the events were described in a counterclockwise direction. The "inverted triangle" is thus the "grand finale," and the events described tell how that event came about. Thus starting from the left side of the triangle, and proceeding counterclockwise, the first symbol we find is that of the Vulture. Since this is a representation of a constellation, it does not depict an event, but a period of time. We are about 60,000 to 50,000 B.C., and the population has emerged from the "genetic bottleneck" due to the "Great Cold." As we mentioned earlier, about 75,000 years ago the Sapiens were affected by this catastrophe as they moved from North Africa to Asia. They therefore passed right through Göbekli Tepe. Both time and place coincide.

The next constellation counterclockwise, Fox, would take us around 50,000 to 40,000 BCE. The next one, Scorpio, would indicate about 40,000 to 30,000 BCE. Proceeding counterclockwise, we find the constellation Ant, which would indicate a time period around 30,000 to 20,000 B.C. The last constellation is the Mixopterus constellation, which would take us to around 20,000 to 10,000 B.C., which is exactly the time period in which this stele is thought to have been carved.

Parallel to these five constellations, five events were engraved on the stele, which evidently were of utmost importance to the local inhabitants. If you look at the stele, you can see that these five events are not precisely between one constellation and another but scattered somewhat within them. This makes it even more obvious that it was not the intention of those who made the stele to create a true "calendar" or "clock" to leave for posterity. Dating has to be done "by eye," and thus is largely inaccurate. One can only get a general understanding of which millennium the various events refer to.

The reading of an ancient tale

The first "event" that appears counterclockwise after the Vulture and Dog/Fox constellations is a "snake." On the stele, however, this symbol is partially covered by a small wall. We said that the snake symbol represents a comet or a meteorite. This would mean that, during that time period, a meteorite or comet came down that was large enough that it should be mentioned among the "memorable" events.

To date, three different craters have been found to have formed around 45,000 B.C. as a result of the impact of celestial bodies with the Earth: the Meteor Crater in Arizona, the Xiuyan in China, and the Lonar in India. It appears that these craters were formed as a result of the impact of an asteroid/cometary between 1 and 2 kilometres in diameter. The explosion resulting from the impact must have been extremely violent, equal to a powerful hydrogen bomb of several megatons. The "small" snake in the stele may refer to one of these impacts, or to some other we do not yet know about. However, according to the Crane Stele, this comet also would have broken into a thousand pieces, bombarding the ground surface.

After the constellation Fox, the constellation Scorpio appears. Then around 30,000 B.C., the second "noteworthy" event in the history of the builders of Göbekli Tepe occurs. A small headless man riding a huge bird appears in the stele. Probably this engraving refers to the encounter of the ancestors of the builders of Göbekli Tepe with humans riding large birds, perhaps Genyornis. Several clues seem to indicate that they came from Southeast Asia, from the Sundaland and Sahuland area. Contact with that population somehow must have profoundly affected the lives of the inhabitants of Göbekli Tepe. They were probably carriers of new knowledge, or new cults. This would confirm that Sundaland explorers, in addition to coming to Central America, came to much of the known world.

Continuing counterclockwise, we find the constellation Ant, which takes us to around 20,000 BCE. The next constellation, the constellation of Mixopterus, takes us to around 10,000 BCE. Between these two constellations, we see a real "overlapping of symbols," corresponding to an "overlapping of events." Evidently, according to those who engraved the stele, a series of events of an "epochal" nature occurred during that period. Starting from the left, the first event described is that of the two half-bird half-man beings, the archetypal "angels." The artist indicates that, in some way, his ancestors had come into contact (real or presumed) with these entities. Who or what were they? Regardless of whether there really was this contact, or whether it was just a popular legend, this event is quite different from the one described by the small headless man riding a large bird. Men riding birds are basically described as human beings, probably very culturally advanced, and therefore perceived as semi-divinities.

Conversely, birdmen are no longer human beings. They are human-like beings, but capable of flight. They were therefore something not human. We can consider them deities, or beings from other planets. From the point of view of the humans of 10,000 years ago who inhabited Göbekli Tepe, there would have been no difference between the two. What role did these entities play? Another stele, the "Crane Stele," deals with answering this question. We will analyse it later.

Immediately to the right of the two "angels" is the symbol of a large snake. That engraved symbol tells us that, according to the author, after the appearance of "the angels," the Earth was struck by a large comet. (More precisely, according to researchers, it would be a swarm of comets that broke into a thousand pieces before reaching Earth, creating a real bombardment of fragments.) We know that we are at this point in time about 12,740 years ago. The cities and villages that were along the trajectory of the comet fragments were disintegrated. Those that were in the vicinity of the impact sites were razed to the ground by the shock wave. Those that remained standing had to face the frost of the Younger Dryas.

Even further to the right of the serpent is the symbol engraved contained in the belt of one of the two monoliths. It is placed between the comet and the two constellations. This is a clear reference to something that was in space. The snake's tail is bent in such a way that it appears to come from the symbol of the monoliths. Thus, according to the artist who made the stele, the comet's tail seemed to come from the second monolith. Could this be an allusion to the possibility that the impact was caused by the monoliths, as a kind of "divine retribution"? It is highly likely that is the sense of the story. The whole scene could be seen as a kind of chronology, useful not to keep track of time, but to have a kind of "list of events not to be forgotten."

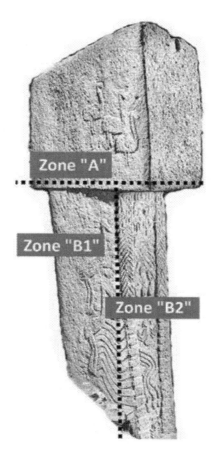

The Tale of the Crane Stele

We now turn to analyse the second stele, the "Crane Stele." Looking at the broad side of the Stele of Cranes, the scene is virtually identical, even in detail, to that which appears in the upper right area of the Vulture Stele. On the broad side of the Crane Stele, two winged beings are seen, virtually identical to those described in the Vulture Stele. They are two crane-like birds but have clearly human legs. They are thus half-human, half-bird beings, the archetypal "angels." They are beings who are considered deities, or who came from "beyond the Earth." This stele shows how this iconography, namely the two winged half-human beings, was a fundamental theme in the culture that produced Göbekli Tepe. It is evidently a deeply imprinted memory in their history.

Immediately next to the two "angels," as in the Vulture Stele, appear the symbols found on the belt of monolith B. The symbols are repeated several times, although the rock, which is rather worn at that point, makes them somewhat difficult to visualize. Also according to this stele, these two groups of entities (the "angels" and the monoliths), were present during the same time period while the comet that later violently struck the Earth was visible in the sky.

This engraving detail can have two meanings. The first explanation is temporal. Let us imagine that the stele depicts a timeline running from left to right. In this case we could say that the two winged figures and the two monoliths appeared immediately before the comet swarm, but that the two events overlapped at least for a period. This would explain why one of the two winged beings is seen superimposed on the swarm of snakes/comets.

A second possible meaning, however, is much more disturbing. If the superimposition did not indicate a chronological aspect, the carving seems to mean that a swarm of snakes (in the thin part of the pillar more can be seen), seems to have come from one of the two winged beings. In the latter case, the sculptor believed (rightly or wrongly, but that is not what interests us at the moment), that part of the comet bombardment was caused by these celestial beings. The Vulture Stele, although it starts the "snake" from the two monoliths, and not from the two "angels," basically says the same thing. In the Vulture Stele we can clearly see how the "tail of the great serpent" is bent to one side. In this way the animal seems to come from the symbol of the two monoliths. It would be like saying that the comet originated from those celestial beings. In the Crane Stele, the exact same concept appears. of comets would have been caused or driven by the two winged beings.

Regardless of the cause of the phenomenon, the fact remains that the comet fragments precipitated at that time were absolutely real. Assuming for a moment that the two winged beings must have belonged to legend, and that the same can be said for the two monoliths, what about the rest? Although the conclusion that comets originated from celestial beings may have been their own inference, the details contained in these stelae are too many, and too far removed from the lives of men 12,000 years ago, to be merely the stuff of legend

The little "Ice Age" triggered by the comet impact, the Younger Dryas, generated yet another "reload." The culture

14 - A tale in a stone

that produced Göbekli Tepe disappeared quickly after those events, and we do not know how many others went the same way. We should not forget that Göbekli Tepe was found entirely underground. Who knows how many other similar structures still lie buried, waiting for someone to find them.

PART 8

Dating:

About 12,000 ago to 7,000 years ago

Occurrence:

The desertification of the Sahara

The end of the 'Exiles of Mount Atlas

Involved populations:

Exiles of Mount Atlas

Progenitors of the Egyptians

15 - Desertification of the Sahara

Slowly Earth and the Sapiens recovered from the effects of comet bombardment and the Younger Dryas frost. Unfortunately, the creators of Göbekli Tepe could not survive those events for long. It seems that even in North America, the Clovis culture did not survive. Nan Madol, too, had probably already been abandoned. We do not know how many other cultures came to the same end at that time.

As we saw earlier, the Deglaciation had led in North Africa to the formation of the giant Tamanrasett River, which extended below the Mount Atlas mountain range. The path of the river created a kind of "island" in North Africa. Since the Mount Atlas range was in the middle of this "island," the writer Plato, about 9,000 years later, called this land by the name "Land of Atlas," or "Atlantis." According to him, a thriving civilization, the Atlanteans, developed in this really existing geographical area.

Although the geographical region that corresponds to Atlantis did indeed exist, to date no city or artifacts have been found that can be traced back to Atlantis. The only objective evidence concerns what Plato calls the "Sacred Island" of Poseidon, which must have been located in the vicinity of what was the Tamanrasett River. This island was a large circular natural structure, alternating two "circles" of Earth with three "circles" of sea, and in the centre was a small island. In the entire earth's crust, there is only one natural structure in all respects similar to the one described by Plato, and it is located right next to the path of the Tamanrasett River. In our days, this structure is called the "Eye of the Sahara" or the "Richat Structure."

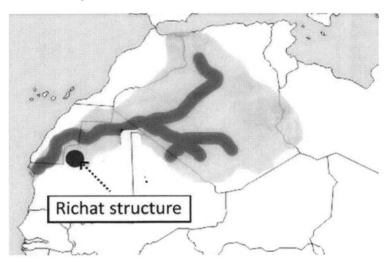

Richat structure

An "eye" in the desert

The Sahara Eye, also known as the "Eye of Africa," is located in Mauritania, in the Sahara Desert. It is a massive geological dome, which lies within a "crater" bordering its edges. Depending on where it is measured from, this crater has an estimated total diameter of 38 to 50 km. The most recent satellite images suggest a diameter of 44 km. For millennia, no one had been aware of its existence. In fact, the Sahara Eye is fully visible as a whole only if the observer is at high altitude, or in space. Viewed from ground level, on the other hand, the "Richat Structure" blends easily with the rest of the landscape. This "eye" was first briefly described by Richard-Molard in 1948. But it was not until 1965, when the crew of the Gemini IV spacecraft took photos from space, that we realized what it actually was.

Seen from space, this structure appears to be formed by a series of concentric rings, strangely precise and regular, spreading outward from the centre. The "rings" are formed by rocks up to two hundred meters high. The different composition of the rocks in the "ridges," compared to the surrounding land that has been eroded, probably caused these "ridges" to appear as a series of circular rings. What is surprising is their symmetry. They are so regular that they look almost "artificial."

At one time, the "Richat Structure" was thought to be a kind of "crater" formed by the impact of a meteorite with the Earth. In fact, the surrounding, outermost walls draw a crater, while a kind of earthen "bubble" rises from the centre of it. But recent surveys have ruled out the possibility that it could be a meteor-type crater. Two Canadian archaeologists have advanced the hypothesis that it is an ancient natural structure. Its formation, according to them, would be similar to that of a "pimple." Due to volcanic activity that occurred underground in what is now the Sahara Eye, the earth would have "swelled" at that spot. But this pressure, over time, ceased without the creation of a volcano. Without the pressure holding it up, this sort of "bubble of earth" would have collapsed in on itself in a perfectly symmetrical manner, giving rise to the characteristic rock rings. The central mound, after a time, would also have collapsed. According to these two scholars, the formation of this "dome" dates to between 94 and 104 million years ago. But this remains a hypothesis to be confirmed.

A 2011 study entitled "Étude paléoenvironnementale des sédiments quaternaires du Guelb er Richât (Adrar de Mauritanie) en regard des sites voisins ou associés du Paléolithique inférieur" concluded that this structure was traversed and shaped by torrential waters. In short, there must have been water there that contributed to the formation of the crater. In addition, there are fossils of brackish water molluscs within the Sahara Eye. The study says, "Numerous radiocarbon dates indicate that part of these sediments accumulated between 15,000 and 7,730 years ago." Based on the sediments, it is likely that a lot of water flowed in the Sahara Eye between 13,000 B.C. and 4,730 B.C., during the Last African Wet Period.

This structure seems to faithfully trace the "Sacred Island" of Poseidon, described by Plato. So let us leave it to Plato himself, from the pages of his dialogue "Critias," to tell us what he thought the civilization that lived at the foot of the Mount Atlas range was like. For ease of reading, we have divided the diverse topics into sections, assigning a subtitle to each section.

Beginning citation -

The source of the tale about Atlantis - If I have not forgotten what I heard when I was a child, I will tell you the character and origin of their opponents. For friends should not keep their stories to themselves but have them in common. However, before I proceed further in the narrative, I would like to warn you that you should not be surprised if you perhaps hear Greek names given to a people of foreigners. I will tell you the reason for this oddity. Solon, who intended to use the narrative for his poetry, investigated the meaning of the names (of the Atlanteans) and found that the early Egyptians, writing them down, had translated them into their own language. Later Solon recovered the meaning of the various names, and translated them into our language, copying them back into the text. My grandfather had these writings, and they are now in my possession. I carefully studied them when I was young. Therefore, if you hear names like those used in this country, you should not be surprised, because I have told you how they were added. The story, which was of great length, begins as follows.

The origins of the "Big Island" of Atlantis - As we said, regarding a lot of the deities who divided the whole Earth into lots, some larger, some smaller, these same deities instituted offerings and sacrifices in their own honour. So did Poseidon, who received the island of Atlantis as his lot. Poseidon established his own human children at the head of a certain place on the island. These were begotten with a mortal woman.

The creation "of the Sacred Island" of Poseidon - In the central part of the [Great] Island, near the sea, there was a plain, which is said to have been the most beautiful ever and was very fertile. At a distance of about nine kilometres (50 stadia), near the plain but in the middle of it, was a small mountain. This mountain was inhabited by one of the first men born there from the earth, whose name was Euenor, and who lived there with his wife named Leucippe. The two had an only daughter, Cleitus. By the time her mother and father died, the girl was old enough to marry. Poseidon, who liked the girl very much, then had relations with her.

Next, he made the hill in which he lived well-fortified. He made it steep all around and made circular belts of sea and land that wrapped around each other. Some were larger, some smaller. Two were of earth and three of sea. He carved them as it were from the centre [of Sacred Island] outward. These belts were at regular distances on all sides, so that they were impassable for man. For at that time there were no boats or navigation.

Poseidon himself then beautified [the Sacred Island] in its central part. He accomplished everything as only a god can. He caused two springs of water to gush out of the earth, one gushing forth hot water, the other cold. He made the earth produce nourishment of all sorts in abundance.

Poseidon begat with Clio five pairs of sons and raised them. After dividing the whole island of Atlantis into ten parts, he assigned to the eldest son of the sons his mother's dwelling and the plot of land surrounding it, which was the biggest and best. In addition, he constituted him king over the other sons. The other sons he constituted rulers, and to each he gave power over a considerable number of men and over a vast territory. He gave them all names. The eldest was called Atlas. From his name was then named the whole [Great] Island and the sea, called Atlantic. The twin brother born after him was called

Gadiro. In Greek, his name was Eumelo, while in the local language it was Gadiro. He had received as his lot the end of the [Great] Island toward the Pillars of Hercules, opposite the region now called Gadirica. From his name the whole region was in fact named.

To the two sons born in the second birth Poseidon gave to the first, the name Amphere and to the second, the name Euhemon. To the third pair of sons he gave the name Mnesea to the one born first, and Autoctone to the one born later. Concerning the fourth pair of sons, Elysippus was the first and Mestore the second. The fifth pair was given the name Azae to the first, and Diaprepe to the second.

All these and their descendants, for many generations lived in Atlantis, exercising command over many other islands in that sea. Moreover, as we mentioned earlier, they ruled regions on this side of the Pillars of Hercules, as far as Egypt and Tyrrhenia (Italy). The lineage of Atlas, therefore, was numerous and honoured, and since it was always the firstborn who passed on power to the firstborn of his sons, they preserved the kingdom for many generations. They were able to amass riches in such quantities as there had never been before in any domain on earth, nor will there easily be in the future. They disposed of everything that was needed in the city and the rest of the country.

Description of the Sacred Island - Due to their rule, many necessary resources came from other countries. But most of the goods useful for the necessities of life were offered by the island itself. First of all, there were all the metals, both hard and metals that can be melted down, which were extracted from the mines. There were also the metals that today are known only by name, but were then more than a name, as there were mines to extract them in many places on the island. Among these should be included orichalcum, which was the most valuable of the metals then known, except gold.

There was an abundance of forests that provided everything needed for carpenters' work. All the produce of the land was abundant, and it fed enough domestic and wild animals. In particular, the elephant species was very numerous in Atlantis. In fact, pastures for animals living in swamps, lakes, and rivers, and so for those grazing on mountains and plains, were all abundant. Equally so were they for this animal, despite being the largest and most voracious of all the others.

To all this we can add the production of the fragrant essences that were found in the land of Atlantis. We can also include roots, shoots, wood, nectar from flowers and fruits. Everything was very abundant. Both cultivated and dried fruit was produced. All species of the product we call grain, which we use to make bread, were present. The woody fruit was present whose nectar we use to make drinks, or fragrant oils. There was also hard-fleshed fruit, used for fun and pleasure, which was difficult to preserve. Also present was the fruit which, as if it were a kind of dessert, we serve after dinner when we are tired of eating. The sacred island offered all these beautiful and wonderful products in endless abundance.

The Island of the Metropolis - Taking therefore from the land all these riches, they built their temples and their royal residences, their harbours, and their docks, and all the rest of their country, ordering everything in the following way. Firstly, bridges made the three maritime strips around the ancient metropolis viable. In this way they formed a way outside, toward the royal palace.

They made the royal palace from the beginning in the residence of Poseidon, and of the ancestors, passing it on as an inheritance from generation to generation. Adding ornaments to ornaments, they always tried to surpass, as far as they could, the predecessor who had owned it. In the end, they produced a dwelling that was extraordinary to behold, both in grandeur and in the beauty of the work.

Starting from the sea that lay beyond the city, they dug a canal that reached to the outermost sea circle, the third. These were the measurements of the channel: ninety meters (three picks) wide, thirty meters (one hundred feet) deep and 9,000 meters (fifty stadia) long. In this way they created on the second circle of land a kind of harbour. They opened a way large enough for the largest ships to pass through, and thus made it their entrance to the sea.

They also cut the two circles of land, which were sandwiched between the three circles of sea, so as to open a channel at the height of the bridges. This channel continued the path of the bridges and led from one circle to the other. It was large enough for a single trireme to pass through. This channel was also covered by a kind of bridge placed at the top so that ships would pass under it. It was possible to do this because the land circles were high enough above sea level.

The largest of the three sea circles, which connected with the open sea via the artificial channel, was 540 meters (three stages) wide, and the land circle next to it was the same width. And regarding the second pair of circles, the sea circle was 360 meters (two stages) wide, and the one made of land was the same size. The sea circle that went around the central island was about 180 meters (one stage) wide.

The island, in which the king's palace was located, was about nine hundred meters (five stadia) in diameter. Now the central island, the various circles, and the bridge, which was about thirty meters (a pick) wide, were surrounded by a stone wall on this side and that side. Defence towers and gates had been built on the bridges on each side of the artificial passage leading through the circles to the sea.

The buildings of Atlantis - And the stone they quarried from under the central island, all around it, and from under the earthen circles, both on the outer and inner sides, were some white, some black, and some red. And as they quarried them, they built two inner docks with these stones, like arsenals, dug into the rock of the place and built with the quarried material.

And about the buildings, some were adorned with stones of one simple colour. In others, however, they mixed ornamental stones, obtaining patterns of many colours. In this way they gave the buildings a natural charm. And they covered the whole circumference of the wall surrounding the outermost circle with brass, as if it were plaster. The inner part was coated with molten tin. The part that enclosed the Acropolis itself, however, was coated with orichalcum, which sparkled like fire.

The royal palace - Within the Acropolis, the royal palace was arranged in this way. The centre, a shrine consecrated to Cleitus and Poseidon, was regarded as "sacred ground," and surrounded by a golden wall. It was there that they originally conceived the lineage of the ten heads of the royal dynasties. To that place they brought from year to year from all ten districts their seasonal offerings to make sacrifices to each of those princes.

The Temple of Poseidon - The Temple of Poseidon was about 180 meters long (one stadium), ninety meters wide (three picks). To look at it, it seemed that its height was symmetrical to the rest of its dimensions. There was something foreign about its appearance. The entire exterior of the temple was clad in silver, except for the pinnacles, which were clad in gold.

Inside, the ceiling was entirely ivory, variegated with gold, silver and orichalcum. The other parts of the temple, namely the walls, columns, and floor, were completely covered with orichalcum. They placed gold statues there, one with Poseidon standing on a chariot while driving six winged horses. The statue of Poseidon was so large that his head touched the ceiling of the temple. All around him were a hundred Nereids on as many dolphins (for that was the number of them as men then believed). And there were also many other images, including ex-votos of private men. And outside, around the temple, there were gold images of all the sons of the kings, both themselves and their wives, as many as there were descendants of the ten kings, along with many other ex-votos, both from the kings and from private men. These came not only from Atlantis, but also from all the foreign peoples over whom they ruled. The altar, because of its size and the refinement of the work done, harmonized with the palace and everything else, and reflected the grandeur of the empire, and the splendour of the temple itself.

The water sources of Atlantis - As for the source of cold water and hot water, they were very abundant, and because of the pleasantness and virtue of the waters, each was extraordinarily suitable for its use. These baths were surrounded by buildings and plantations of trees, as was convenient.

There were separate baths for kings and privates, as well as others for women. Still others for horses and all other beasts of burden, each arranged appropriately. These were located around water cisterns. Some were open-air, others had a cover so that warm baths could be taken in winter. And the water that came out of that spring led to the sacred forest of Poseidon. This contained trees of all sorts, which were beautiful to look at and of considerable height, due to the richness of the soil in which they were planted. By means of canals this water led to the outer circles near the bridges.

Facilities for horses - In each circle of land around the island they had built many temples for the gods, and many gardens. There were also places for exercise, some for men and others, separate, for horses. In addition, in the centre of the larger island was a hippodrome, which was about 180 meters wide (a stadium), while in terms of its length, the track reserved for equestrian competitions ran along the entire circumference of the island.

The arrangement of the guards - And all around, on both sides, were the guardhouses and most of the Spear Bearers. But the garrison for the most trusted guards was placed in the smaller circle of land, which was closer to the Acropolis. In addition, those who had distinguished themselves most in loyalty had quarters inside the Acropolis, around the residence of the kings. The arsenals were filled with triremes and their necessary accessories, all prepared in sufficient quantities. Such was then the state of affairs around the residence of the kings.

The city for the common people-After crossing the three outer circles, there was a wall that started from the outer sea and ran in a circle around the city, an even distance of 9,000 meters (fifty stadia) from both the largest circle and the harbour. This circular wall closed toward the mouth of the canal. Over the entire extent of this wall rested many dwellings, while the canal and harbour teemed with boats. The alleys and streets were so full of merchants coming from all sides, that because of the considerable number they made all kinds of voices and din heard day and night.

The geography of Atlantis - Now, as far as the city and surroundings of Atlantis are concerned, we have completed the description as it was originally given to us. But we must strive to remember, in order to convey the whole narrative, also what the rest of the country was like, its morphology, and how it was organized. According to the narrative, the whole region rose rapidly from sea level, so that it appeared to be sheer to a great height. But the summit, where the city was located, was a large, completely flat place. This plain enclosed the city all around, and in turn was surrounded by mountains that stretched down to the sea.

The plain had a flat surface and had an elongated shape like a rectangle, being 540 kilometres (3,000 stadia) long on both sides, and 360 kilometres (2,000 stadia) wide in the middle and stretching upward from the sea. This part of the island faced south and was sheltered from the northern winds. The mountains that surrounded it were famous at that time, both in number and in size and beauty, and were superior to the mountains that exist today. There were rivers, lakes, and meadows there, capable of feeding all sorts of domestic and wild animals, as well as many wealthy villages with inhabitants. There were numerous forests, inexhaustible in what they could produce.

An artificial water system-Now, as a joint result of the forces of nature and the labours of many kings who undertook to modify it in many ages, the condition of this great plain was as follows. Originally it was a rectangle, mostly straight and elongated, or oblong. Where its outline deviated from the straight line, the plain was straightened by means of a ditch dug all around it. Now, as to the depth of this ditch, its width and length, it seems incredible that it should be as large as we are told. We must not forget that it was done by hand, and in addition to everything else. But we still have to report what we heard. This ditch was dug all around the plain to a depth of thirty meters (one pick) and a uniform width of 180 meters (one stage). And because the ditch was dug all around the plain, it resulted in a length of 1,800 kilometres (ten thousand stadia).

This huge moat received the streams of water that descended from the mountains and caused them to go around the plain. After discharging them toward the city on this side and the other, it made them flow out toward the sea. And toward the inner part of the island, toward the city, straight channels had been dug, about thirty meters wide, cut across the plain. These flowed back into the moat by the sea, at a distance of about eighteen kilometres from each other.

In this way they transported lumber from the mountains to the city. They also transported seasonal agricultural products on boats, creating cross passages from one canal to another to the city. And they ploughed the land twice a year, taking advantage of the rain from the sky in winter and the water that flowed from the earth in summer, using the streams that came from the canals.

Military ordering - As for those who were eligible for military service, each of the lots provided a leader who organized that group. The lot had a size of 1.8 x 1.8 kilometres (ten stages by ten stages). Within the plain, bounded by the moat, there were 60,000 lots.

The number of men living both in the mountains and in the rest of the country was innumerable. According to their districts and villages these people were assigned to the various lots under their respective chiefs. Each of these chiefs was to contribute the sixth part of the equipment of a war chariot to the formation of the army. In this way a total of about 10,000 war chariots could be equipped, together with two horses and their riders. He also had to provide a chariot without a seat and two horses, which had a soldier capable of fighting on foot, and who wielded a small shield. He was also to provide a charioteer for both horses. The contingent was to be completed with two hoplites, two archers, two slingers, three light-armed soldiers capable of throwing stones, and three javelin throwers. To these were added four sailors to complete the crew of the one thousand two hundred ships at their disposal.

Such were then the military arrangements in the capital. Those of the other nine districts varied in many ways, but it would take too long to explain everything in detail.

Political order - As far as magistracies and honours were concerned, each of the ten kings, in his own division and city, had absolute control of the citizens and, in most cases, of the laws. He could punish with capital punishment anyone he wished.

But their mutual rights and duties, and the power they exercised over each other, were governed by the precepts written by Poseidon. These principles were handed down to them from the law and records that had been engraved by the first kings on a column of orichalcum, which was placed inside the temple of Poseidon in the centre of the island.

In that temple the kings would gather every fifth and sixth year alternately, thus giving equal honour to the even and odd number. And when they gathered, they would consult on public affairs. They would ask each other if anyone had transgressed in any way and made an erroneous judgment. And before passing judgment, they would promise each other the following.

In Poseidon's sacred precincts sacred bulls grazed freely. The ten kings, being alone, after praying to Poseidon that they might capture a victim that was to his liking, would go out to hunt these bulls, using sticks and logs, but no iron weapons. Whichever bull they managed to capture, they would carry it up to the pillar of the Law and slit its throat over the top of the pillar, causing the blood to drip onto the inscription that contained their Sacred Law. On the pillar, in addition to their

Basic Law, was an oath that invoked powerful curses on those who broke the covenant of obedience.

After they had offered the sacrifice and consecrated all the bull's limbs, according to the dictates of their laws, they would mix in a bowl some wine and a lump of the bull's blood, poured out on behalf of each person. The rest of the victim they would burn in the fire, after purifying the column all around. Then using golden goblets they would take the wine mixed with the blood out of the bowl and pour part of what they drew as a libation on the fire. They also swore that they would always judge the people according to the sacred laws carved on the pillar and would punish the one who at any time transgressed them.

They also swore that from then on, they would not voluntarily transgress any of the sacred laws, nor would they rule by any edict that was not in accordance with those laws, nor would they submit to any such edict. And when each of them had made this invocation both for himself and for his descendants, he drank part of the chalice of wine mixed with blood, while part offered it as a gift in the temple of Poseidon.

After they had all dined together, when it was getting dark, and while the fire around the sacrifice was still fresh, they all wore beautiful blue robes. During the night, sitting on the ground, having put out all the fires around the temple, the kings would give audience and judgment over the embers of the sacrifices by which they had sworn. And after placing their judgments, at dawn they would write their decisions on a golden tablet, and offer it to the temple, together with their robes, as a memorial.

And there were many other special laws concerning the legal right of the ten kings. The most important were these: they were never to take up arms against each other. In addition, if anyone tried to overthrow their royal house in any city, all the kings were to lend aid as allies. They would always make decisions by mutual agreement, like their forerunners, on politics, war, and other matters, giving supremacy to the royal descendants of Atlas. Finally, the king did not have the authority to put any of his brother princes to death except with the consent of more than half of the ten.

The degradation of Atlantis - The power that Poseidon bestowed in the lost island of Atlantis was vast indeed. And this enormous power was directed against us Greeks for several reasons, if we are to heed the various traditions that have been handed down. As long as the divine nature had the upper hand in the Atlanteans, they were obedient to the laws and remained attached to the will of their god, whose children they were. For they possessed in them true spirits, and that they were in every way great. They combined gentleness with wisdom in the various events of life, and in their dealings with each other. They despised everything but virtue, caring little for their contingent condition in life. They thought lightly of the possession of gold and other goods, which seemed to them to be only a useless burden. They were not intoxicated by luxury, and wealth did not deprive them of their self-control. They were sober people, and they clearly saw that all these goods can increase virtue and friendship with each other. But if one pays too much attention to them, one can even lose friendship with others. Because of these reflections and the permanence of the divine nature in them, the qualities we have described grew and increased among the Atlanteans.

But when the divine quality began to fade in them, and was diluted with the mortal quality, human nature took over. Then, no longer able to bear the weight of their glory, they became ugly to those who are able to observe things intelligently. They lost the most beautiful of their precious gifts. But to the eyes of those who are unable to look at what really makes us happy in life, the Atlanteans appeared even more glorious and blessed, just at the time when they were full of ambition and lawless power.

The punishment of Zeus - And Zeus, the God of gods, who rules according to the Law, and has the gift of perceiving such things, became aware of how this righteous race was in a wicked situation. He therefore wanted to inflict punishment on them so that they could improve themselves. Therefore he gathered all the gods together in that abode which they honour most. When he had gathered them together, standing at the centre of the whole Universe, and observing all things that participate in becoming, he spoke thus: -

- End Quote.

The rest of the dialogue "Critias" remained unfinished or was lost. In the dialogue "Timaeus," however, Plato speaks of a cataclysm that within a brief time, destroyed both the territory of Greece and that of North Africa, where Atlantis stood. In the "Timaeus" it is said:

Quote beginning - "But at a later time there were violent earthquakes and floods. In a single day and night all the [warriors] of Greece sank together into the earth. And the island of Atlantis similarly disappeared into the depths of the sea. That is why the sea in those parts is impassable and impenetrable, because there is a shoal of mud that closes its access. This was created by the subsidence of the island." - *End quote*

Climate change

Regardless of the veracity or otherwise of Plato's account, whatever population lived in North Africa some 11,000 years ago underwent another "reload" at some point in its history. Indeed, climate change gave the Sapiens no respite. Again, in North Africa, the climate was making itself extremely dangerous. About 75,000 years ago it had been the cold that had decimated them to the point of near extinction. Now, about 8,000 years ago, some 4,000 years after the Younger Dryas, North Africa had to deal with the sudden rise in temperature.

As quickly as North Africa had literally filled up with water in the period following the Deglaciation, the exact opposite was now being witnessed. Rapidly, all the freshwater reserves located in North Africa were depleted. The giant lakes dried up. Of the great Tamanrasett River only a memory remained. Its disappearance confused researchers for millennia who wanted to identify the geographic place Plato called Atlantis. And the fertile land where, according to Plato, the Atlanteans built their cities soon became a vast and boundless desert: the Sahara. So, assuming that indeed an advanced population inhabited North Africa some 11,000 years ago, their remains would now lie beneath the sand dunes of the Sahara. Let us analyse this phenomenon in more detail.

Desertification

Recent studies by climatologists have firmly established that the area south of Mount Atlas, that is, the area between present-day Morocco, Algeria, and Tunisia, i.e., the Sahara, has not always been an arid desert. On the contrary, there is a true "climate cycle" concerning North Africa, called the "African Wet Period." This cycle, in alternating phases, has made the Sahara at times a verdant plain full of lakes and animals, and at other times an arid desert as it is today. Several factors influence the cyclical change in the Sahara's climate.

Serbian civil engineer and mathematician Milutin Milanković has proposed a theory in this regard that, although not fully refined, helps to explain the phenomenon. According to this theory, the orbital eccentricity, axial tilt, and precession of Earth's orbit vary periodically due to the gravitational perturbation exerted on Earth by the Moon, and the other more massive planets in the Solar System.

All these interactions induce periodic changes in the Earth's orbit, in which three cycles interact, which although they occur simultaneously have different durations. Thus there would exist a first orbital cycle of 100,000 years, a second orbital cycle of 41,000 years and a third orbital cycle of 20,000 years. All three orbital cycles-known as "Milanković cycles"-affect African climate on long time scales. The most important of these orbital cycles is the phenomenon of "precession," or the oscillation of the tilt of the Earth's axis, which changes cyclically between 22 degrees and 24.5 degrees.

In addition to the Earth's orbital cycles, another key factor in the cyclical mutation of the Sahara's climate is the strength of the African Monsoon. This name is used to identify the humid currents that reach African territory from the South Atlantic. The stronger the African Monsoon is, the greener the Sahara is. At the stage when the African Monsoon is weak, the Sahara tends to dry up. But the variables at play are many, and perhaps not all known.

In addition to "Milanković cycles," other theories have been proposed, all of which are based on more or less the same mechanisms but propose slightly different results from each other. According to Professor David McGee of the Department of "Earth, Atmosphere and Planetary Sciences" at MIT (Massachusetts Institute of Technologies), the Sahara would change its state from "dry and dry" to "green and wet" every 20,000 years or so. According to this theory, the last drying of the Sahara would have occurred about 5,000 years ago, around 3,000 BCE. This would mean that the Sahara should turn green again in about 15,000 years.

Other scholars provide slightly different dates. According to Dr. Kevin White of the University of Reading and Pr. David Mattingly of the University of Leicester, whose thoughts are contained in the paper "The Lakes of the Sahara," it would appear that "over the past 10,000 years there have been two distinct wet phases [in the Sahara], separated by an interval of highly variable, but generally drying, conditions sometime between 8,000 and 7,000 years ago. Another drying trend occurred about 5,000 years ago, leading to today's arid environment."

Their paper contains a whole series of dates of the alternations of dry and wet periods, which can be summarized as follows: (the outline is obviously very simplified).

> 400,000 BC to 70,000 BC. - Predominantly wet and verdant Sahara, with the creation of huge lakes
>
> 70,000 BC to 12,500 BC. - Dry and desert Sahara
>
> 12,500 BC to 8,000 BC. - Wet and green Sahara
>
> 8,000 BC to 7,000 BC. - Dry and desert Sahara
>
> From 7,000 B.C. to 3,000 B.C. - presence in the Sahara of the sub-pluvial, humid, verdant Neolithic climate
>
> From 3,000 BC to the present day - Dry and desert Sahara

After the Great Lakes had dried up, and after the Tamanrasett River had completely disappeared, what happened to the people who lived at the foot of Mount Atlas? They too, like the inhabitants of Sundaland did millennia earlier, became true "environmental refugees." The "exiles of Mount Atlas" headed for the only major source of fresh water available, the Nile River. They then became the "Zero Dynasty," from which the Egyptians would later arise.

16 - The 'Mount Atlas Exiles'

In analysing Egyptian history, it is evident that their civilization did not start completely "from scratch." Some of the greatest masterpieces of Egyptian civilization were created when this people were just at the beginning of its development. It thus becomes quite evident that the "early Egyptians" relied on the technology of someone who lived in the same geographical area before them. Let us give a few examples.

Based on the reconstruction of history made by Egyptologists, the "Step Pyramid of Djoser" is a kind of "touchstone" for all pyramids found in Egypt. This is the first pyramid of which we are reasonably certain to know the builder, the client and the period of construction. It was built on the orders of Pharaoh Djoser, based on the design of his famous official Imhotep, around 2,630 BCE. On this pyramid, therefore, everyone is in rather good agreement.

The Djoser pyramid has a stepped structure 62 meters high, and with a base of 109 × 125 meters. This means that its faces are not smooth but are like remarkably high steps that continue to the top. It is a rather crude pyramid and not very difficult to build. Recent examinations of the internal structure of Djoser's pyramid indicate that its construction was progressive, and was done by repeatedly expanding, in successive periods of time, a "mastaba," the classical Egyptian tomb. At an early stage, the "mastaba" in question was enlarged three times horizontally. Later it was enlarged vertically, adding several "terraces" on the mastaba itself, making it into a small, stepped pyramid. At a still later time this small pyramid was expanded until it became what we see today. According to the story in vogue today, on a trip to Elephantine, a certain Imhotep, servant of Pharaoh Djoser, allegedly saw the small pyramid, and urged his lord to make a much larger one. We find ourselves around 2,630 BCE.

Until a few years ago, it was believed that this was the first ever pyramid to be built on Egyptian soil. According to scholars, all other pyramids located in Egypt are later than that of Djoser and could be considered as "evolutions" of this ancient pyramid. But is this really the case? Was Djoser's pyramid really the first pyramid to appear in Egypt? Can all the other pyramids really be considered an "evolution" of the "Step Pyramids"?

On the basis of this reasoning, any pyramid that, hypothetically, would be on Egyptian soil but would turn out to be "earlier" than the "Step Pyramid of Djoser," built around 2,630 BCE. , could not be considered "Egyptian" in the sense we give that term today. It would have been built by someone who came before the pharaohs. The pharaohs, therefore, would have merely "taken" possession of it, making it appear as "their stuff." Did things turn out that way? Let us give some examples based on the latest findings of science.

The mystery of the temple of Qasr-el-Sagha

In recent years we have had to completely reconsider "who" and "when" built the temple of Qasr-el-Sagha. This temple, located about one hundred kilometres south of Cairo in the Lake Fayyum area, was until a few years ago considered by many archaeologists to have been built by a "New Kingdom" pharaoh around 1400 BCE. But it is now realized that the archaeologists were completely wrong on this point. In a survey using the method of "Optically Stimulated Luminescence (OSL)," carried out by the Department of Archaeometry of the University of the Aegean, Greece, it was found that the limestone rock of the temple of Qasr-el-Sagha may date as far back as 5550 B.C. (mean date: 4700 ± 850 B.C.).

This formidable discovery tells us that that temple was built between 1,200 and 3,000 years before Djoser's Pyramid. This is far too great an interval of time to consider the temple of Qasr-el-Sagha as belonging to "the Old Kingdom" of the Egyptians. But if it is now certain that the Egyptians did not build it, then who did?

The very ancient "Little Pyramid"

Let's take another example. In a survey using the "Optically Stimulated Luminescence (OSL)" method, carried out by the Department of Archaeometry of the University of the Aegean, Greece, it was found that the Pyramid of Menkaure, one of the three famous pyramids of Giza, commonly dated around 2,500 B.C., is centuries or millennia older than once believed. Red granite used to cover the base of the facade of the Small Pyramid (Pyramid of Menkaure), examined with this modern dating system returns 4,400 B.C. as the earliest date (Mean date 3450 ± 950 B.C.). Even if the earliest date is excluded and the mean date (3450 B.C.) is taken into account, the pyramid would be at least 1,000 years older than the traditional dating. That block of granite has been located on the Small Pyramid

16 - The 'Mount Atlas Exiles'

(Pyramid of Menkaure) since between 1,000 and 2,000 years before Cheops!

It also takes as the "birth date" of the unified Egypt of pharaohs 3,100 BCE, when Narmer, the first pharaoh of united Egypt, was crowned. With this dating, the Pyramid of Menkaure turns out to be older than the oldest known Egyptian pharaoh. It is therefore a scientific fact, proven in the laboratory, that the Small Pyramid (Pyramid of Menkaure) has nothing to do with any Egyptian pharaoh. This is no longer an opinion: it is a fact proven by science.

But that is not all. It must be remembered that the granite placed on the outer layer of the Small Pyramid (Pyramid of Menkaure) is only the "last stone" of the construction. So the beginning of the pyramid's construction must be backdated in time. By exactly how much? Examining the Small Pyramid (Pyramid of Menkaure), scholars give for certain that it contained another pyramid inside it, on which the one we see today was built. This means that a smaller pyramid was first built, which was later enlarged into what we now call the "Pyramid of Menkaure." This "inner pyramid" is therefore necessarily older, perhaps by centuries or millennia, than the one we all admire today.

For all these reasons, a date close to the earliest (prior to 4,400 BCE) seems to be the one to be preferred regarding the construction of the Small Pyramid (Pyramid of Menkaure). But it is clear that it cannot have been the Egyptian pharaohs who built it, since at that time their dynasty had not even begun. In fact, it was probably not even the Egyptians we know today who were in control of that land at that time.

The Sphinx perpetually under the sand

The Sphinx is a stone colossus in the centre of a "basin" enclosed on three sides, particularly on the back side and the two sides. It is clear from the latest research that it was originally a "yardang" that was shaped to be a kind of parallelepiped with a head. It had no front legs, no hind legs, and no tail part. Nor did it have the classic "Egyptian headdress," which was added only much later. It therefore did not represent a lion, but most likely depicted a female deity.

But this is not the most interesting aspect. Since sand in Egypt has been moved continuously by the wind over the past millennia, under normal conditions the wind carries the sand into the "basin" of the Sphinx, filling it completely. The sand then covers the entire "basin" up to the height of the statue's neck, whose head is roughly at the height of the surrounding ground. Under normal conditions, therefore, the Sphinx's head remains the only visible part of the statue.

This was in fact the condition in which the Sphinx was found in the 19th century, completely buried in the sand except for the head. It was archaeologists who dug it up and showed it to us as we see it today. If we even see the Sphinx's body today, it is only because of the maintenance work that is continuously being done on the grounds. With this in mind, it is extremely unlikely that the builders of the Sphinx decided to use a "yardang" as a rock to carve when it was already covered with sand. The builders would have deduced that even if they shovelled the sand away, it would reappear punctually in a brief time.

The simplest and most plausible explanation is that, evidently, when it was decided to use a "yardang" to make a statue there, the area around the rock was not at all covered with sand as it is today. This would explain in a simple and reasonable way why the builders did not consider the possibility that the sand might invade the "pool" and bury the Sphinx. Sand at that time simply did not exist! So sand was not a problem to be considered.

This reasoning, shifts the decision to use the "yardang" that was in Giza to make a statue, to a time when the Sahara was green, and sand was not a problem, the so-called "African Wet Period." At that time, the "yardang" that was located near Giza, and overlooking the Nile, was turned into a statue, the "first Sphinx." So the original statue cannot have been carved by the pharaohs. The "original Sphinx" may have predated the pharaohs by as much as 10,000 years. What the pharaohs did instead was to add the legs, tail, headdress, and "stubble" (which later collapsed) to the original statue.

The "regress" of the pyramids

According to many archaeologists, the vast majority of the Egyptian pyramids, about sixty of them, or two-thirds of the total, would have been built during the "Old Kingdom," that is, at the dawn of Egypt, between 2630 BCE and 2190 BCE. These first sixty pyramids (including the smaller pyramids, or "satellite" pyramids), which include the largest Egyptian pyramids of all time, according to many archaeologists should have been built during a rather limited period of time: about 400 years.

Doing two quick calculations, we understand that we are saying that that ancient population built a pyramid every 6-7 years, without ever stopping. Honestly, that seems a pace not only excessive, but probably impossible to maintain for a population of that time. Indeed, while the "New Kingdom" Egyptians knew, for example, about iron and the use of the wheel for transportation, this knowledge was completely absent in the "Old Kingdom" Egyptians. How could those populations, without the knowledge of the wheel and iron, build a pyramid every 6 to 7 years?

This would mean that most of a nation's financial resources, human resources and workforce would have been constantly directed to building the pyramids. But what nation, past or present, can afford the luxury of using all its resources only for monument construction? And who would have taken part in the army, the cultivation of fields, fishing, and all the other activities that keep a nation on its feet? Indeed, it should not be forgotten that Old Kingdom Egypt consisted of only a few hundred thousand inhabitants, perhaps a million at most. The adult male labour force, therefore, was limited. Building sixty pyramids over the course of four hundred years seems to be beyond their actual capabilities.

In the next 2,000 years of Egypt's history as an independent nation, perhaps only about 30 pyramids were built. We can thus see the numerical disproportion between the "ancient" and later pyramids. The "ancient" Egyptians, with less building skills, less workforce, and fewer economic resources, would have built the most impressive pyramids, and in large numbers. Conversely, the "later" Egyptians, despite having superior technology, more workforce, and more economic resources, built very few pyramids and all of inadequate quality. This makes no sense and is not supported by any logic.

This first analysis of the facts makes us ask: but is it really possible that the first sixty pyramids in Egypt's history were all built in the four hundred years "of the Old Kingdom"? Is the first Egyptian pyramid really the pyramid of Djoser, built in 2630 BC? Or is it more logical to think that at least some of the pyramids found in Egypt were built in the "dark period" of thousands of years that preceded Narmer, the first pharaoh of the united kingdom of Egypt, crowned in 3150 BCE? If so, those pyramids could not be considered "Egyptian" in the common sense of the term. That is, they would not have been the result of the pharaohs and their people, but of someone who was there before them. Logic and the latest findings of science lead us to believe that several of the pyramids attributed to "the Old Kingdom" actually predate Djoser's pyramid, and consequently cannot be considered "Egyptian."

The nòmes of Lower Egypt

When can the first settlements by the "exiles of Mount Atlas" in Egypt be traced back to? Not much is known about the history of that area in the period before the pyramids. The climate change that turned a verdant area into a desert must have "buried" the past of that people under the immense sand dunes.

Before unified Egypt was formed, the Rostau (Giza) area was known to the Pharaohs as Ta-Mehu, whereas we commonly call that area by the name "Lower Egypt." This part of the country was divided into "nomo," or provinces, which were almost entirely autonomous. Each "nomo" was ruled by a monarch (or provincial governor) who answered directly to the pharaoh of Lower Egypt. There were twenty "nomo" in Lower Egypt (while there were twenty-two in Upper Egypt), and the main one of these was Aneb-Hetch, where the capital Memphis was later built. In time this city became the capital of the whole of Egypt. The history of Memphis seems to begin around 3100 BC with King Menes (or Narmer) who unified Egypt. Conversely, the history of Lower Egypt understood as a "kingdom" is traced back to 3600 BC.

But the history of "nòmi" can go back even further. In fact, according to several studies, the drying up of the Sahara is thought to have begun in parts of North Africa as early as 6,000 BC. The lack of water pushed many Saharan peoples into a veritable "environmental migration" in search of a water-rich area. Most of the North African peoples who migrated eastward found this "water source" in the Nile River and settled there. So it is entirely likely that the first "nòmi" were formed as early as the Neolithic period, probably before 6000 BC. The Rostau (Giza) area, therefore, was already inhabited by these "environmental exiles" millennia before the date when the construction of the pyramids is commonly indicated to have begun.

A vanished ancient people

All of this suggests that before the "Old Kingdom" of the Egyptians began, before Egypt was unified in 3,100, Giza already had a probably multi-thousand-year history behind it. On May 30, 2017, a study titled "Ancient Egyptian mummy genomes suggest an increase of Sub-Saharan African ancestry in post-Roman periods" was published in the journal Nature Communications, which can be translated as, "Ancient Egyptian mummy genomes suggest an increase of Sub-Saharan African ancestry in post-Roman periods." This study, using DNA recovered from more than a hundred Egyptian mummies, sought to determine what ancestry the ancient Egyptians were from.

The results tell us that at least as early as 1500 B.C. the ancient Egyptians were mostly from the Middle Eastern areas, and not from Black Africa. It was only later, after the Roman conquests, that the population acquired many people from southern Africa. You can see this very well if you look closely at the statues of the pharaohs. Practically none of them have African features. They all seem to have European, or Middle Eastern features.

Further confirmation that the "exiles of Mount Atlas" were probably more "European" than "African" can be had by consulting ancient historical documents. Lanzarotto Malocello was, among other things, an Italian explorer of the Republic of Genoa. He is regarded as the discoverer of the Canary Islands, which lie across from Morocco in the Atlantic Ocean. In fact, in 1312 AD. Lanzarotto Malocello landed on an island that was later named after him: Lanzarote, in the Canary Islands. As we saw earlier, it is likely that this group of islands was part of what Plato called the "empire of Atlantis," which included a "Big Island," a mainland area and other smaller islands. The Canary Islands, and other archipelagos that before the Deglaciation were located between Mauritania and Spain, may be included among these "smaller islands."

The original people who inhabited the Canary Islands before the arrival of Europeans are known as the "Guanches People," now extinct. The term "Guanches" is derived from the native term "Guanchinet," which literally means "inhabitant of Tenerife." The term, in fact, is composed of Guan (meaning in the local language "person or inhabitant"), and Chinet (the original name of the island we call "Tenerife"). From a DNA analysis carried out on some Guan remains by researchers, it would appear that the humans to whom the analysed remains belonged arrived on the island at least 6,000 years ago. Of course, there can be no absolute certainty as to who the owners of those remains were since they have not been alive for centuries.

In fact, there is nothing to deny that prior to the Guanches, there were other peoples on those islands, who have since completely disappeared. In fact, the Roman historian Pliny the Elder, quoting the king of Mauritania, Juba II, wrote about an expedition that took place on the Canary Islands, around 50 BC. According to him, the explorers found only the ruins of large buildings, but the places appeared uninhabited. What large buildings was Juba II referring to? The Guanches in this respect were more like "cave dwellers" than "Roman" citizens, since many of them inhabited natural caves, or dug artificial ones in the tuff.

16 - The 'Mount Atlas Exiles'

The Canary Islands were visited by a number of peoples in recorded history, including the Numids, Phoenicians, Carthaginians, and then the Romans. It is therefore possible that there was some "contamination." But when the Spanish conquered the Canary Islands, they found no evidence of the ability of the local inhabitants, the Guanches, to build or use boats of any kind. This is indeed peculiar for a people living on islands. If this were true, the Guanches would have lived as "prisoners," locked up in water walls, until 1312 AD. From this we can see that until that year, both their ethnicity and customs remained quite similar to those they had when their ancestors somehow landed in the Canary Islands.

A second aspect that leads us to believe that until 1312 A.D. the Guanches did not mix extensively with other peoples is the description of them by both the Romans, who visited those islands, and the Spaniards. They are described as a white-skinned people with blond or reddish hair, blue or grey eyes, very tall and strong. The women were extremely beautiful. Some Spanish-era paintings that have come down to us confirm these characteristics. A white-skinned population settled in the sea opposite North Africa, the "dark continent" par excellence, is not a common thing at all.

The white complexion, especially at that time, would immediately suggest a Northern European, perhaps Viking, origin. Yet DNA tests carried out on samples belonging to the Guanches, and analysis of their writing system, made it clear that this was largely a population derived from the "Berbers," who settled in North Africa, the region from which the "exiles of Mount Atlas" came. According to DNA tests, this is the same population that existed in Egypt before the Romans occupied those lands. Thus, what Plato called the "Atlanteans," the ancestors of the "Guanches," and the actual builders of the first pyramids who arrived in Egypt because of the desertification of the Sahara, were largely the same people, now gone.

17 - Technology of the 'Exiles'

What level of technology did the "exiles of Mount Atlas," or as Plato called them, the "Atlanteans," possess. Obviously, no artifacts have been found that are with certainty attributable to them. But by analysing some structures found in Egypt that can reasonably be associated with their work, we can get an idea.

Djoser's collection

Less than a kilometre away from the Saqqara Serapeum, about thirty meters below Pharaoh Djoser's "Step Pyramid," lies another question mark in history that still has no certain answer. It is probably the first art collection in history. It seems that Pharaoh Djoser, who lived around 2,800 B.C., collected 40,000 vases in one of his private collections. This collection also includes the famous "schist disc," one of the most enigmatic artifacts in history. Pharaoh probably collected all these "wonders" so that they would not be lost. So we only know the date when the collection was made, around 2,800 B.C., but we do not know for sure either what era these vessels belong to or who created them. In all probability they may be among the remains of the "exiles of Mount Atlas."

They are undoubtedly the finest and most artistic objects ever found up to that time. But it is not only their great beauty that attracts attention. Before explaining what the uniqueness of these objects consists of, let us recall how we humans usually produced our vessels. First of all, when it comes to artistic vessels (for example, amphorae with elongated necks, or with very thin and finely worked edges) we have always used the most ductile and malleable material possible. We have used alabaster, clay, terracotta, or even expert glassmakers have used glass still liquid to be worked by blowing. This is necessary because only with extremely malleable material can the most artistic and refined decorations be made. In addition, we used some kind of wheel that served as a lathe. The clay, for example, turning on the lathe, gradually took shape and became a vase with a circular base.

Many of the vessels in "Djoser's Collection" are made of alabaster, a soft stone that is easy to work with. Others, however, are made of granite or diorite. On the Mohs Scale (which describes the hardness of stones) diorite is in the 6 - 7 position. To get an idea of what hardness this is, just see that on this scale steel is in the 4 - 4.5 position. This means that a steel tip cannot scratch diorite. Of course, we are not talking about strength, but hardness. If we take a steel hammer and hit the diorite, we will smash it without much trouble.

In fact, in our days to work granite artistically, sculptors use steel chisels of many sizes to detach small pieces of the block to be worked. In this way they slowly give the block the desired shape. But while this method may work for making a statue, it certainly cannot work for a vase. This is because although the outside of the vase could theoretically be worked in this way (but to give the perfect roundness one would have to be a "Michelangelo"), this becomes materially impossible when trying to work the inside of the vase. The narrower the neck of the vase, the more impossible it becomes to carve the inside of a granite or diorite vase. To work the inside of a hard stone vase that way requires a lathe and circular brushes made of quartz or diamond that gradually wear away the diorite. But the Egyptians of 2,800 B.C. had none of this. Also, for vessels with very narrow necks, or with a very wide "belly" compared to the neck of the vessel, this system would not work either.

In fact, it is not an opinion, but a fact, that after Djoser's "collection," Egypt for at least 1,000 years (and according to other researchers for an even longer period of time) failed to produce similar diorite vessels. There is no find after Djoser that can even remotely compare to the vases he collected. So it is clear that it was not Old Kingdom artists who produced them, otherwise they would have continued to do so.

The more time passes, the stronger the idea becomes that Pharaoh Djoser, in a sense, was the first "archaeologist" in history. Evidently during that period of time, there were artifacts in Egypt with exceptional artistic workmanship, the remains of a people who had lived before the Egyptians, and whose remains were lying around in the desert. Djoser had the undeniable merit of realizing the artistic importance of that treasure abandoned in the sand, and he ensured that at least 40,000 pieces were saved, storing them thirty meters below the surface of his pyramid.

With the exception of the "diorite vases" found at Saqqara, it appears that the earliest documented use of diorite in antiquity is the stele containing the famous "Code of Hammurabi," dated around 1750 BCE or at a later date. (But the artifact is not Egyptian, and the dating is not certain.) We thus note that there is a leap of more than a thousand years between the "diorite vessels" from Saqqara, and the stele containing

Hammurabi's codex. In addition to this, while the slab containing Hammurabi's codex is a single piece, the "diorite vessels" number in the thousands. The technique used for a single diorite slab, the processing of which could take months or years, cannot be replicated for the processing of vases numbering thousands of pieces. For those who made those pots, working with diorite was something commonplace, like working with clay for us today. But this should be objectively impossible, because clay can be made ductile, diorite cannot (or at least, we cannot).

According to many researchers, the working of diorite using the means possessed by the Egyptians, namely through tools made of wood (or copper) and quartz powder, would not be sufficient to produce the diorite vessels found under the Djoser Pyramid. Even assuming that Egyptian artisans armed themselves with "holy patience" to use quartz powder in their workmanship, how would they have made the inner cavity of these vessels? Technically speaking, the hollow part inside the vase could not be larger than the diameter of the neck of the vase itself. So how to explain the "hollow belly" of the diorite vases? Also, with what equipment was the quartz used that shaped the handles, the "petals" possessed by some of the vases, and all the little structures that we are used to seeing in a vase made of molten glass, but that would really be almost impossible to make with a rock harder than steel. And all this in series--and also, with what "tip" did they make the exceptionally fine carvings? (Some say that, at least in some cases, a 0.12 millimetre bit was used.) And how did they make almost perfectly circular surfaces?

To many scholars, it seems evident that those who were able to mass-produce these kinds of vessels had some "secret" in working with diorite, some kind of knowledge that has been lost over time. One could hardly explain the vast production of diorite vessels in any other way.

The "Serapeum" of Saqqara

The hand of the "exiles of Mount Atlas" is not only evident in Giza, but also reaches to Saqqara, the necropolis located in Egypt 30 km south of the modern city of Cairo. This trace can be seen in a structure named the "Serapeum." Not even archaeologists can indicate who built the Serapeum, and for what it was used. The oldest burials found at this site are attributed to the reign of Amenhotep III, the ninth pharaoh of the 18th Dynasty, who reigned during 1350 B.C. But there seems to be no direct connection between the "Serapeum" and this pharaoh.

The "official version" teaches that tombs for "sacred bulls" (hence the name "serapes," which connects to the sacred bull "Apis") were located at this site. How did they come to this conclusion? Since a series of nearby galleries, called "Lesser Galleries," were used by the Egyptians to bury sacred bulls, some archaeologists have advanced the hypothesis that the Serapeum's huge sarcophagi were also designed to house dead bulls. This would also seem to be partly justified by the enormous size of the burials. But with the exception of a few ox bones found in one of the granite parallelepipeds, no finds have been made that would confirm this theory, and the space inside each parallelepiped is enormously larger than the body of a bull. In addition, while the Lesser Galleries is a crude structure, the Great Serapeum Gallery is meticulous in every detail. Thus they look like two completely different structures, built by different hands and for two completely different purposes.

Observing the inside of the parallelepipeds, both the open ones and the closed ones, it was found that no one, neither human being nor animal, has ever been buried in there. So the "field test" tells us that they are not graves. But besides this "funerary" hypothesis, no other possibilities are advanced by archaeology. Beyond that, darkness falls on the Serapeum. Let us try to figure it out.

What is actually the Serapeum? It is a series of tunnels that draw an underground structure. (Some say it is even a multilevel structure, of which only the first level is accessible to the public. In fact, the man who discovered the site, Auguste Mariette, told that there was another tunnel that could not be entered for security reasons. But that gallery, at least officially, was never later found again.) The total structure is just under three hundred meters wide, is located completely underground, and consists of an irregular path. The width of the tunnel varies from place to place, but in general it is about three meters wide, while the average height is just over five meters. Although it took many years to create this series of tunnels, there are no signs of smoke caused by flashlights on the walls and ceiling, and there do not appear to be any spaces with which to let light in from the outside, even with a play of mirrors. It would appear that the workers worked completely in the dark unless they were able to use some kind of artificial fluorescence to get the necessary light. Or even some form of electric lighting.

In several places, on the sides of the various tunnels, there are large "niches" carved into the rock, located on both sides, an average of 6-8 meters deep. In particular, in the area east of the Serapeum there is a tunnel with 12 "niches" located on both sides. The floor of the "niches" is not on the same level as the floor of the tunnel, but is located at a lower level, about 1 to 2 meters below it. So to enter the niches one has to jump, to land about two meters below. The total height of each niche is about 6 to 7 meters.

Huge "parallelepipeds" were placed in many, but not all, of these niches. It seems that only three of these giant objects have hieroglyphs engraved on them, but they are of inadequate quality and absolutely inaccurate. According to many, these hieroglyphs are a clumsy attempt to associate these giant parallelepipeds with Egyptian civilization. But the attempt is poorly successful and has had the opposite effect.

These "parallelepipeds" are called "sepulchres" by many, but it is a fact that they were found completely empty and there is no hint that they were graves. (There are those who claim that Mariette's notes said that the archaeologist found the remains of a mummy of human features, and only some remains of ox bones. But today these notes cannot be found. So there is no way to confirm or deny this rumour). Therefore, not being sure that they are sepulchres, it is more correct to call them by the term "parallelepipeds." It seems that a total of twenty-four of these parallelepipeds were found in the "Serapeum" (according to others, twenty-five were found instead). Some of these parallelepipeds, no more than three, were not found while lying in one of the niches but seemed to have been hastily "abandoned" in the corridors of the tunnel (At least a couple of them are still visible today in the same position in which "someone" left them there, abandoned, despite their enormous weight).

Like the parallelepiped in the "King's Room" of the Great Pyramid, many of these parallelepipeds were carved from a single block of granite. Others were carved from single blocks of gabbro-diorite, granodiorite, syenite porphyry and diorite. All the parallelepipeds thus have in common that they were made from a single block of awfully hard rock, with a hardness between 6 and 7 on the Mohs hardness scale, a hardness higher than that of steel.

Externally, the average measurements of a parallelepiped are the following: length about 3.85 meters, width about 2.32 meters, and height about 2.32 meters. The interior dimensions are the following: length about 3.17 meters, width about 1.46 meters, and height about 1.73 meters. The longitudinal walls of the parallelepiped are forty centimetres thick, the bottom about forty centimetres, and the transverse walls are about thirty centimetres. The dimensions of the various parallelepipeds vary from each other, but they are still huge measurements. In each of these parallelepipeds four adult men could lie side by side.

Being granite or similar rocks, whose weight is about 2.8000 kilograms per square meter, it is estimated that the original blocks from which the parallelepipeds were quarried weighed on average about 30 to 50 tons, depending on size. Subtracting from this weight the inner part that was hollowed out, the total weight of which is about twenty tons, the various parallelepipeds should weigh an average of 10 to 30 tons each, depending on size.

Each of the parallelepipeds has a kind of "lid," whose average measurements are the following: length about 3.85 meters, width about 2.32 meters, height about 0.91 meters. Each lid, made of the same material as the parallelepiped on which it rests, should weigh on average about twenty-five tons or more, depending on size. According to some estimates, the largest parallelepipeds, together with their lids, can weigh as much as 50 to 70 tons. As a comparison of the difficulties involved in lowering one of these parallelepipeds two meters into the "recess," one need only recall that the elevators on modern aircraft carriers used to get fighter-bombers up and down from the flight deck to the interior area of the ship can lift only forty tons of weight.

The mystery of these structures lies precisely in their size, their weight, and the very narrow spaces in which they were arranged. The Serapeum tunnels are only slightly larger than the parallelepipeds. Inside the tunnels there would have been only forty centimetres left and right manoeuvring space to move these containers. So how would they hold them up to move them? Not to mention the difficulty of lowering objects of such weight into the niches, having no room to build cranes, scaffolding, or whatever helped them lift such a huge weight. If they had been moved by sled, or on carts, the marks would still be present at their bases today. The difficulty of moving the parallelepipeds inside the Serapeum is so great that many have brought up "magnetic levitation" with "superconductors" to explain it. Conversely, it is really not understood how they managed to move those extremely heavy containers inside such narrow spaces. There are no other theories to that effect. Were the "exiles of Mount Atlas" able to do such things? We may never know.

Geopolymers

What is a geopolymer? "Geopolymer" refers to a category of synthetic materials based on aluminosilicates that can potentially be used in many areas, but especially as a replacement for Portland cement. Simply put, a geopolymer is a kind of "synthetic rock" that can be created at room temperature with relative ease. It seems that in the modern era, the first to create "geopolymers" were Russian scientists in the ΄50s, although they called them by the name of "soil cements." But they were not the ones who discovered "geopolymers." Today we understand that this material comes to us from the distant past.

Professor Michel Barsoum is a world-renowned scientist, a leader in research on the design of materials developed from ceramics, holder of the A. W. Grosvenor at Drexel University. He received the 2020 International Ceramic Materials Award from the World Academy of Ceramics. According to Professors Michel Barsoum and Gilles Hug (of the National Aerospace Research Agency), the covering of the Great Pyramid of Giza (not the limestone covering that covered it and was removed, but what is underneath it) would consist of two types of stone: one from the limestone quarries, as has always been believed. The other, however, was artificially created by man on site. Part of this cover, in fact, would consist of geopolymers. Their study was published in the Journal of American Ceramic Society . So a material believed to have been first synthesized by the Russians in the '50s is actually at least 5,000 years older. This is not an opinion: these are laboratory-proven facts.

How come the researchers are so certain? One of them said, "Until recently it was difficult for geologists to distinguish between natural limestone and a geopolymer, which is an artificially created limestone. But with advances in science made even in the field of chemistry, thanks to modern equipment, this difference is now apparent." The two professors compared small fragments taken from the pyramid with others taken from the quarries, using X-rays, a plasma flashlight, and an electron microscope. The scholars found "evidence of a rapid chemical reaction that did not allow natural crystallization. The reaction would be inexplicable if the stones had been extracted from a quarry of natural origin. But this reaction would be perfectly understandable if it were accepted that it was a kind of cement."

But before Professor Michel Barsoum, another famous scholar had been claiming for at least 30 years that part of the limestone blocks used to build the Great Pyramid were geopolymers, that is, artificial rock. Joseph Davidovits is a French chemist who inaugurated a new branch of Chemistry, "Geopolymer Chemistry," and for this he was awarded the "Ordre national du Mérite" by the French President. Professor Joseph Davidovits was the first to express the idea that the blocks of rock used by some past peoples, including the builders of the pyramids, might actually be geopolymers, i.e., "synthetic" rocks built on site. In September 1982, the professor had proposed an experiment. Using substances and materials that would also have been available in ancient Egypt at the time of the pyramids, he had "constructed" a geopolymer identical to a block used in the construction of the pyramids, weighing about one ton.

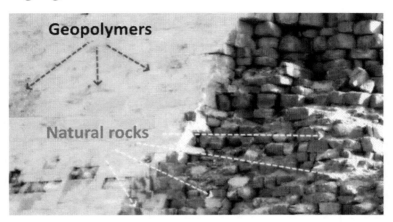

The experiment performed had been rather simple. A small pool about 4 x 4 meters had been made, and it had been filled with water to a certain level. Two types of material had been poured into the pool: red sandstone and natron (sodium carbonate decahydrate), and everything had been mixed thoroughly. After evaporating the water, a kind of mud had been left in the pool. With containers this mud had been poured into some wooden forms and pressed with mortars. After a while, the forms had been removed, and the mixture had been left to dry in the sun.

After a few hours, a block of limestone rock had been obtained that was apparently identical to that extracted from a quarry. The idea of building geopolymers directly on site in the shape of approximately 1-ton blocks of stone, rather than moving blocks of similar weight from quarries, thus seems to have been successfully tested by Professor Joseph Davidovits. According to the professor, this was essentially the way the builders built at least part of the pyramids, bringing the material in the form of topsoil directly to the place where the block was to be placed, and building it "in situ."

But the Great Pyramid of Giza was not the only one to have been built in part with the help of geopolymers. Until recently it was believed that the Rhomboidal Pyramid was made, like most other pyramids, of common limestone rocks, brought up to the construction site in some way. There seemed to be nothing more to say on this subject. There was only one detail that puzzled everyone. The rocks of the outer facing of this pyramid are not similar to regular bricks laid on top of each other. Rather, the outer facing of this pyramid is composed of irregular, trapezoidal-shaped bricks, but they fit perfectly into each other, creating a kind of "jigsaw puzzle." No one could understand how the engineers of that time managed to create this kind of construction.

On July 14, 2011, an article appeared in the prestigious scientific periodical "Materials Letters" entitled "Were the casing stones of Senefru's Bent Pyramid in Dahshour cast or carved? Multinuclear NMR evidence," which can be translated as "Were the casing stones of Snefru's Bent Pyramid in Dahshour cast or carved? Multinuclear NMR evidence." This paper bears the signatures of a team of internationally renowned scholars, including Pr. Kenneth J.D. MacKenzie (professor of the MacDiarmid Institute for Advanced Materials and Nanotechnology, Victoria University of Wellington, New Zealand), Professors Mark E. Smith, Alan Wong, John V. Hanna (from the Department of Physics, University of Warwick, Coventry, CV4 7Al, UK), Pr. Bernard

Barry (of the Institute of Geological and Nuclear Sciences, Lower Hutt, New Zealand), and Pr. Michel W. Barsoum (of the Department of Materials Science and Engineering, Drexel University, Philadelphia).

The main point of their research says, "The NMR results suggest that the stones of the [Bent Pyramid] cladding are made of limestone granules from the Tura quarry, cemented with an amorphous calcium silicate gel formed by human intervention, with the addition of additional silica, possibly diatomaceous earth, from the Fayyum area." Briefly, the study asserts, bringing as evidence an awfully long series of chemical and petrographic analyses, that the lining of the Rhomboid Pyramid is not made of limestone, but of geopolymers, or synthetic rock.

Why it was preferred to create geopolymers to build the outer covering of the Rhomboid Pyramid rather than using classical rocks is an as-yet-unresolved mystery. Only hypotheses exist. For example, this would explain how the ancient Bent Pyramid builders managed to construct the outer facades of their monumental complexes with stones that are not joined like bricks, but like "jigsaw puzzles." The stones of the Bent Pyramid's exterior facade are in fact irregular trapezoids, each one different from the others, but fitting together perfectly. To do this work with stones to be carved from time to time would be impossible even for us today. Conversely, creating wooden shapes that are filled with "slurries" that then become rock would make it much easier.

Or this would explain how the builders had managed to move extremely heavy rocks. With the use of geopolymers, it would not have been necessary to move any rocks. They would simply have had to bring along "bags" containing the material to be mixed and create the mixture on the spot. Of course, this is only speculation, and any properties that the geopolymer coating imparted to the structure are unknown.

Opponents of this theory point out that the limestone blocks have different shapes from each other, and therefore the 'moulds' were not all used in the same way. They add that a huge amount of limestone plaster and burned wood would have been needed to finish the work by this method. Indeed, it is still unclear how the builders shaped the blocks. The fact remains, undeniable because proven in the laboratory, that those rocks are artificially created geopolymers. This is now an established, undeniable fact. How they did it is still not entirely clear.

Similar research has not yet been conducted on the other pyramids; therefore, we cannot go as far as to say that the same technique was used in the creation of all the pyramids. However, these discoveries made in the laboratory tell us plainly that whoever created the outer facade of the Great Pyramid and the Rhomboidal Pyramid had sufficient knowledge of chemistry to synthetically "recreate" the limestone rock using geopolymers, giving them the desired shape.

One thing is certain: the more evidence that the use of geopolymers by the "exiles of Mount Atlas," the original builders of some pyramids, has been extensive, the more all explanations made so far about the construction of the Egyptian pyramids collapse. It is beginning to be understood that they were monuments built not with muscle, but with brains and chemistry. This scientific data, and not subject to human opinion, tells us that centuries or millennia before the Egypt of the pharaohs there was a civilization in Egypt capable of creating and using geopolymers, a technique that we only "rediscovered" around 1950.

Technical capabilities out of time

The Great Pyramid of Giza has an enormous weight, probably approaching or exceeding 6,000,000 tons. It is a pretty easy thing to imagine that under such a weight, the ground underneath could have subsidence. There are not many areas on Earth that bear such weight. If, for example, this pyramid had been built in Bangkok, the underlying alluvial soil would have given way over time, and the pyramid would have at least partially sunk in places, damaging it beyond repair. In contrast, over thousands of years, and despite some very violent earthquakes in the area in the past, the Great Pyramid appears not to have experienced any significant subsidence.

In our days, every architect includes the variable of "subsidence" in his design. Careful geological studies and static calculations are made, and it is considered acceptable for a building to experience a subsidence of fifteen centimetres every one hundred years. Well, so far, the Great Pyramid, despite its incredible weight, has suffered a subsidence of less than 1.5 centimetres in at least 5,000 years! Such a result, bordering on the paranormal, cannot be due to chance.

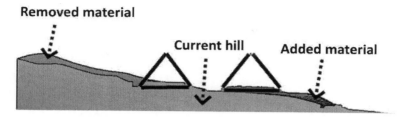

Whoever decided on the exact site where the Great Pyramid was to be built knew exactly what they were doing. Likewise, they knew exactly what they were doing by the ancient engineers who levelled the ground below, with a margin of error of one centimetre in 230 metres. So the suspicion that ancient geologists and engineers "with flakes" worked in that area becomes very pressing. But, normally, a civilization thousands of years ago, fresh out of the Neolithic period, should not have had this kind of knowledge. If that pyramid were really built by the Egyptians, the workers would have made everything using only copper chisels and wooden logs, having virtually no knowledge of geology or static calculations. Is it possible that with those poor means the men of thousands of years ago were able to do better than the man of the 21st century?

External precision

Despite the "cyclopean" dimensions of the Great Pyramid, these disfigure, becoming little compared to the precision with which it was made. Let us give some details, just to give an idea of what levels of precision we are talking about.

Perimeter of the Great Pyramid: - Compare the length of the four sides of the base of the pyramid.

The north side of the pyramid measures 230.2505 meters

The west side of the pyramid measures 230.3565 meters

The east side of the pyramid measures 230.3905 meters

The south side of the pyramid measures 230.4535 meters

It should be remembered that in ancient times the meter was not used as a base value for measurements. We do not know exactly what reference value the builders of the pyramid used (the Egyptian "cubit" measurement, proposed by many, applies only if this pyramid was made by the Egyptians, which is highly doubtful, if not impossible). Therefore, to detect the accuracy of the construction, it is more practical to measure the variations in measurements between its four sides. The average value we obtain is 230.35 meters. Compared to this value, we note that the maximum margin of error in the construction is about ten centimetres along each of the 230 meters on each side.

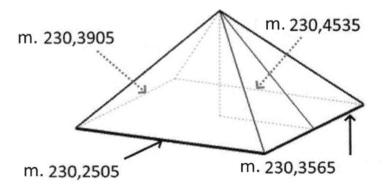

m. 230,3905

m. 230,4535

m. 230,2505

m. 230,3565

It does not appear that the blocks at the four corners of the pyramid were cut "on purpose" to achieve such precision. This means that each of the two hundred or so blocks that made up each side of the Great Pyramid were exactly the size required so that, placed together with the others, they could achieve the desired size. Moreover, the blocks are all perfectly aligned on the line that traces the edge of the pyramid. We should not forget that this precision was not achieved on a wall of plaster or made of bricks, whose "defects" can be easily corrected at the end of the work. This precision was achieved with blocks that weighed between 1.2 and 4 tons at the base, which were exceedingly difficult to move once placed.

With what instruments were measurements made to achieve such precision? The instruments in the possession of the Egyptians would have been only strings and reeds. Over short distances these instruments, if used very accurately, can give some accuracy. But over long distances (230 meters x 4, the perimeter of the Great Pyramid, is an awfully long distance) these methods suffer from the inevitable "laws of physics." Ropes stretch or shrink by a few millimetres per meter, depending on the heat, cold, humidity or tension exerted on the rope. But multiplying that small value by 230 meters leads to large inaccuracies. Even measuring with rods, over long distances, has similar problems that leads to large margins of error. The counterevidence that this is the case is that all other civilizations, including the Egyptians, using these methods for centuries have never again reached even close to a similar level of accuracy. It is therefore a "scientifically proven" fact that the builders of the pyramid used something other than rods and strings for the measurements of the Great Pyramid.

The Great Pyramid, in almost one kilometre total perimeter (230 meters of each side multiplied by 4) has a margin of error of only twenty-four centimetres. To get comparable results, we use laser gauges today. What kind of gauges the builders of the Great Pyramid used to have such accuracy is something that, objectively, we cannot explain at present.

Inside corners at the four sides: - Let us briefly analyse the accuracy of the four corners at the base of the Great Pyramid of Giza.

Southeast interior angle: 89° 56' 27"

Northeast interior angle: 90° 03' 02"

Southwest interior angle: 90° 00' 33"

Northwest interior angle: 89° 59' 58"

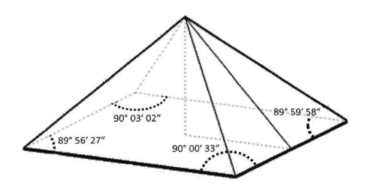

The interior angles of the base of a "perfect" pyramid should each measure exactly 90°. We note that in the case of the Great Pyramid, the northeast corner and the southwest corner are virtually perfect, measuring exactly 90°. The other two corners have a margin of error of less than 0.1 percent. Even for us today, it is difficult to fit two walls perpendicularly perfectly, so there is always a small margin of error in measuring the angle. Yet, this margin of error is almost absent in the Great Pyramid. Such precision is not found in any other monument of antiquity, either Egyptian or of any other people, and it is extremely difficult to find even in the skyscrapers of the 21st century.

This problem is multiplied out of all proportion for a 230-meter wide construction. With compasses and a square, it is relatively easy to draw a 90° angle on a small sheet. But to make two lines each 230 meters long continue throughout to be at 90° to each other at all times, without the slightest variation, is another matter. There are only two methods to achieve something similar. Either the two perpendicular walls are corrected at the end of construction, or they are made perfect as they are built. Since the base of the pyramid is made of rock blocks weighing an average of several tons, it is extremely unlikely that they could have corrected anything at the end of the work. So the blocks were placed already perfectly. No one else, either before or since, has ever managed to repeat this feat (Our modern era "maybe" has exceptions).

Angle of inclination: - "Perfect." It cannot be defined by any other word: the inclination of the pyramid is simply perfect. The angle of inclination is 51° 50' 35" for all four faces of the pyramid (There is only an "almost imperceptible" 1 degree inward variation in the centre of the four faces of the pyramid, which we will discuss later). Not only is it impressive that all four faces of a pyramid with a base of 230 meters and an apothem of 186 meters are tilted identically and perfectly. It is equally puzzling that this inclination was consistently maintained throughout the entire 186 meters or so length of its apothem, with no perceptible deviations along the line, for each of its four faces. But it is even more puzzling to realize that such a peculiar angle, exactly 51° 50' 35", was consciously sought and achieved, on all four faces! It is therefore not a random angle, but this particular angle was strongly intended, sought, and found. Moreover, it is evident that the makers had the technological means to repeat it on all four faces with virtually zero margin of error. What these "technological means" were is a mystery.

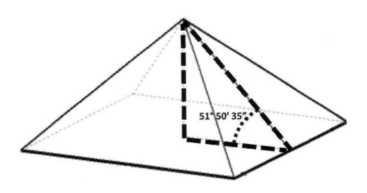

When asked how it had been possible to make something like this in the distant past, many famous architects candidly stated that it would be "almost impossible" for most modern-day construction firms to make something like this today, and they had no idea how it could have been done in the past. The Great Pyramid was built with about 210 levels of stones. It would have taken only the slightest mistake in any one of these levels to compromise the perfection of the entire structure. In fact, the slightest error in the lower rows would have been matched by a progressively greater error as one ascended to the upper rows. Then it would have been necessary to correct it. But none of this can be seen on the faces of the Great Pyramid.

This meant that there had to be a series of suspended "guidelines" that reached from the base of the pyramid to the top, about 150 meters up, tracing the surface of the pyramid. This was the only way for each face to consistently hold the correct inclination. But these guidelines would literally have to "cover" the outside of the pyramid, since the structure is precise at every point.

But, assuming that these "guidelines" had been ropes in use in ancient times, what would they have "clung" to in order to stretch them from the base of the pyramid to a summit located almost 150 meters away? Human constructions did not reach this height until about 1880 AD. Also, what material would these ropes have been made of? The apothem of the pyramid was about 186 meters, and a rope stretched over such a distance (unless we are talking about steel cables) loses strength and tends to "sag," becoming completely useless for accurately indicating the correct angle. It is therefore impossible that these were the means used to create the fantastic angle of the Great Pyramid. It is something simply astounding.

Eight-sided pyramid: - Although it is hardly noticeable to the naked eye, as we mentioned earlier, each of the four faces of the pyramid has a change in surface inclination of about 1 degree toward a hypothetical imaginary line that bisects each face of the pyramid. But this is not an error. On the contrary, it is yet another "masterstroke" of the mysterious builders. In this way, the outer structure of the Great Pyramid of Giza has not four faces, but as many as eight faces. Because of the Earth's shift relative to the Sun, two days a year the true "eight-sided" shape of the Great Pyramid becomes visible to the naked eye. This happens during the spring and autumn equinox days. On those two days, for a truly short interval of time, the relative position of the Sun with respect to the pyramid is such that half the side of the pyramid is illuminated, and half is in shadow. In this sense the Great Pyramid "marks" the two equinoxes.

However, what we see today is only part of the original structure of the pyramid. The outer white limestone covering was literally "stolen" over the centuries and used in other local constructions. There is no way of knowing whether even with the outer covering the same phenomenon occurred as it does today during the two equinoxes. Bearing in mind the maniacal attention to detail that the builders took in the construction of this pyramid, it is difficult to think that this phenomenon was simply due to chance. If indeed this pyramid was built to "mark" the two equinoxes, it would further increase its already incredible precision of construction to insane levels. The "fusion" of such astronomical knowledge with geometric and mathematical knowledge is objectively impossible to have been found in a people who had recently emerged from the so-called "stone age."

By the way, according to a great many experts, this way of constructing the pyramid walls, combined with the way the structure was built, by stacking boulders at a precise angle of advancement, makes this construction a real bunker. The Great Pyramid has seen very violent earthquakes, such that most of the buildings in Cairo collapsed. According to archaeologists, inside the Great Pyramid virtually nothing has moved....

Aligned with the Geographic North Pole

The planet Earth possesses a Magnetic North Pole and a Geographical North Pole. The Magnetic North Pole is a point on Earth where the action of its magnetic field causes a magnetic needle (such as, for example, a compass needle) to be attracted in that direction. At that precise point, the flow of the magnetic field is perpendicular to the ground. The Magnetic North Pole is generated mainly by the iron core that lies beneath the Earth's crust. Since the Earth's crust and the iron core do not have a perfectly symmetrical rotational motion with each other, it follows that the Magnetic North Pole slightly changes its position with respect to the Earth's crust over time. The Magnetic North Pole is therefore not fixed but varies over time.

While the Magnetic North Pole is something that exists "physically," the Geographical North Pole is just a conventional geographical point, a concept. At that point passes "the imaginary axis" around which the Earth rotates. It follows that if we stood exactly at the Geographical North Pole and looked around us, we would not see the stars set and rise as they do in the rest of the world. At that point, the stars in the sky would rotate around us in an apparent 360-degree motion. (Obviously because of other motions of the Earth around the Sun, and of the Sun around the galaxy, even if slowly, over time the appearance of the sky nevertheless changes even at the Geographic North Pole.) The Geographic North Pole and the Magnetic North Pole, although they are often in a fairly close area, rarely coincide perfectly.

From this it follows that, a star that lies in its apparent motion on the perpendicular of the Geographic North Pole is a star that, compared to an observer on Earth, has less apparent motion than other stars. For a certain period of time, which can be estimated in centuries, it is therefore a kind of "fixed star." (Obviously due to Earth's motions, the star that is on the perpendicular of the Geographic North Pole will also change its position over time.) For this reason, in every age, the star that was closest of all to the Geographic North Pole in that time period has always been taken as a reference point for orientation. In our days it is commonly called the North Star.

Of course, this is just our convention. In fact, rarely has a star perfectly indicated the perpendicular on the Geographic North Pole. Moreover, as stars in the firmament shift over the millennia, over time the star indicating the perpendicular over the Geographic North Pole changes. In some time periods, in fact, no star has indicated the Geographic North Pole with relative accuracy. But given the rather simple needs of ancient navigators, knowing the star that was "approximately closest to the Geographical North Pole" was more than enough to be useful in orienting themselves in their travels.

We have made this brief explanation to better understand one of the most remarkable features of the Great Pyramid. This pyramid turns out to be aligned with the Earth's Geographic North Pole, with an estimated margin of error of about four-tenths of a degree. For comparison, the astronomical observatory in Paris has an orientation error twice that of the Great Pyramid. This observatory was built in 1671, just over three hundred years ago. If Bronze Age men made the Great Pyramid, the precision with which this construction points to the Geographic North Pole raises several questions that are not easily answered.

The first question to answer is, how did the builders of the Great Pyramid know exactly where the perpendicular on the Geographic North Pole was. The most obvious answer is that they referred to the stars in order to correctly determine this point. The Egyptians were great observers of the sky. Their system of measuring time gave rise to the solar calendar that underlies our own, and they drew a complete star map. As we have said before, usually in the apparent motions of stars there has almost always been a star that seems almost "fixed," and that points to what we call "the North." Using that "fixed" star, one can orient oneself with respect to a geographical map or using other landmarks.

The ancient Egyptians regarded Seshat, the woman dressed in cheetah skin, as the one who inspired the construction of new temples and new architectural complexes. In fact, when anything of any importance was being built, the pharaoh ideally accompanied by his divine companion Seshat, was expected to attend the "rope-tending" ceremony. Using the stars of Ursa Major as a reference, the pharaoh would look for the Geographical North, and then place four ropes corresponding to the four cardinal points, planting a stake in the ground for each of them. He would then lay the foundation stone of the construction. It appears that this ritual dates back to at least the 2nd Dynasty, that is, 2,900 BCE.

But these claims we hear in various documentaries, although true in substance, cannot be entirely correct. Why? Planet Earth is subject to the cyclical "precession of the equinoxes," which is a movement of the Earth that causes the orientation of its axis of rotation to change slowly but continuously with respect to the ideal sphere of fixed stars. Based on this motion, the arrangement of certain groups of stars observable from Earth changes cyclically about every 25,772 years.

One of the most obvious effects of the precession of the equinoxes concerns the star that marks the Geographic North Pole. In our days, the star that comes closest to the perpendicular on the Geographic North Pole is the North Star (or Polaris star), in the constellation Ursa Major. But because of the precession of the equinoxes no star can be said to always point to the Geographic North Pole, except in a narrow window of time. For example, according to calculations, the star Polaris will indicate the North Pole with the highest possible accuracy only in 2,100 A.D., when it will have a margin of error of only 0.4 degrees with respect to the Earth's Geographic North Pole.

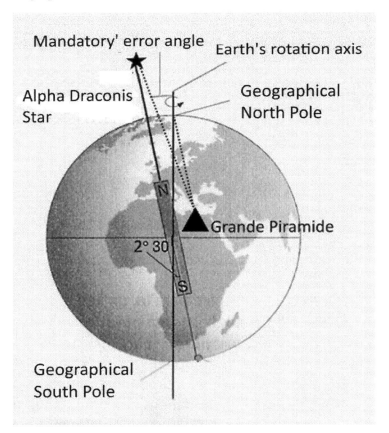

What was the star that indicated the Geographic North Pole at the time when the Great Pyramid is thought to have been built? The "pole star" at that time was Alpha Draconis, a star belonging to the constellation Dragon, which is known by the name Thuban. The closest Alpha Draconis came to the North Pole was in 2787 B.C., when it was only 2 1/2 degrees from the perpendicular on the Geographic North Pole.

This detail is a small "earthquake" for those who think that the builders used the stars to orient the Great Pyramid. Alpha Draconis could never precisely point to the North Pole because it had a "natural" margin of error as a minimum of 2 1/2 degrees. And since its period of "maximum accuracy" with respect to North does not coincide with the period when the Great Pyramid is thought to have been built, it is only obvious to infer that the margin of error in calculating the Geographic North Pole using that star could only have been larger, not smaller.

With this in mind, one would expect the Great Pyramid's error in indicating the Geographic North Pole to be at least 2 1/2 degrees, like that of its "reference star." But the Great Pyramid is much more accurate than Alpha Draconis, having an error of only four tenths of a degree. How is this possible?

Before we launch into the various hypotheses about how the pyramid builders were able to "correct the error" in alignment, an even more pressing question needs an answer: how did the builders know that the star Alpha Draconis did not "perfectly" indicate the Geographic North Pole? In fact, "theoretically," they should not have even known that the "pole star" of that time contained a margin of error. Based on what had they realized that Alpha Draconis did not perfectly indicate Geographical North? They had to know that the Earth is a sphere spinning on itself, and therefore has a "Geographical

North Pole." They would have had to calculate this "North" in their map, and only then would they have realized that the star Alpha Draconis was not perfectly perpendicular on Geographical North. But were the Egyptians of 2,500 B.C. able to do all this? To the best of our knowledge, no.

In fact, it is assumed that people 2,500 years ago did not know the nearly spherical shape of the Earth. It is also assumed that they did not know that the Earth revolves around its own axis. Therefore, they could not plot the Earth's geographic North Pole on a globe. And consequently they could not see that Alpha Draconis had a margin of error of 2 1/2 degrees on the axis of the Geographic North Pole. This is not theory; these are hard facts that leave little room for doubt.

It follows that, if the builders really used the stars to orient the Great Pyramid to the Geographical North Pole, it should have an error "as a minimum" of 2 1/2 degrees. How is it possible for the Great Pyramid to be aligned with the Geographical North Pole with a margin of error of less than 1/20 degree? Why did the builders not "trust" their "North Star"? Is it possible that they had such accurate observation instruments to detect such a small variation in the position of that star? If they had them, where did they go?

Others propose the alternative that the Great Pyramid was built by imagining a symbolic line that crossed two stars, Mizar in Ursa Major (the Big Dipper) and Kochab in Ursa Minor (the Little Dipper). For a period of only 9 years, between 2485 B.C. and 2475 B.C., according to Kate Spence of Cambridge University, these two stars aligned with each other indicated the straight line touching the Geographic North Pole.

17 - Technology of the 'Exiles'

But even this explanation leaves something to be desired. First, there is ample evidence that the Great Pyramid was built centuries before that time. Moreover, this kind of indication serves us, who "already know in advance" where the Geographical North Pole is and try to figure out how to calculate it using the stars. But this was not the case for the ancient builders. They supposedly did not know that there was a 'geographical North Pole' at all and relied on the 'fixed star' for orientation. They could not use the stars to find something that they, "theoretically," did not even know existed. It cannot even be assumed that they were using some form of compass, since the Geographic North Pole and the Magnetic North Pole do not coincide perfectly.

It must be accepted that, from a strictly scientific point of view, the builders of 3000 B.C. could not have been able to correctly calculate the Geographical North Pole using the stars or some kind of compass unless they knew the sphericity of the Earth and its correct dimensions. This is a fact that can hardly be questioned. Normally, the Great Pyramid should contain an alignment error of about 3 degrees, simply because their "pole star" had a similar alignment error at that time. Only then would it have been a construction belonging to "that time period." Since it did not contain a similar alignment error, the construction of that structure raises awkward questions. What kind of astronomical knowledge did the builders of the Great Pyramid possess? Did they know the sphericity of the Earth? The Egyptians certainly did not know it, and so the builders could not have been the "Egyptians" we know. Evidently, the "exiles from Mount Atlas" knew this as well.

17 - Technology of the 'Exiles'

Taking stock

What kind of scientific knowledge did the "exiles of Mount Atlas," or "Atlanteans," as Plato called them, possess. We analysed some of what might be "their remains," particularly the Great Pyramid of Rostau (Giza). What we discovered left us astonished. The angle of inclination of all four faces of the pyramid, 51° 50′ 35″, perfectly researched and found for all four faces of this construction, identical on all four apothem, tells us that the builders were architects with chops.

Its builders possessed considerable chemical knowledge, since some of the stones of which it is constructed are geopolymers, or synthetic rock (this has also been established for the Rhomboidal Pyramid). In practice, these builders shaped the rocks directly on the construction, to give them exactly the shape they wanted, down to the smallest detail. Perhaps this is why the Great Pyramid has perfect shapes.

By analysing the incredible precision of its measurements, we understood that its builders were experts in geometry and mathematics. They were also accomplished astronomers, since at least two pyramids, the Great Pyramid and the Central Pyramid have their bases oriented toward the Earth's Geographical North in an almost perfect manner. This is despite the fact that the star that was commonly used to indicate North had more than 2 degrees of error with respect to the Earth's Geographical North Pole. This detail suggests to us that their makers knew the sphericity of the Earth. Conversely, it is not clear how they knew that the Earth had a shifted "North point" relative to the star they used to calculate the Geographic North Pole.

17 - Technology of the 'Exiles'

We also understood that these were people who could move blocks as heavy as five hundred tons without too much trouble. (This has been established for the Central Pyramid, called the Pyramid of Khafre). It is hard to imagine that they did this with sleds pulled by workers, as the Egyptians did. A 500-ton block would have simply refused to move by those means. Just to make a simple comparison, a modern fighter-bomber, such as the F35 aircraft, weighs about thirteen tons.

We also understood that they were able to process hard stones, such as granite, even on an industrial scale. The Great Pyramid alone has at least 8,000 tons of processed granite inside it, at least 1,000 of which with a margin of error of less than a millimetre. No known people of the past, prior to 2,000 B.C. at a minimum, possessed the technological and logistical means for the industrial processing of granite. This is an established fact that even the most conservative of archaeologists dare not argue about. The question then remains as to who processed those thousands of tons of granite.

Lastly, most surprising of all, the latest laboratory analysis tells us that these builders had at least some knowledge of physics, as the Great Pyramid of Rostau (Giza) concentrates electromagnetic energy in its inner chambers and the area below. Professor Peter Grandics went as far as to say that it is actually "a broadband antenna for atmospheric electrostatic discharge pulses," which would allow the conversion of electrostatic energy from the atmosphere into alternating current. Other professors, such as those at Itmo University in St. Petersburg and the Laser Zentrum in Hanover, however, simply note that the Great Pyramid has this characteristic, which can be measured in the laboratory, and that this can be useful for producing highly efficient "antennas."

The ability to interact with electromagnetic phenomena places the Great Pyramid of Rostau (Giza), and all other pyramids where it will be proven to possess the same feature, on a different plane from the rest of the ancient ruins found around the world. By now we no longer speak of archaeology, but of "technological marker." A technological marker is an object that possesses technological features that, based on the time period in which it was believed to have been built, it should not possess. Very often we have heard well-known scientists who are somewhat sceptical say, "If one day we find a remote control among Egyptian mummies, then we will believe that non-terrestrial civilizations visited Earth." Well, it seems that the researchers have not found a remote control, but they have found an antenna. And what an antenna! It is 230 meters wide and over 150 meters high. If this research is confirmed, it will probably be the greatest discovery in human history. But precisely because the stakes are so high, we await further confirmation.

PART 9

Period:

From about 7,000 years ago to 5,000 years ago.

Occurrence:

The "reload" of the Y chromosome

Involved populations:

Probably all the people on Earth

18 - The reload of the Y chromosome

We have seen how the "exiles of Mount Atlas" were severely affected by the desertification of the Sahara, which forced them to abandon their land. But according to a group of researchers, that was not the only cause of the last "reload" that we know of. Something else must have affected the world at that time.

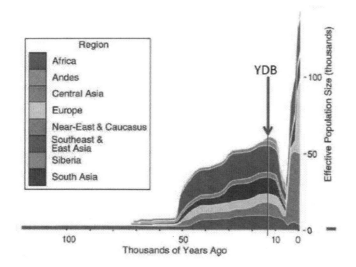

In 2015, a group of more than one hundred researchers from around the world, coordinated by Dr. Monica Karmin , on behalf of Genome Research, published a study from which the table you see on this page is taken. The subject involved, among other things, a measurement of the variation in the Homo Sapiens male human population throughout history.

From this graph we can see that the male human population of Homo Sapiens, about 75,000 years ago, was recovering from something that had almost "reset" it to zero. In fact, looking at the graph, it appears that before that date there were no Sapiens males on Earth. But the graph is meant to explain that at that date, there were simply too few Sapiens males to leave a historically relevant trace. But we know that Homo Sapiens has existed for at least 200,000 years. So to have a numerically irrelevant population means that 75,000 years ago the first "Genetic Bottleneck" had occurred.

Dr. Monica Karmin's graph shows how between 75,000 and 50,000 years ago, the population of Homo Sapiens males grew slightly, but something prevented a significant population increase. Then from about 50,000 years ago until 12,800 years ago, there was a real "population explosion" among Homo Sapiens males. But at this point, exactly from 12,800 years ago, there was a new vertical collapse in the population of Sapiens males, a new "Genetic Bottleneck."

As we saw earlier, this period coincides perfectly with the bombardment of comet fragments, which hit the whole Earth. In addition, we recall that subsequently there was the Younger Dryas, a small ice age, which suddenly hit the Earth. The sharp decline in the male population of Homo Sapiens, highlighted by Dr. Karmin's graph, can give us an idea of how many civilizations disappeared during that period.

But this graph also tells us something else. The human population did not recover immediately after the comet bombardment, or even after the Younger Dryas. For some reason unknown to us, the population continued to decline at an accelerating rate, until it nearly halved about 7,000 years ago. It was a real carnage, a true "Armaghedon" of the past. What could have caused it?

The Y chromosome

A unique aspect of this "Bottleneck," at times inexplicable, is that the population decrease was not uniform for males and females. This "extermination" affected almost exclusively males of the Homo Sapiens species. It reached the point of having seventeen females for every male. What could have caused "selective" death in the human race? Dr. Monica Karmin proposed the possibility that it was a period of widespread warfare. Usually, especially in the past, it was men who fought wars, while women and children remained safe in towns or villages. Thus, according to Monica Karmin, a period of prolonged wars would bring as a side effect a sharp decrease in the male population. This conclusion makes sense. But can it be enough to explain the halving of the world population, and the near extermination of the male gender?

All researchers are unanimous in accepting the results of this study, which everyone considers "excellent." But not everyone agrees with the reason for this decrease in population. According to Dr. Karmin's explanation there would have been a kind of episodic World War, made up of a myriad of internecine wars. But that would mean that the populations of 12,800 years ago had to be developed enough to be able to move war against each other on a large scale, as happened, for example, in the last century with the two world wars. Was the world of that time already divided into "zones of influence," or "empires," which fought against each other? Conversely, it is difficult to imagine a human world divided into many small tribes deciding to exterminate each other. Even any problems such as food shortages would hardly bring war across the globe if only individual tribes were fighting.

This explanation baffles many people. The point of view of the "perplexed" is this: internecine wars have always been there, and they have not produced comparable results in other periods of human history, not even during the century of world wars. Why would wars have such catastrophic results 12,800 years ago?

By studying the decrease in the male population of Sapiens, exemplified in the graph proposed by Dr. Monica Karmin, one can understand in which areas the "Genetic Bottleneck" has hit hardest. (1) The male population of the Andes has almost disappeared. (2) The male population of Siberia has almost disappeared. (3) The male population of Southeast Asia, including Oceania, has shrunk by two-thirds. (4) The male populations of Central Asia and South Asia have halved. (5) The male population of Europe, the Middle East, and Africa also declined by a large amount. After "bottoming out" about 7,000 years ago, the world's male population began to grow exponentially again, as is still happening now.

A climatic explanation

According to others, since the population decline coincides with the beginning of the short ice age called the Younger Dryas, the explanation must be found there. Moreover, it should not be forgotten that this period spanned about 5,000 years, during which time the world population continued to decline. Is it possible that, in addition to wars, something else prevented the males of the Sapiens species from staying alive? According to some, it seems that the problem was not so much that males were dying, but that not enough were being born.

Can climate affect the birth rate of a population? According to some researchers, in an article in PNAS of Feb. 12, 2008, a prolonged period of particularly low temperatures can decrease the population of unborn males very significantly. It is therefore likely that, at least in the ancient period from 10,900 B.C. to 9,700 B.C., the sharp decrease in the male population was due to the intense cold caused by the Younger Dryas. This, however, does not explain why the male population continued to decline afterwards, when the global temperature became as it is today. Evidently there is an as yet unknown "external cause."

A hidden cause

It is evident that attempts to find an answer to the "Y Chromosome Catastrophe," although they have succeeded in giving some reasons, fail to explain the phenomenon in its entirety. It is obvious that the death of the males of the species will not have left the peoples of the past indifferent. What did they think about what was happening? Is there a tradition, or a legend, in which the death of the males of the human species is mentioned? In fact, a famous story tells us about something like that: the story of Moses.

18 - The reload of the Y chromosome

In the book of Exodus, in chapter 1, verses 8 to 19, it is said, 'With time in Egypt there was a new Pharaoh, who had not known Joseph. He said to his people, 'The people of Israel are more numerous and stronger than we are. We must be smarter than they are. Otherwise they will continue to multiply, and if a war were to break out, they would be on the side of our enemies to fight against us, and they would leave the country'.

[...]

Afterwards, Pharaoh spoke to the Hebrew midwives, whose names were Sifra and Pua, and said to them, 'When you help the Hebrew women give birth, and you see them ready for childbirth, if a boy is born you must put him to death; if it is a girl, however, let her live'. - End quote

There is no historical basis for this account. There was no attempt by any pharaoh to genocide the Hebrew children. In fact, the Jews had not only not been captives in Egypt but had never even resided there. Where did the scribes of the past get this story of the attempted genocide of only the male children? This fictionalized account illustrates for us how the death of male children only had been perceived by the general population in the past. According to the creators of this story, male sons died violent deaths, as during "ethnic cleansing." Is it possible that in the past an "external element" of an intelligent type contributed to or caused a sharp decrease in the human population, particularly affecting the male gender?

19 - The Missing Wonder

The famous Roman historian Pliny the Elder, referring to the "Labyrinth of Fayyum" (for us today the "Labyrinth of Hawara"), in his book Hystoria Naturalis, book XXXVI, in verse nineteen says "factus est ante annos, ut tradunt, III DC," which translates to "they say it was made 3,600 years ago." According to Pliny that structure had been built about 3,600 years before his time. Since Pliny died around 75 AD, that would mean we are talking about a 5,500-year-old construction. Definitely not a structure built by the Egyptians, since the first pharaoh, Narmer, was crowned as pharaoh of unified Egypt in 3,100 BCE.

The main clues to attribute this construction to are the "exiles of Mount Atlas." In this case, the "Labyrinth of Fayyum" may be one of the last megalithic constructions of this incredible civilization. Pliny also says that the Egyptians dated this construction to a time before the pharaohs, and attributed this construction to Petesuchis, or Petsuchos. According to Wikipedia, "the term Petsuchos is the phonetic rendering of the name of the sacred crocodile of the temple of Sobek at Crocodilopolis in Ancient Egypt. The term Petsuchos is the Greek interpretation of an Egyptian word meaning ´he who belongs to Suchos´, and thus can be translated as ´son of Sobek´" - end of quote.

In Egyptian, "Sobek" is the term used for "Crocodile." In the list of Egyptian pharaohs, the first pharaoh ever, the one who came before all of them, is called the "Crocodile King," from whom the "Scorpion King" descended. These rulers formed the so-called "Zero Dynasty," that is, those who came "before" the first dynasty of pharaohs. (According to Herodotus, ten others were added, all of whom predated the "Crocodile King.") So it is highly likely that by the term "Petsuchos" the Egyptians of Pliny's time were not pointing to a real Egyptian ruler, but to the legendary "Crocodile" or "Crocodile King" from whom the Egyptians made their history begin. It was a way of saying that even they did not know who had built that structure, and that it came from a past that predated Egypt.

As we mentioned, Herodotus adds that Petsuchos, or "King Crocodile," was only the last of twelve kings who built this giant labyrinth. Since "the last king" predates the first of the pharaohs, the other eleven kings also had to predate the era of the pharaohs. We can make a calculation. Since a pharaoh ruled an average of 20 years, according to Herodotus it took about 240 years, if not more, to build the labyrinth of Meris. This detail is surprising since, again according to Herodotus, the entire structure of Giza, including the pyramids, was built in less than one hundred years. The "Labyrinth of Hawara" according to him, was therefore something even larger than the entire structure of Giza found above ground. Moreover, the beginning of its construction must necessarily have preceded the era of the pharaohs by at least several centuries.

Describing the Labyrinth, Herodotus says, "Indeed, there are twelve covered courtyards, with doors facing each other; six facing north, six open to the south. Its courtyards are contiguous, and a single wall encloses them on the outside. The rooms are on two levels. Some are underground. Others are on the ground level, above the former. In all there are 3,000 rooms; 1,500 on each level." So we are talking about a 2-story building: one ground level and one basement level below the ground. In the area above the ground surface, twelve courtyards had been built, with several colonnades. Some have suggested that it could cover an area of at least 70,000 square meters, but if the rooms were particularly large, the entire labyrinth could have been even much larger.

In his writings Pliny says he was amazed that the entire labyrinth was built with Parian marble, a highly prized white marble found not in Egypt but in Greece. The columns, on the other hand, would have been made of syenite, an extremely hard rock similar to granite but lacking quartz. The historian Strabo (64 B.C. - 19 A.D.), in his 17-volume work "The Geography," in Book 17, in paragraphs 1, 3, 42 and 47 marvels at the materials with which the structure had been created. He says, "But the extraordinary thing is that the ceiling of each room is made of a single stone. Likewise, the galleries are covered for their entire width with monolithic slabs of exceptional size, without supporting beams or any other material."

From Strabo's words, we note that in this very ancient structure, built according to Pliny at least 5,600 years ago, we find the common element of all "impossible" constructions located in Egypt: huge marble blocks, raised several meters above the ground, cut and placed with such precision that no glue was required to bind the blocks together. There are many engineers today who have no idea how it is possible to build a roof with a single slab of granite, without any supporting beams. One of them said, "If it were true, it would be a miracle." This type of construction seems to be the unmistakable signature of those who had been in Egypt "before" the pharaohs.

Virtually all ancient historians who have dealt with Egypt speak of the "Labyrinth of Fayyum," which was 50 percent a completely underground structure. Among them we can mention Herodotus, Strabo, Diodorus Siculus, Manetho, and Pliny the Elder.

Ancient historians are unanimous in saying that this half-subterranean Labyrinth was a work of such grandeur that it even ridiculed the pyramids of Giza. For a great many years, the existence of this incredible structure had been considered by a great many scholars to be a mere "exaggeration" of past historians, if not an outright legend. Nowhere in Egypt seemed to be the remains of anything that could even remotely compare to the description made by ancient historians of this Labyrinth. But not everyone was of this opinion, and some continued to search for the remains of this ancient wonder. In time these efforts were rewarded.

The historian Herodotus (484 - 430 B.C.), in Book II of his "Histories," beginning in verse 148, tells us that the Labyrinth was built in the vicinity of a lake, opposite the ancient city of Crocodilopolis, or Arsinoè, today's Fayyum, located about 90 km from Giza. This prompted some archaeologists, including Flinders Petrie (1853 - 1942) to search for the "Labyrinth" near Lake Qarun in the Hawara area.

These archaeologists hypothesized that the building mentioned by Herodotus was connected to the funerary temple of the pyramid of Hawara, attributed to Amenemhet III, who lived around 1800 BCE. This hunch, though partly correct, played a trick on the willing researchers. In fact, when the world-famous Flinders Petrie arrived in front of the remains of the Hawara pyramid in 1889, he realized that beneath the sand was a homogeneous, hard structure, apparently resembling a man-made floor, about 304 meters long and 244 meters wide. Some remains of ancient artifacts, not particularly important, surfaced from the sand. Thus the celebrated archaeologist became convinced that he had found the floor of the legendary Labyrinth, but that it had been completely dismantled by the Romans. So that imposing construction had ceased to exist for at least 2,000 years. The story of the "Labyrinth of Fayyum," better known today as the "Labyrinth of Hawara," seemed to have ended there. And this belief in the scientific community has lasted well over one hundred years.

But not everyone gave up. Between February 18 and March 12, 2008, with the permission of the Supreme Council of Egyptian Antiquities, a Belgian team, funded and coordinated by the renowned artist Luis de Cordier (aka Cosco) was able to begin a series of investigations. This group included several Belgian researchers working on behalf of Ghent University, and other Egyptian researchers working on behalf of the NRIAG (National Institute of Geophysics and Astronomy) in Helwan. This multidisciplinary group of researchers made an "epic" discovery. Using georadar, they discovered something that could revolutionize everything we know about Egypt's history.

Scholars, in what was called the "Mataha Expedition" discovered that what Flinders Petrie had mistaken for the "floor of the Labyrinth," was actually the "roof of the Labyrinth." Not realizing this, the famous archaeologist had managed to find none other than the roof of the "Hawara

Labyrinth," located about 8 to 12 meters below ground level. All indications are that, under that roof, the Labyrinth still exists virtually in one piece. (Unfortunately, the area suffers from highly saline water infiltration, which is inevitably deteriorating the structure, reasoning that work should be started immediately to save what can be saved.)

Georadar revealed that underneath that "slab of rock" about three hundred meters long, walls of extremely strong shape and structure, which seem to be almost certainly made of granite, could be seen. Furthermore, researchers found that all the ruins found so far "above" the large rock slab did not belong to the "floor" of the Labyrinth at all. Rather, they were ruins that were several meters away "on its roof." Those ruins were part of a village built in Ptolemaic times when the remains of the labyrinth were probably used as a cemetery.

According to georadar scans, the roof of the Labyrinth is now on average under five meters of earth, and its floor is about 8 to 12 meters underground. If, as past historians say, the labyrinth also had an underground zone, the floor of this zone should be about 12 to 16 meters deep. The entire structure was covered by at least twelve meters of earth and sand in about 1,300 years (in fact, it seems that at least until the seventh century AD, the ruins of the Labyrinth were visible at ground level). Incidentally, this is a reminder of how many structures, even gigantic ones, perhaps entire cities, are still buried under the sands of Egypt, waiting for someone to find them.

Researchers were also able to reproduce an early three-dimensional model of the Labyrinth. It looked like it would be one of the most important archaeological revelations in history. But, for reasons unknown, after giving permission for the work, the Supreme Council of Egyptian Antiquities not only "froze" the project but enjoined all the researchers involved (the majority of whom are Egyptians) not to disclose the results of the research. Of everything the researchers found, there remains the video presentation of the conference held in Belgium immediately after the discovery, and a short NRIAG paper that "escaped" censorship. Beyond that, for more than 10 years there has been total silence about this exceptional find.

Why, as in the case of "Mastaba 14" or "Tomb of the Birds," are Egyptian authorities blocking research that has to do with the underground world of Giza? What are they afraid of? Or what do they want "not to know"?

A megalithic site

Very few people today have all the results of the analysis of the Hawara Maze at their disposal. But from the data that have been leaked through "oblique ways," the outlines of this mega-structure can be sketched. It seems that, from what can be seen through georadar, the shape of the Labyrinth traces rather closely what was described by past historians. Given the tight time frame the expedition had, only two surfaces were scanned with georadar. One of these has a width of about 150 meters x 100 meters. A second, located beyond the Bahr Wabi canal that flows nearby, has the dimensions of eighty meters x 100 meters. At present no one can say exactly how large the entire complex is, but it appears that the affected area covers several hectares of land. Extensive investigations are needed, which, unfortunately, have not yet been done, and no one seems to be doing them.

Thus, the main structure consists of a two-story building, originally conceived with one floor above ground and one underground. (Now, of course, it is all underground). The main area consisted of "twelve zones," each built around twelve huge courtyards. Each of the courtyards was surrounded by about 125 rooms in the area above ground level, and 125 rooms in the underground area. In all, there were at least 1,500 rooms on each level, for a total of at least 3,000 rooms and twelve courtyards. (Since the courtyards were on the ground level, it is unclear what was in their place on the underground level.)

All ancient writers agree that each of the 3,000 rooms had a roof formed of a single stone. This would explain why the roof, seen from above, fooled even an expert archaeologist like Flinders Petrie, who mistook it for the base of a floor. But if true, this would create a problem for us. Not even we, humans of the 21st century, are able to make the roof of a rather spacious room using a single slab as a covering. How did they manage to do it?

From the surveys made, at least one area of the Labyrinth appears to be located exactly opposite the remains of the pyramid of Hawara, attributed as we have said to Amenemhat III. It is highly unlikely that the Labyrinth has anything to do with the pharaoh's funerary complex, otherwise it would not explain what such a large structure is doing below ground level while the rest of the complex is still above ground. But, of course, until the remains of the Labyrinth are seen with the naked eye, there can be no certainty. Today the lower part of the pyramid appears to be inundated by water, so it is inaccessible. Most likely, therefore, this highly saline water must have flooded the underground remains of the Labyrinth as well. Considering the size of the cities of that time, usually very modest, rather than an underground temple this Labyrinth can be considered a true underground citadel.

An underground bunker?

The historian Strabo in his writings explains what the structure looked like, saying that all the courtyards were "lined up in a single row on just one of the walls, almost as if it were one long wall where the courtyards rested on the facade. The streets leading up to that point ended right in front of the wall." Then he adds, "In front of the entrances to the courtyards are numerous long underground tunnels, connected with each other by winding passages." The underground structure described by Strabo, combined with the architecture of the complex above ground, seems to give the idea that rather than a temple, it was a bunker. Normally, bunkers consist of a single central gallery, from which secondary galleries branch off. This seems to be exactly the structure described by Strabo for the surface buildings, and it is possible that this structure was replicated for the underground buildings. The twelve surface entrances corresponded to courtyards, or plazas. This is also a typical bunker structure. On the surface, close to the entrances, there are always assembly yards. The fact that there were the same number of rooms both underground and above ground may indicate that there was an area located at ground level for "calm" periods, while the area for "crisis" periods was located underground. Of course, all this may just be coincidence, but it is useful to note.

Diodorus Siculus (who lived in the first century B.C.), in Book I of his "Bibliotheca historica," in verses 61.1-2 and 66.3-6, adds, "This king did not get glory for wars but for the construction of a tomb, the so-called ´Labyrinth´. This construction was known not only for its grandeur but for its inimitable art." It makes a certain impression to read that in the heyday of classical civilizations, such as Greece and Rome, there was something that was considered "inimitable" even for them.

Who were the builders?

What civilization was able to build this marvel? As we have read, the Egyptians themselves were unanimous in saying that when the reign of the pharaohs began, this imposing and mysterious construction already existed. So it is not an Egyptian construction. From what the various historians of the past write, it is clear that the construction skills of those who made the Meridian Labyrinth (built at least 5,600 years ago), were far superior to what, at that time, the peoples known to us could do.

It is therefore likely that the "exiles of Mount Atlas" were the builders of the Fayyum Labyrinth. It was probably their "swan song," their last great work, before the "Y-chromosome catastrophe" put a final end to their glorious civilization.

What was the point of having hundreds and hundreds of underground rooms? As we saw earlier, the people of Nan Madol built their houses "high up," placing them on about one hundred artificial islands, to protect themselves from something. Perhaps they were protecting themselves from the sudden floods caused by the Deglaciation. Similarly, the Labyrinth builders had built a vast number of rooms underground to protect themselves from something coming "from above." Was it the heat of the Sun? Or the cold? Or something of which we are not aware?

The maze-building period coincides with the peak period of the "Y chromosome catastrophe." According to Dr. Karmin's studies, at that time "it reached the point of having 17 females for every male." The world male population was less than half of what it was 12,000 years ago. The level of depopulation was such that, to this day, there seems to have been almost no civilization before 3,000 BC. Whether Egyptians or Mesoamerican Peoples, from Africa to Oceania, the entire present civilization seems to have been "reborn" since 3,000 B.C., after the events of the "Y chromosome catastrophe." It is therefore probable that the Meridian Labyrinth might have been intended to "protect" itself from something that was reaping victims to no end on Earth's soil.

Unfortunately, the Fayyum Labyrinth, like all the other constructions of the "Mount Atlas exiles," ended up under the desert sand. This means that, regardless of intentions, the attempt to seek protection underground failed.

PART 10

Period:

About 3,500 to 2,000 years ago

Occurrence:

Akhenaten

Yahoshua ben Yoseph from Nazareth

Involved populations:

All of us

20 - The first "facilitator"

The "Y chromosome catastrophe" was over. Around 3,000 B.C. throughout the world civilization was flourishing again, albeit very slowly. Ancient ruins, as in Egypt, Asia, and Central America, stood as reminders of what humanity had done but was no longer able to do. Some peoples of the past, such as the Egyptians, tried to reuse or adapt the majestic ruins they found in their territory. Others were simply "taken apart," and the resulting material was used to build dwellings. Others were simply forgotten, and ended up covered with soil, sand, or submerged by water.

It seems that as the centuries passed, after things had proceeded more or less the same for a long time, at some point there was a real "explosion of civilization." What does this mean? As we analysed at the beginning of this book, it is evident that, at some point in human history, the evolution of our species "exploded," making real leaps, leading to the birth of Homo Sapiens, Neanderthals, Denisova, and perhaps other "human families" whose existence we do not yet know. According to the latest research, most likely these "leaps" are due to viruses that injected genes into some specimens of humankind, which allowed for very rapid evolution, effectively creating what we are today.

But we are only talking about DNA evolution. Unfortunately, viruses, however powerful, cannot trigger cultural evolution. Well, analysing our history, it is evident that at some point, after the "Y-chromosome catastrophe," characters appeared who, like social viruses, helped humankind make a real "evolutionary leap," not in DNA, but in the mind, in one's moral, ethical, and social values. They acted as "facilitators," allowing those who wished to do so to greatly speed up the evolution of their thoughts.

It seems that particularly in the fourth to fifth centuries B.C. , a veritable "patrol" of "facilitators" appeared on the scene, from Plato in the West to Confucius and Buddha in the East, just to mention a few. Instead, we want to focus on the "first" and "last" of the "facilitators" of that time. Indeed, some of the remains of their bodies pose "intriguing" questions for us, to say the least.

The first facilitator: Akhenaten the heretic

He has been described as "enigmatic," "mysterious," "revolutionary," "the world's greatest idealist," and "the first individual in history," but also as a "heretic," a "fanatic," and "possibly insane." Who are we talking about? We are talking about Akhenaten, whose original name was Amenhotep IV, the most controversial Egyptian pharaoh in history. This ruler ruled his reign from approximately 1353 BC to 1336 BC. The famous pharaoh, belonging to the Eighteenth Dynasty, then reigned during the New Kingdom, a time period of approximately five hundred years (1550 B.C.E. to 1069 B.C.E.) in which Egypt reached the height of power and wealth for the third time in its history.

About 5 years and 7 months into his reign, Amenhotep IV became "a legend" or "a fool," depending on your point of view. At that time, in fact, he took on a new name, and called himself Akhenaten. At the same time, he repudiated the whole plethora of Egyptian gods, their traditions, and their priests. He affirmed that "life" comes "from the Light," and that only to this "Light" should one be devoted. Akhenaten modified an Egyptian religious symbol of a pre-existing solar god and made it the symbol of "Aton," the "Light." "Monotheism" was born.

Unlike almost all deities of that time, Egyptian or otherwise, the deity Aton, or "the Light," was never represented by Akhenaten in a human manner, or by any animal. The "heretical" pharaoh represented this "god" as a disk from which emanated numerous rays of light ending in hands. Each hand carried the symbol of life, or "Ankh," at the level of the nostrils of human beings, mainly members of Pharaoh's family. The message, then, was the following: from the "Light" comes the breath of life. Such original, complex, and profound symbolism was an absolute novelty for the world of that time.

In the "Stele of the Sphinx" commissioned by his grandfather Thutmose IV, located between the legs of the colossal Sphinx at Giza, the Sun had been represented as a disk from which branched two arms embracing the royal scroll, the symbol of the pharaoh. Akhenaten took this symbol dedicated to the Sphinx and made it a central element in Egypt. As we shall see later, this direct reference to the "Sphinx Stele" by Akhenaten is by no means accidental.

Akhenaten was the consort of Queen Nefertiti, a mythical Egyptian ruler considered by many scholars to be one of the most beautiful women who ever lived on Earth. Akhenaten's beautiful consort supported him across the board in what was for all intents and purposes the greatest "religious revolution" in history, at least up to that time.

To initiate a "new Egypt" under the sign of "Light," Pharaoh Akhenaten gave orders for a new capital to be built, called "Akhetaten" (Horizon of Aton), in the Amarna region. It became a city without statues of the various deities or war scenes. Nothing like this had ever been seen on Earth until that time. The city of Akhetaten (Horizon of Aton), was to be a "Florence ante litteram." From that city, in Akhenaten's intentions, a true "Renaissance" for Egypt and for the entire world would begin.

As long as this extraordinary character was alive, things proceeded according to his plans. The temples of the gods were closed, Egypt did not declare war on its neighbours and the new capital attracted crowds of Egyptians who began to convert to this new idea. But with the demise of Akhenaten, things changed quickly and drastically. The powerful priests of the cults proscribed by the rebellious pharaoh, joined by representatives of the army, reared their heads again.

After his death, Akhenaten's monuments were dismantled and made untraceable. His statues were torn to pieces, and his name was erased from the descendants of the pharaohs. Even one of his direct successors, named Tutankhaten, whose name meant "Living Image of Aton," was forced to change his name. He had to call himself Tutankhamun, meaning "Living Image of Amun," to honour the traditional Egyptian deity, which had been restored after Akhenaten's death.

20 - The first "facilitator"

The records of later pharaohs refer to Akhenaten as "the enemy" or "that criminal." In particular, Pharaoh Horemheb, who succeeded Pharaoh Ay, initiated a true "iconoclastic" campaign to erase any trace of Akhenaten and his "circle" from Egyptian history. Horemheb's destructive fury did not spare even the sarcophagi where the dead were buried, a gesture that would have horrified every Egyptian of that time, even the most abject. Akhenaten's name was to be erased from history. So what is known today about Akhenaten is only what managed to survive the "censorship by fire" practiced by Horemheb and his other peers.

Of the cult "of the life that comes from the Light," there was no trace left in Egypt for millennia, until archaeologists found the few remnants of this incredible story, which almost seems to us like something out of an adventure movie. This cult was reborn in Israel as the "cult of Yahweh," or the Jewish religion.

Man or woman?

So far, we have written about what, with reasonable certainty, is known about Akhenaten and his wife Nefertiti, and their extraordinary attempt at cultural and religious "revolution." But in reality, the things we do not know about Akhenaten are many more than what we do know. In fact, the "erasure" from history of Akhenaten and his family by the pharaohs of "restoration and counter-revolution" was very profound and, unfortunately, highly effective. Only scraps of information have remained, escaped by pure chance from the destructive fury of the pharaohs of the "ancient religion," and which archaeologists try to reconstruct as best they can. But they themselves admit that, in most cases, these are only guesses or mere clues.

What things do not we know about Akhenaten? One of the mysteries surrounding both Akhenaten and his family concerns their physical appearance. Their representations are unique in Egyptian history, and perhaps even in world history. While all pharaohs are portrayed with perfect, young, slender, and strong bodies, the statues of Akhenaten and his family members completely escape this norm.

For example, Akhenaten's statues, from the time he assumed his "new name," are strongly "androgynous." This means that while depicting a male, his sculptures possess undeniably feminine elements. In fact, in some statues the pharaoh's chest appears to be much more like that of a woman than that of a man. His belly is protruding and flabby, like that typical of a woman after childbirth. Her hips are wide and prosperous, similar to those of a full-fleshed woman. His lips are also very fleshy, to the point that some believe Akhenaten was actually a woman.

It would certainly not have been the first time that a woman "pharaoh" passed herself off "as a man." Queen Hatshepsut (who lived about 150 years before Akhenaten), who ruled in her own right as "pharaoh" after the death of her husband, had herself depicted with the beard typical of pharaohs, despite being a woman. We do not know whether she did this for "reasons of state," whether she wanted to fool her subjects by passing herself off as a man, or whether she even did it to "mock" the customs of her time. Likewise, no one can know exactly why Akhenaten's statues have this strong androgynous connotation. But Akhenaten's strongly androgynous appearance is not the only mystery surrounding his figure.

An uncommon family

Not only Akhenaten, but his entire family are portrayed with truly bizarre physical attributes, to put it mildly. Both he and his beautiful wife Nefertiti, and even at least one of his daughters, are portrayed with an exceptionally elongated skull. It appears as if the skull extends backward at more than twice the normal length. The eyes tend to be almond-shaped and strongly elongated. Akhenaten's face is much longer than normal.

The rest of the body of Akhenaten's family is also highly abnormal. The limbs are very thin, especially in comparison with the rest of the body. In addition, the fingers of the hands are thin and at least twice as long as normal. In addition, the last phalanx of the index finger of the hand seems to have a "natural dislocation," not being in line with the rest of the finger. The same is true for the toes. The forms of Akhenaten and his family members are so unusual that Professor Bob Brier, a world-renowned Egyptologist, and Egyptian language teacher at "New School" University in New York, used these words in one of his documentaries, "It is as if a creature from another planet had been catapulted into the Egyptian desert."

One element further complicates the picture. In the paintings in which Akhenaten and his family are portrayed near other Egyptians, the rest of the people have normal features, like those visible in all the rest of Egyptian artistic production. Only the "royal family" is portrayed so abnormally, almost "alien." Why? Basically, there are two kinds of answers to this question, which guide the two main schools of thought on the subject.

The first school of thought tells us that this is just a new artistic expression that matured with the advent of Akhenaten, a new way of depicting the pharaoh and the royal family. But this approach to the problem turns many people's mouths. In fact, several writings from that time that have been found, as well as all the art of that period, suggest that it was Akhenaten's will that court artists portray himself and his family as they really were. They did not want to be "idealized" like the rest of the Egyptian pharaohs, who were always depicted as perfect human beings. So the idea that court artists "deformed" the pharaoh's body in pursuit of a new style of painting seems rather unlikely.

But if the pharaoh encouraged a realist art, then he, his wife and daughters really appeared as they were portrayed by court artists. This brings us to the second and most likely school of thought, which tells us that Akhenaten and his family members really did have those forms. According to several researchers, some genetic defects and other diseases had produced deformities in Akhenaten's family, such as a much longer than normal skull, exceptionally long fingers, and an elongated face. Moreover, according to these scholars, Akhenaten, assuming he was a man and not a woman, really had "androgynous" forms.

But how come the whole royal family was affected by these "deformities"? The mummies of Akhenaten and Nefertiti have disappeared (more on this later). Therefore, it is not possible to conduct a DNA examination of these people to know whether they were subject to some genetic mutation or other disease. One can only speculate from the statues and paintings depicting them.

Prominent physicians have proposed "clinical" reasons for this mystery. For example, Dr. Irwin Braverman specializes in determining the health of individuals based on their portraits and teaches at Yale University School of Medicine. According to him, Akhenaten's androgynous form was due to a genetic mutation in the pharaoh that caused him to produce female hormones rather than male ones. Wanting to use technical language, Braverman attributed the pharaoh's "bisexual" form to "familial gynecomastia," brought on by a hereditary syndrome called "aromatase excess syndrome." Egyptologist and archaeologist Donald B. Redford said he supports Braverman's belief. Other equally famous doctors hypothesize different diseases, such as "Frohlich syndrome," "Klinefelter syndrome," or "Marfan syndrome."

But the "hereditary disease" theory runs up against a rather obvious, and easily provable, fact. Assuming that Akhenaten was indeed ill with one of these diseases, and that by heredity this was also transmitted to his daughters, this does not explain one detail. That is, why Queen Nefertiti, who according to all evidence was not a blood relative of Akhenaten, also had the same abnormalities in the depictions. How Akhenaten's "hereditary disease," whatever it was, could have infected his consort, no one can explain.

In fact, the mystery of the "anomalous body" of Akhenaten and his family has never found a definitive explanation. If the profound physical diversity from the rest of the Egyptians is added to the profound diversity of thought from everything Egypt stood for at that time (coupled with the fact that his statue never appears while he was a teenager, but only as an "adult"), it has prompted more than one scholar to wonder if Akhenaten was really "someone from outside."

A dead body never found

After Akhenaten, no other pharaoh was depicted in that way by court artists. By comparing the skeleton of his mummy, it would have been possible to understand whether the deformed appearance given to the statues depicting Akhenaton was real or just an artistic representation. But not even the most accredited of Egyptologists can tell us without fear of being wrong whether Akhenaten's mummy has been found or not. Let us see why.

According to some scholars, Akhenaten ruled as pharaoh about 17 years, five of them under the name Amenhotep IV, and the remaining twelve under the name Akhenaten (but it is thought that during the last year of his reign, while the pharaoh was still alive, two other figures ruled in his stead, probably his wife Nefertiti and his brother Smenkhara). It is not known exactly when Akhenaten was born. He is thought to have died in 1334 BCE at the age of about forty. So some think he was born around 1374 B.C., but even that is only a guess. Other scholars think that Akhenaten was as much as ten years younger than previously thought, so his reign lasted much less.

We know for sure that Akhenaten had a few daughters, but it is not known precisely how many. About any sons, however, we know truly little. Previously, two sons, Smenkhara and Tutankhamun, were attributed to Akhenaten. But with the use of modern diagnostic techniques that can compare human DNA, it was definitively ruled out in 2010 that Smenkhara was Akhenaten's son. He was actually his carnal brother. Whether Tutankhamun was indeed Akhenaten's natural son, however, still remains a big question mark, one that can probably never be fully clarified.

In fact, the only mummy clued in as "probably belonging" to Akhenaten, referred to by scholars as "Mummy 61074," found in the tomb named KV55, is shrouded in mystery. Although it has been subjected to DNA testing using the most futuristic techniques, the results have not completely clarified who really owned that mummy. They have only come to the certain conclusion that mummy 61074 is Tutankhamun's biological father, and that he fathered him with one of Akhenaten's secondary wives. But that the mummy in tomb KV55, that is, Tutankhamun's "biological father," is really Akhenaten, cannot be proven. In fact, Akhenaten's "secondary wife" may have fathered Tutankhamun with another member of the royal family, perhaps after Akhenaten had died. Several archaeologists lean toward this second hypothesis.

As we have seen above, several have advanced the hypothesis that Akhenaten suffered from some kind of syndrome or disease that made him deformed, and this would explain in part why he was kept "hidden" when he was a child, and why he was depicted in statues depicting him with physical oddities. But CT-assisted examination of mummy 61074 and other definitely related mummies showed that neither the owner of that skeleton nor his family suffered from hereditary physical defects. This conclusion leads several archaeologists to believe that mummy 61074, because it lacked physical defects consistent with Akhenaten's appearance, did not belong to him, but to his brother Shemkara.

Moreover, Mummy 61074's sarcophagus is a "reuse" of a sarcophagus prepared for a woman, which was then adapted only later for use by a man. It appears from the findings that it was a job done with some haste. This is very unusual for a pharaoh. In fact, practically from the very moment a member of the royal house was crowned pharaoh, preparations for his future funeral began. Egyptian tombs are famous for their pomp and grandeur. How is it that upon the death of one of the greatest pharaohs in history, his body was "hastily" placed in a tomb prepared for a woman and then "readjusted" to accommodate a man? This undeniable detail makes many believe that that is not Akhenaten's tomb, but that of a pharaoh who reigned briefly, too briefly to have time to arrange a sarcophagus "worthy" of a king.

From this point of view, it is more likely that the sarcophagus belonged to Smenkhara, who ruled only 1 year, and not Akhenaten, who ruled about 16 years. The sudden end of Smenkhara's reign after only 1 year of rule may have found his burial attendants unprepared, and they were forced to "improvise," quickly readjusting what they had. In this case, Smenkhara, Akhenaten's brother, who was co-regent during the last year of Akhenaten's reign, became pharaoh himself. He would therefore be the father of Tutankhamun, who was fathered by one of Akhenaten's secondary wives. This would explain, according to several scholars, why Tutankhamun is not mentioned until his appearance on the throne at the age of nine. As Akhenaten's grandson, and not his carnal son, he never appeared portrayed with the Pharaoh's other daughters.

All these clues lead one to think that the mummy that some say "might have belonged" to Akhenaten is actually that of his brother. "Genetic defects" seem to be completely absent in this mummy, which further complicates the whole scenario. How is it possible for a genetic defect to "turn on" only for a single member of a family, and then never reappear, either before or after, in any other member of the family? The researchers are puzzled.

Appeared suddenly

Despite being the son of a pharaoh, as a child Akhenaten is never portrayed with the royal family of which he was supposed to be a part, not even once. Akhenaten as a child and teenager simply does not exist in the official portraits of the royal family (as would also happen later for Tutankhamun). Along with his supposed parents, only his sisters appear, but no male. (Conversely, of his "brother" Thutmose, who should have become pharaoh instead of him, had death not struck him at an early age, some accounts would exist.) Why does the young Akhenaten never appear in "family portraits"?

Some scholars suggest that this absence of the young Akhenaten's representation in the royal family was due to some physical defect, which the royal family did not want to make obvious. But other equally celebrated scholars point out that Akhenaten may not have been the only pharaoh who had a physical defect as a boy. For example, analysing the mummy of one of his successors, the young Tutankhamun, it was discovered that he had a "club foot" and was lame. Perhaps he had other ailments as well. But official depictions of Tutankhamun report a proud and perfect-looking young man, even though he is depicted sitting, not standing, while performing some royal functions. Could not the same have been done with the young Akhenaten?

According to others, Akhenaten was not depicted with the royal family for a quite simple reason: when those statues were made, Akhenaten was not part of the royal family, or at the very least, not in his full capacity. So Akhenaten already appears as an "adult" for the simple reason that he approached the royal house, or at least the pharaoh, while he was already that age. Somehow Akhenaten "came from the outside." But in this case, was he really a member of Pharaoh's family?

Did he really die in Egypt?

In 2021, in a limestone quarry near present-day Dayr Abū Ḥinnis, an inscription was discovered that reads, "Great Bride of the King, His Beloved, Lady of the Two Lands, Neferneferuaton Nefertiti." The inscription is dated to the "16th year of the reign, 3rd month of Akhet, 28th day" of Akhenaten's reign. This inscription confirms that in the 17th year of Akhenaten's reign, the "Lady of Egypt" was still Nefertiti. She is called the "bride of the king," and thus it is implied that Akhenaten was still alive at that time. This disproves earlier theories that Nefertiti died before her consort. But why is the pharaoh not mentioned by name, while the figure of his wife is given great prominence?

Moreover, in one of the "Amarna letters," an official correspondence between Pharaoh and other individuals, the signature of Pharaoh Neferneferuaten, not Akhenaten, is given. According to several scholars this is a woman's name, probably that of Nefertiti. Since it is written in official correspondence, this would mean that Nefertiti, at least for a period of time toward the end of Akhenaten's reign, held the position of pharaoh. How is it that Nefertiti briefly reigned as pharaoh, and not as regent, in Akhenaten's place during the last months (perhaps a year) of his reign, if he was still alive?

If Akhenaten had died at that time, there would have been succession to the new pharaoh, and in the vacant period Nefertiti would have been only a "regent." But from the found correspondence it is understood that Neferneferuaten (Nefertiti with the title as pharaoh) was a pharaoh in her own right. What had happened? Everyone knows that something must have happened in the last period of Akhenaten's reign, but there is no direct evidence to indicate what really happened in Amarna's court. One can only speculate.

Let us try to imagine what might have happened, stressing that there is currently no direct archaeological evidence on these hypotheses. When Pharaoh Akhenaten was about forty years old, his life was at a crossroads. As a political leader, there were now many who wanted him dead, and he knew that very well. They wanted him dead were the priests of the ancient Egyptian religion, who had been ousted by him and the Amarnian Heresy. The various commanders of his own army wanted him dead, because of his disinterest in foreign policy, which at that time was essentially implemented by war. Akhenaten hated war, and for that reason his military hated him. They wanted him dead, all those whose economy had gone to hell because of the pharaoh's new religion. In fact, religion, in Egypt, was one of the engines of the economy and the redistribution of wealth. Except for those who had followed him to his new capital, Akhetaten (Amarna), the whole of Egypt had isolated

Pharaoh Akhenaten. Pharaoh was thus alone, with his wife as his last ally, locked up in his desert capital of Amarna.

Although Akhenaten was now isolated as a political leader, no one would ever dare to publicly raise his hands to the pharaoh. Not out of loyalty to him, but because the entire Egyptian government rested on the idea of the pharaoh's absolute untouchability. Thus there was a kind of unwritten covenant that forbade the use of violence on any pharaoh, even the most hated. There were less conspicuous and absolutely more effective methods of getting rid of "unwieldy" pharaohs, the most widely used of which was surely poison. Akhenaten probably expected to be poisoned at any moment. He probably realized that he was living in a now dead-end situation. What would he have done? Would he have waited for someone to hand him "the last cup of wine," obviously poisoned? Or would he have tried to fight back?

A revealing clue in this regard may be the "absence of the corpse." Although Akhenaten's burial place has been found, unlike his family members, his mummy (and thus his body) has never been officially identified definitively because some details do not match. But if so, what happened to Akhenaten?

According to the opinion of some scholars, Nefertiti should have ruled as pharaoh for at least a year while her husband was still alive. This would mean that at that time Akhenaten was not dead, but was unable to rule, or perhaps no longer wanted to rule. So he ruled his wife in his place. What prevented Akhenaten from ruling until the time of his supposed "official death"?

It is possible that "to poison" Pharaoh Akhenaten chose "life." In what sense? It is highly unlikely that Akhenaten would have wanted to retrace his steps, restoring the polytheistic cult of deities, and renouncing his pacifist policy. It is equally unlikely that his enemies would have let him live much longer. It is therefore possible that, perhaps uniquely in Egypt, Akhenaten decided to renounce his position as pharaoh in order to continue simply as the "high priest" of Aton. After all, his entire history indicates that this was what was really close to his heart. The role of pharaoh, on the other hand, left him rather indifferent. This would explain why Nefertiti (and perhaps also her brother Shemkara) reigned in his stead before his "official death."

The idea that Akhenaten abdicated the throne so that he would not end up poisoned is not borne out by any Egyptian findings. It is therefore only an argument that may have its own logic, but which never seems to have official confirmation, since almost nothing remains of this pharaoh's history. But wanting to continue this line of reasoning, if indeed Akhenaten had wanted to abdicate his role as pharaoh, then one can imagine that as soon as the news reached Thebes (the Egyptian capital where the most important priests resided), the priestly caste will have "demanded" news of an "official death" of Akhenaten. (The "official death" served the bureaucracy of the time to start the process of appointing a new Pharaoh.) In fact, for the ancient Egyptian religion, the pharaoh was the embodiment of divinity, and one could not "resign" from this position. One could leave that role only by dying. Whether such death was then "real" or only "official" was a less important matter.

If indeed Akhenaten had decided to vacate his throne in favour of his wife, Nefertiti, it is therefore entirely possible that at some point news was given that Pharaoh had died. However, Akhenaten's "official death" would have quickly become a "royal death" if he had not quickly left Egypt, perhaps in disguise. Indeed, the hatred brooded by the religious and military caste toward Akhenaten was too deep, too radical to allow him to live at large as High Priest of Aton. Now that he was deprived of his "untouchability" as pharaoh, the priests of Thebes must have wanted his blood as well. (It should not be forgotten that even this was not enough. They went as far as to erase his name, smash his statues, desecrate his family sarcophagi, and burn any papyrus that spoke of him.) Akhenaten was probably left with nothing but escape. This may explain why his mummy does not appear to be in Egypt.

An "alter ego" for Akhenaten

If indeed Akhenaten fled to have his life saved after "resigning" as pharaoh, serving as a kind of "High Priest" for the god Aton, this detail of his life would correspond to that of an equally famous personage, albeit for completely distinct reasons. We are talking about Moses, the mythical character described in the Bible, commonly believed to be the founder of Israel.

Who was Moses in fact? For several scholars he is a legendary character, a figment of the imagination of those who wrote the Exodus account. According to others, he is a real-life character, whose name is inextricably linked to the Ten Commandments he received while leading the Jewish people through the desert, beginning in 1613 B.C. (but religious tradition shifts his supposed existence between 1500 B.C. and 1200 B.C.).

20 - The first "facilitator"

According to the traditional account, for the first 40 years of his life, Moses had been an Egyptian prince, after which he was forced despite himself to flee Egypt to save his life. Do you notice a similarity with the story of Akhenaten's life?

But the similarities between the two characters do not end there. Both Akhenaten and Moses were in fact Egyptians. In fact, the name "Moses" is Egyptian in origin, not Jewish. This name is derived from the Egyptian word "Moses" and means "son" or "protégé." In fact, it would not make sense for a child, described in the Bible as the adopted son of Pharaoh's daughter and therefore a possible heir to the throne, to bear a Hebrew name. It was only later, after generations of Jews heard the story of the "Egyptian prince rescued from the waters of the Nile River," that the Egyptian term "Moses" also acquired the meaning of "rescued from the waters," a meaning it retains to this day in the Hebrew language.

Both Akhenaten and Moses had a similar story. In fact, it is said of Moses that he belonged to Pharaoh's family as an adopted member. It is said that Moses, while only a few months old, was found in the Nile River, placed in a small floating basket. This was a fairly common custom for Egyptian noblewomen, especially those of Thebes, who entrusted in this way "to fate" an illegitimate child who could not be raised as their own. Similarly, many scholars advance the hypothesis that somehow Akhenaten was also adopted by the pharaoh's family. In fact, as we have said, the infant Akhenaten does not appear in statues depicting the royal family before his accession to the throne.

20 - The first "facilitator"

It is said of Moses that he had a physical defect in his mouth, which prevented him from speaking fluently. Statues of Akhenaten depict him with such features that many people think he had a physical defect in his face, which was very elongated. Moses went down in history for teaching the Jews about the existence of one true God. For his part, Akhenaten went down in history for teaching the Egyptians the worship of Aton as the "one true God," repudiating the plethora of Egyptian deities. He was the first "monotheist" in recorded history.

Of Moses it is said that he was the mediator between Yahweh and his people, just as of Akhenaten it is said that he was the mediator between Aton and his family, and thus between Aton and the Egyptians. Moses taught that God was not similar to any existing creation, neither human, animal, vegetable nor inanimate. The only time Moses "saw God," according to the account he saw a formless being as bright as the Sun (See Exodus 33:19-22; 34:5). It is also said of Akhenaten that he saw an apparition of the solar disk of Aton in the desert. And Akhenaten also did not depict the god Aton using any other living being, neither human nor animal. Rather he used the symbol of the Sun, to indicate an extremely powerful source of light.

This is indeed a singular fact, since in traditional Egyptian religion the various deities were systematically represented as humans who had animal heads. Aton, on the contrary, was represented by the solar disk, a physical symbol for indicating light. In fact, Aton was seen as "the god of light." For Akhenaten, the god Aton was "light," just as for Moses he was Yahweh.

20 - The first "facilitator"

As we read in the text of the "Book of the History of the Heavens and the Earth," contained in the book of Genesis, Elohim (the god of the earliest part of Genesis) is the sole creator of all things. Likewise, Akhenaten taught that Aton was the creator of all things, and he was a benign god who cared for all his creatures. One of the Hebrew appellations used to address God in the Torah is "Adonai." According to some scholars, this name has the same root as the name of the ancient Syrian god "Adon," which in turn would have a strong assonance with the god worshipped by Akhenaten, namely "Aton." (Other scholars, however, disagree with this explanation, and say that there is no correlation between the two names.)

Akhenaten ordered the names of traditional gods to be erased throughout Egypt, and many Egyptians changed their names if they contained the name of a deity. Akhenaten himself changed his own name, which was originally Amenhotep IV since the previous name included the name of the Egyptian god Amun. This attitude seems to follow the "first Commandment" given by Yahweh to Moses in the Hebrew version proposed by the priests, namely to "have no other gods but me."

According to some commentators, Psalm 104 dedicated to Yahweh contained in the Hebrew Tanakh seems to have similarities with the "song of Aton," attributed to Akhenaten, the Pharaoh who dared to set aside the gods of Egypt to promote the worship of one "God." According to others, these similarities are merely coincidental and insubstantial. Although they may not belong to the period when Akhenaten was alive, some Egyptian literary works recall certain passages contained in the Ancient Hebrew Scriptures. For example, several scholars see in the famous account of "Sinueh the Egyptian" a direct reference to the story of Joseph's son of Jacob who became prime minister in Egypt under the name Zaphenat-Panea.

Moses is considered the founder of the nation of Israel. The detail that Moses had grown up as a "hated" Egyptian would never have been included in his "official biography" had it not been something absolutely certain and in the public domain at the time. Thus, this detail argues in favour of the historical existence of an Egyptian who had become "Moses." Had this character been only the figment of the writer's imagination, this "inconvenient" detail, his Egyptian nationality, would probably never have been included.

Rabbinic Judaism asserts that Moses lived in a time period between 1391 B.C. and 1271 B.C. It is indeed peculiar to note that the time period in which the Jews believe Moses was born overlaps with the time period in which Akhenaten is thought to have been born, around 1374 B.C. Thus, during the time period when according to Jewish tradition Moses proclaimed to Pharaoh the existence of "one god," according to Egyptian chronicles it was Akhenaten himself who taught his subjects to believe in the same concept, monotheism.

The similarities between the two characters are about the time they lived, the place they lived, their childhood, their adult lives, their rank, their deeds, and why the entire world remembers them. The similarities are too pronounced and detailed to be accidental. It is clear that the same person is being talked about, from two different points of view. There is a historical point of view, the Egyptian, and a religious point of view, the Jewish.

But there is also a fundamental difference between Akhenaten and Moses. Despite the desire of his successors to literally erase him from history, we today have ample historical and archaeological evidence of the existence of the "heretical pharaoh," Akhenaten. Conversely, of the existence of Moses there is no evidence, either historical or archaeological. About him we have only a traditional religious account: the Bible. Of the two characters, the "original" one is therefore unquestionably Akhenaten. Moses is his fictionalized "transposition" from Jewish tradition.

The cloud

Making Akhenaten coincide with Moses is anything but a detail. If the "mutant" features of Akhenaten and his family have caused many to cry "alien," this doubt becomes even stronger if the figure of Moses is substituted for that of Akhenaten. Indeed, according to the Bible, Moses was able to perform superhuman feats. But not only this. We are also told that, during the Exodus in the desert, this character was perpetually followed in his every move by a small "cloud,"

20 - The first "facilitator"

which at night was as bright as fire. And from within that cloud, as from within a ship, someone spoke to him.

We quote below some passages from the biblical account to clarify what we are talking about:

Exodus 19:9 "And Yahweh said, `Behold, I am about to come to you *within the cloud*, that the people may hear when I speak to you [*from the cloud*], and they may believe your words when you yourself speak."

Exodus 24:18 "Moses *therefore entered into the cloud*, and afterward went up into the mountain."

Exodus 34:5 "And Yahweh *came down from heaven, being in the cloud*, and spent time with [Moses], and spoke to him."

Exodus 33:9 "And as soon as Moses entered the tent, *the cloud descended, it stopped at the entrance of the tent*. And from the cloud Yahweh spoke to Moses."

Exodus 40:36-39 "At each stage of their journey, *when the cloud rose from the tent*, the Israelites would raise their camp. If the cloud had not risen, no one would have set out. For *Yahweh was in the cloud* during the day. Instead, during the night [in the cloud] there was something like fire, visible to all the house of Israel, all the time of their journey."

A first consideration when reading these verses is that the "entity" behind the cloud was not speaking to the people, but to Akhenaten/Moses. This is a further similarity between the two characters. In fact, in all the paintings of Akhenaten together with the god Aton, it is observed that Aton's attention is always directed to Pharaoh and his family. It is then the pharaoh who is the "spokesman" for the rest of the Egyptians. The same thing is noted with the Exodus account. Yahweh speaks only to Moses, and it is he who then repeats his words to the nation.

Moreover, as we have seen, in the Hebrew account of the events of the Exodus, the same element returns almost obsessively, namely, the "cloud" that followed and protected Moses/Akhenaten. This cloud thus moved independently of the wind. It was very dense and did not allow one to see what was inside. At night, on the other hand, it was bright, like fire. The cloud went up and down, like a helicopter, and could even "stop on the ground," allowing those inside it to talk to Moses/Akhenaten while standing in front of the tent. In another passage, it was again the "cloud" that said that Moses' body should never be found. Moses went up the mountain to meet the one who spoke "from the cloud," and nothing more was heard of him. (See Deuteronomy chapter 34). The same can be said of Akhenaten, whose body was never found.

We could go on and on with this theme, but the concept is quite clear. We are accustomed to thinking of Moses as a gentleman of a certain age, with a white beard, covered in Hebrew clothes leaning on a staff. But what if, instead of the "Hebrew Moses," we substituted the historical figure of Akhenaten? What would we think about seeing a tall man in his forties, with an unnaturally elongated face, a skull stretched almost twice as long as normal, the fingers of his hands very long, his limbs slender, approaching something dark that looks like a cloud, but reaches to the ground? What would we have thought if inside the cloud was something bright like fire, and that from that "something" came a voice speaking to

Akhenaten? To what would we have compared the one who would emerge from the cloud to speak to Akhenaten? If we substituted the "Jewish" figure of Moses for the historical figure of Akhenaten in the Exodus narrative, we would seem to see something akin to Spielberg's "Close Encounters of the Third Kind."

Is it all the result of incredible coincidences, intertwining legends, hereditary genetic diseases, and other such stories? Of course, it could be. The time that separates us from these events, more than 3,000 years, is too long, and there is too little evidence to venture firm conclusions. It could be that Akhenaten and his family were indeed ill, or had genetic defects, which would be the cause of their "alien" features.

In addition, the biblical account of Exodus is full of inaccuracies, or outright "historical falsehoods." (For example, all research has shown that no "slave" Hebrew people who could have numbered several million ever resided in Egypt. Moreover, there is no record of any "slave people" wandering for 40 years dying of hardship on the plains of Sinai, as Exodus relates.) Therefore, one cannot take this story for "fool's gold." It follows that it is possible that the story of the 'cloud' told in Exodus is the product of a mind capable of imagining the behaviour of a 'half-alien hiding in a cloud' more than three thousand years before modern times. All of this cannot be ruled out, and objectively may be a valid answer to the various questions on this subject.

But similarly, it cannot be ruled out either that, at least in its essentials, there is "also some truth" in the Exodus account of the mysterious "heretic" pharaoh, Akhenaten/Moses.

Probably a young Egyptian prince really did encounter in the desert a strange light, described as "the bright cloud" in the Bible, or as the "rising sun of Aton" in the Egyptian account. Perhaps that encounter really did change his life forever. Even, one may go as far as to say that the change of name, the change of physiognomy, and the total change of politics and religion that took place in that Egyptian, literally from night to the day, may lead one to suspect that Amenhotep IV and Akhenaten were not the same person, but only resembled each other. It would be the first case not only of "abduction" but also of "alien substitution" in history. And we might go as far as to think that "the substitute" travelled with "the sun of Aton," in the manner of the Egyptians, or with "the luminous cloud," in the manner of the Hebrews. But of course these are only suppositions, which can neither be confirmed nor denied.

In fact, at least about Akhenaten, it is rather easy to speculate, since it is really difficult to find someone who can disprove or confirm them. The truth is that we simply do not have evidence about many hidden aspects of this extraordinary personage's life, and we can only try to reconstruct what might have happened, but without being able to give these ideas any proof that would turn them into certainties.

But one thing we know for sure. Akhenaten/Moses changed the history of the world, and we still feel that influence today. He was therefore no ordinary personage. The combination of the historical details of Pharaoh Akhenaten with the fictional story of Moses argues in favour of an Egyptian pharaoh who found something far greater than himself in the desert. The continuation of that life indicates the deliberate attempt of a clear mind to change the social foundations of the greatest world power of the time, Egypt. And to change society, he attacked the very basis on which it rested: its religion. The fact that after more than 3,000 years the cult of the "one god" embraces more than half the world's population indicates that that attempt was at least partially successful.

21 - The Last

But the best-known and most influential "facilitator" in recorded history is undoubtedly Yahoshua ben Yoseph from Nazareth, known throughout the world as Jesus Christ. Both admirers and detractors say the man really changed the world. Where did he come from? Was he just the son of a Jewish woman, as the story tells us? Or, as his disciples say of him, did he come "from another world"? Let us try to figure that out by examining the only "physical trace" he, perhaps, left on this earth.

The Shroud is a linen sheet woven in a herringbone pattern measuring about 4.41 x 1.13 meters, preserved in the Turin Cathedral. This sheet has a peculiarity that is more unique than rare. Due to a chemical-physical process that is still not entirely clear, the fabric has a large pale yellow stain that possesses the obvious appearance of a life-size human being.

The image depicts a bearded man, dead. The marks of nails driven into his hands and feet can be seen. A blow received on the side of the deceased is also glimpsed. On the body we see evidence of about 120 Roman scourge blows, a number about six times greater than that received by those sentenced to death by the Romans at that time. On the scalp are marks consistent with a "bramble helmet" pressed on the head. The man's nose appears to have been violently struck by something. In short, this body appears similar to that described in the gospels in connection with the torture and killing of Jesus of Nazareth.

The shroud of the Shroud wrapped the human figure both from the back and on the back. So the image is repeated twice, both front and back. The image is in negative, so it must be made "positive" in order to see many of the details contained in it. Conversely, one would see only a faint yellow halo on a linen cloth, with the faint "shadow" of a face.

A series of independent tests conducted in 1988 at the University of Oxford, at the University of Arizona and at the Swiss Federal Institute of Technology concluded that, with 95 percent approximation, the Shroud material can be dated to around 1260-1390 AD. It would thus be a medieval artifact, created more than 1,000 years after the appearance of Jesus of Nazareth. This dating, on the other hand, perfectly matches the period of the Shroud's first appearance in church history. In fact, the first certain testimony of the existence of the Shroud dates back to 1390 AD. At that time, Bishop Pierre d'Arcis in Lirey, France, wrote a memorandum to Antipope Clement VII (Obedience of Avignon). That writing stated that the Shroud that is now kept at the Cathedral of Turin at that time actually existed but was a fake. Furthermore, the same writing stated that its creator had confessed to the forgery.

Until recently, all of the hypotheses used to challenge the 1988 radiocarbon dating that date the Shroud to the Middle Ages have been scientifically refuted. These include the medieval tissue repair hypothesis (which would have misled scholars). We can add the hypothesis of bio-contamination, and the hypothesis of carbon monoxide released during some of the fires that affected the Shroud (and which some thought might have affected its dating by the radiocarbon method). All this seemed to have put an "end" to the historicity of the Shroud.

That sheet seemed to be for all intents and purposes a medieval "fake."

A new discovery shuffles the cards

On April 11, 2022, an article entitled: "X-ray Dating of a Turin Shroud's Linen Sample," by Professors Liberato De Caro, Teresa Sibillano, Rocco Lassandro, Cinzia Giannini and Giulio Fanti, appeared in the quarterly scientific journal Heritage (edited by CNR). This team of scholars applied to a Shroud sample a new system for assessing the antiquity of a tissue, called Wide-Angle X-ray Scattering (WAXS).

The abstract of this study says verbatim, "On a sample of the Shroud of Turin (TS), we applied a new method for dating ancient linen threads by analysing their structural degradation using "Wide-Angle X-ray Scattering (WAXS)." The X-ray dating method was applied to a TS sample consisting of a thread taken near the 1988/radiocarbon area (corner of the TS corresponding to the foot area of the front image, near the so-called Raes sample). The size of the linen sample was about 0.5 mm × 1 mm. We obtained one-dimensional integrated WAXS data profiles for the TS sample, which were fully compatible with similar measurements obtained on a linen sample whose date, according to historical records, is 55-74 AD, the period of the siege of Masada (Israel). The degree of natural aging of the cellulose constituting the flax in the investigated sample, obtained by X-ray analysis, showed that the TS fabric is much older than the seven centuries proposed by radiocarbon dating in 1988. The experimental results are compatible with the hypothesis that TS is a 2,000-year-old relic, as assumed by Christian tradition, provided it has been maintained at appropriate levels of average temperature s - 20.0-22.5°C - and related relative humidity - 75-55% - for 13 centuries of unknown history, in addition to the seven centuries of known history in Europe. To make the present result compatible with that of the 1988 radiocarbon test, TS would have had to have been preserved during its hypothetical seven centuries of life at an ambient temperature very close to the maximum values recorded on earth."

Briefly, the study tells us that the Shroud, provided it was not stored in exceptionally hot and exceptionally humid places, should be about 2,000 years old, and not about 700 years old as previously believed. Actually, already in the past few years several scholars, rereading the data of the radiocarbon examination carried out in 1988, had raised doubts about the 'accuracy of the analysis carried out. Reconstructing the "raw data" obtained from the 1988 'experiment, some had noted that it was not "consistent," and that therefore the examination should be repeated. But, partly because of the Vatican's reluctance to have the sheet examined, nothing more was done about it. Now, this article that appeared in Heritage magazine about the WAXS technique applied to the Shroud could be a major game changer.

Unexplained aspects

If we delve into the subject from a strictly scientific point of view, putting aside faith and what the Shroud represents for many believers, there are serious doubts that a craftsman from 1390 was able to "create" this sheet. The motivation for these doubts lies in the 'image itself. Let us see why.

Let us ask: from a physical point of view, what creates the yellowed image on the linen cloth? It is true that traces of tempera, i.e. colour, were found on the Shroud cloth. But after analysing the linen fibres that form the cloth with an optical microscope, it was realised that it is not this colour that generates the image. By analysing the individual filaments of the Shroud, it was seen that no colour penetrated inside the fibers of the fabric. Only the outermost layer, on the order of a few microns, is "yellowed." Based on known painting techniques, therefore, it seems impossible that that figure was "painted" in any way by an artist. Indeed, in that case, at least in part, the colour would have penetrated the flax fiber, which did not happen.

So what creates that yellowish image on the linen cloth? According to Prof. Emanuela Marinelli, the image is created neither by a coloured pigment nor by thermal processes. Rather, it would be a "yellowing" of the linen fabric, achieved by dehydration and oxidation of the fabric itself. Although the term sounds complicated, it is actually a process in all respects identical to the phenomenon whereby a delicate fabric of plant origin, exposed to light turns yellow. For example, even the pages of a book, over time, yellow for the same reason. Thus, there would be nothing mysterious about the phenomenon itself since it is a completely natural process. Except for one detail: in this case, the "yellowing" of the cloth "draws" on the linen a human image, with nail marks in the hands and feet, lash marks and other torture marks. In order to make the linen fabric yellow, leaving such an imprint, it would seem that an extremely bright human body was wrapped in that cloth. This body would then have "imprinted" the linen cloth, causing it to "age" in certain places through dehydration, just as light imprints the negative of a film

We are thus at the paradox. The phenomenon that caused the portrait to form seems, at first analysis, entirely "natural": the linen in those places has simply aged through dehydration and oxidation, and has thus "yellowed," as happens to the pages of an old book. But it becomes immediately clear that it is physically impossible for a fabric to age in such a way as to leave a "human" imprint on the cloth.

Failed attempts

Therefore, the "hunt" has begun for the method by which "the creator" of the Shroud, whoever he may be, could have accomplished something similar. Several experiments have been made. In 2009, Luigi Garlaschelli, professor of organic chemistry at the University of Pavia, did a life-size experiment using acid pigmentation on a model, and then putting the cloth in an oven to "age" it. Professor Garlaschelli comments on the result of his experiment this way, "The technique used seems incapable of producing an image with the most critical features of the image of the Shroud of Turin."

Other techniques used have been the use of bas-reliefs mixed with chemicals and heat, applied in many ways. Although several results appear to be similar to those produced on the cloth of the Shroud, none of them seem to come close enough to the final result to be considered "conclusive," especially upon 'microscopic investigation. It is one thing to create an image "similar" to that of the Shroud visible to the naked eye, and quite another to see the effect this image creates on the fibers of the cloth, using a microscope. In this second case, things do not match.

The 'experiment that seems to have come closest of all to achieving an image similar to the one found on the Shroud, both macroscopically and microscopically, was done at the ENEA laboratories in Frascati, directed by physicist Paolo Di Lazzaro, in 2017. Using an ultraviolet laser, and then heating the tissue "bombarded" by the laser, ENEA researchers achieved the closest result so far to the 'image contained in the Shroud.

This result would seem to support the thesis that what "printed" the image of the Shroud on the cloth was a powerful ultraviolet light, of the power of a laser, which also gave off some heat, but not such as to burn the linen. In this regard there are two options: if this "light" was point-like, like the small light of a laser, then someone used it to "draw" the Shroud. Or, if the "lamp" that generated the image of the Shroud was in the shape of a human being, then the linen cloth enveloped this "human lamp."

One step closer to reality

Assuming this hypothesis is plausible, which of the two "possibilities" mentioned above seems more likely? Was the Shroud "drawn" by a point laser, or was it imprinted by a "human-shaped lamp"? Undoubtedly the first hypothesis is the one that comes closest to the Shroud in our possession. In fact, if it is true that it was a light source that created the image of the Shroud, it seems that this light was used as a "brush" on a cloth. Why can we affirm this? The reasons are to be found in the anatomical proportions imprinted on the 'image.

For example, analysis of the two images that appear on the Shroud are compatible with a shroud used to wrap a body 1.75 meters long. But in this regard, the image imprinted on the front side of the Shroud of Turin is 1.95 meters long (part of the excess length depends on the 'anatomy of the human body). In contrast, the image opposite the first, is not exactly the same size as the image on the back, which turns out to be 2.02 meters long. According to anatomy scholars, this disproportion would not be possible if the cloth had covered a real body. Joe Nickell (a paranormal investigator) in 1983 and Gregory S. Paul (an independent researcher) in 2010, state on different grounds that the proportions of the Shroud image are not completely realistic. Gregory S. Paul states that the face and body proportions visible in the Shroud are unrealistic if it were a real human body. According to him, the forehead of the man imprinted on the shroud is too small to be real. The eyebrows are also unnatural, both in size and position. The arms, for their part, are too long. According to him, the printed figure cannot represent a real person, and the posture is also unnatural. According to these scholars, the "wrong" anatomical features of the Shroud can be explained if it was somehow "painted" in the Gothic style.

In addition, a Bloodstain Pattern Analysis (BPA) was performed on the Shroud in 2018. That is to say, simply put, some experts studied the way blood would have flowed from the wounds suffered by the man in the Shroud to see if the bloodstains found on the sheet are realistic or "made up." (It must be said that, at present, studies of the blood appearing on the Shroud have clarified that it is "primate blood," but it is not yet proven to be human blood. Another analysis would be needed to have a definitive confirmation, but at the moment Vatican approval has not yet been granted.)

Comparison of different tests showed that the blood trails on the forearms and the back of the hand are not connected and should have occurred at separate times. In addition, the rivulets on the front of the image are not consistent with the lines on the lumbar area. According to these studies, therefore, the blood that appears on the Shroud would also have been "painted" with real blood but would not belong to the body "drawn" on the linen cloth.

A revolutionary conclusion

Before moving on to hypothesize conclusions, some details should be added. The pollen powders found on the Shroud cloth are compatible with the plants growing around Jerusalem. The aragonite found on the linen is typical of the Jerusalem caves. Traces of Aloe and Myrrh, the ointments that were reportedly used in the preparation of Jesus' body, were also found.

How to put together all these data, which seem so discordant with each other, to understand what the Shroud actually is? Putting all these "scientific" elements together, and not dictated by faith or folklore, we come to a revolutionary, pulse-pounding conclusion. Let us list what we know with "near certainty"

(1)   We have a sheet, the latest analysis of which tells us that it may be about 2,000 years old.

(2)   On the sheet are the remains of aragonite typical of caves near Jerusalem.

(3)   On the cloth are traces of the flowers that sprouted in the spring in Jerusalem 2,000 years ago.

(4)   A human figure appears on the sheet obtained by "fabric aging," probably due to a very strong light source.

(5)   The image on the cloth closely resembles Jesus because it describes him exactly as the gospels report.

(6)   It is quite evident that this is not the "cast on cloth" of Jesus' dead   body, because the anatomical proportions of the image do not match those of a three-dimensional body. Instead, they look like a masterfully done "drawing."

(7)   A powerful, point source of light "then drew" on the cloth the image of a man being tortured and killed. That image vigorously recalls the story of Jesus' torture and killing.

(8)   The 'image is incredibly accurate on so many aspects, even on the marks in the scalp due to the thorns. Yet, it contains enough anatomical imperfections to remind us that it is only a "drawing," not an imprint. This is in keeping with Jesus' thinking, which was against any idol or object of worship.

But if that is the case, and at present there is no evidence to tell us otherwise, the question is: Who "drew" that image on the Shroud with a powerful ultraviolet, laser-like light? It does not appear that at the time of Yahoshua's life from Nazareth, or Jesus, anyone possessed such technology. Nor does it seem that even in the Middle Ages anyone knew how to do work like this. The "litmus test" comes from the fact that throughout the world there is not a single piece of cloth in which such an image was printed. If it were a pictorial or other technique, we would probably have other specimens similar to the Shroud. Instead, with the exception of the Shroud of Turin, there is nothing similar in the world. It is therefore quite clear that we are talking about an object "outside" the society of the past time.

A "self-portrait?"

From the accounts in the gospels, we note that the only being who claimed to have "come from heaven" at that time was Jesus himself. He is therefore the number one candidate to be the real "painter" who made the Shroud. And indeed, if we read carefully what the Gospels say, things cannot be otherwise. In discussing this point, however, let us take for granted what is said about Yahoshua of Nazareth in the gospels, namely, that he "came from heaven" (but never said he was a deity), was born naturally to a woman, after the age of thirty was killed, a few days later returned to life in a tomb, and after a time "disappeared" going back to where he came from.

Let us ask: Was Yahoshua, or Jesus, immortal? Had he been immortal, the Romans would not have been able to kill him. Instead, Yahoshua died under torture at the hands of the Romans, hanging from a Roman stauros for about four hours. Finally, a Roman's spear pierced his lung until it hit his heart, which no longer beat.

When he was resurrected, it was not a heavenly being that was raised, but the same mortal man who was killed by the Romans. The same body that had been carried dead into the tomb, wrapped in bandages, came forth, having freed itself from the burial bandages. According to the story, these bandages were found by his friends at the entrance to the tomb. It was he himself who told his close friend and disciple Thomas. Jesus told him to touch his wounds on his feet, hands, and side, which were still healing. If Jesus' body had not been the same one that was killed by the Romans, his resurrection would have been a hoax, a trick. Moreover, if Jesus' body had not been the same one that lay dead in the tomb, he would have lied to his friend Thomas. The invitation to touch "false" wounds, in addition to being a "hoax," would have been only a gruesome and cruel game.

If all this is true, then the Shroud could be the "signature" or portrait that the "alien" called Jesus left us. Indeed, at this point, we should say that it could be a kind of "self-portrait." Of course, this is a hypothesis, which can probably never be verified scientifically. But on balance, if indeed that cloth is 2,000 years old, and if indeed the human figure was imprinted on the linen by a very intense light, this may be by far the most plausible hypothesis.

While mentioning the various bandages that wrapped Jesus, the gospels do not say that these had any printed images. How so? Evidently that image at that time was not there. What are we saying? Experiments with lasers carried out at Frascati, in the laboratories of the CNR, show that although the image can be imprinted by a laser, it becomes visible to human eyes only later, either because of time, or because of a heat source acting on the cloth.

It is therefore possible that, assuming it really happened, at first Jesus' self-portrait, although imprinted in the cloth, was not visible in normal light. The disciples must have simply kept that sheet for themselves as a "keepsake" of their beloved master. It was only in time, perhaps over the years, that gradually that image became visible, by which time the gospels had already been compiled. This may be a probable reason why they do not mention it.

An alien?

In any case, the idea that the Shroud was drawn "scientifically" with something like a laser, and that it did not "appear" on the cloth for mystical reasons, makes the figure of Jesus much more like an alien than a "Messiah." Of course, we do not mean to say that Jesus was a "little green man," or a being descended from a flying saucer. From what the accounts tell us, Jesus-Yahoshua was in every way a human being. But at some point, in his life, he began to remember that he had "come down from heaven," in his own words. He had phrases like "you are of this world, I am not of this world." Or, he added, "very soon I will go back to where I came from." How can this apparent contradiction be explained?

Jesus' words closely remind us of the famous and beautiful movie K-Pax, which centred on a singular encounter with an extra-terrestrial. In that film, the alien had travelled through space using only his mind. Upon arriving on Earth, his mind "inhabited" the body of his friend. On Earth, therefore, the traveller was physically 100% human. Mentally, however, he was 100% alien. Having finished his mission, Prot (the alien's name), returned from whence he came, leaving only his friend's body on Earth. Well, about 2,000 years in advance, especially the gospel of John describes the coming of Jesus-Yahoshua to Earth in this way. He was in every way a human being (and in fact he died like any condemned man). But his mind was not human. His mind was from another place, or perhaps from another time.

After all, it is obvious that although he was Jewish by birth, Jesus-Yahoshua's teaching had nothing to do with the Jewish religion. It is beyond doubt that the "Abba" of whom Yahoshua spoke from Nazareth, that is, his Father, the very personification of love and forgiveness, could not have been "Yahweh of armies" worshipped in the Jerusalem temple by the Jews. According to Jewish accounts, the god of the Hebrews had been willing to slaughter tens of thousands of Egyptian children at the time of the Exodus, children whose only fault was that they were born in Egypt at the wrong time.

According to their accounts, this deity conducted the first known ethnic cleansing, exterminating all the people living in the land of Canaan, including children, to give that territory to the Jews. The "Law of Yahweh" imposed the death penalty for completely negligible behaviour. That same Law allowed such things as slavery, discrimination against women, religious discrimination, and many other violations of basic human rights. After all, although the canonical gospels portray him as the King of Israel or their Messiah, it is a historical fact that Yahoshua of Nazareth, or Jesus of Nazareth, never became the King of Israel, and that the Jews never recognized him as their Messiah. Therefore, either the Jewish prophecies about him were wrong, or the canonical gospels are wrong in stating that he was the Messiah of the Jews, or both.

But then who was Jesus-Yahoshua really? If he was an alien, what did he come to Earth to do? And if he really left, will he return? In one of the writings in which his words are reported, we read, "There will come a time when on Earth every nation will fight against other nations and every kingdom against other kingdoms, as has never happened before. In the same period of time there will be great earthquakes and, in one place after another, famines and epidemics. Then there will be great and unusual phenomena in the heavens. Attention will have to be paid during that period of time. All the nations of Earth will fall into anguish, seeing no way out of the situation in which they find themselves. People will feel lacking in fear and fearful anticipation of the things that are going to happen on the inhabited Earth, because there really will be a global upheaval. But when these things begin to happen, then the Great Destruction will also be nearby. But liberation from it will also be nearby. [...] At that time I will come back for you."

Was Jesus of Nazareth referring to a new "Reload" of the human species that would happen in the distant future? What does this "Reload" have to do with him? And what did he mean by the phrase "I will come back for you"? That will be the topic of the next book. Stay tuned.

By the same author

List of books by the same author where the themes set forth in this book are deeply explored, and where the material was drawn from.

Atlantis 2021 - Lost continent discovered

318 pages

12,794 Years ago - The visitors of Göbekli Tepe

260 pages

The path of the survivors

246 pages

An Alien named Jesus Christ

240 pages

Abba: Thus spoke Yahoshua of Nazareth

326 pages

The Sphinx and the Black Goddess

209 pages

In search of the book of Yahweh

137 pages

References

livescience.com, December 17, 2018, "Long-Hidden 'Pyramid' Found in Indonesia Was Likely an Ancient Temple," Mindy Weisberge

Nationalgeographic.grid.id, Dec. 19, 2018, "Ilmuwan Ungkap Gunung Padang Sebagai Struktur Piramida Tertua di Dunia" (Scientists reveal that Mt. Padang is the world's oldest pyramid structure), Gita Laras Widyaningrum

Folklore in the Old Testament: studies in comparative religion, legend, and law. London: Macmillan. pp. 362-387

"the History of the Indies of New Spain," 1581, Diego de Duran

"Pyramids Carbon-dating Project," Mark Lehner and Robert Wenke.

"The Lakes of the Sahara," David Mattingly

http://giza.fas.harvard.edu

Nature, November 10, 2015, "African humid periods triggered the reactivation of a large river system in Western Sahara," C. Skonieczny

Nature, March 6, 2020, "Evidence of Cosmic Impact at Abu Hureyra, Syria at the Younger Dryas Onset (~12.8 ka): High-temperature melting at >2200 °C"

Journal of American Ceramic Society, November 30, 2006, "Microstructural Evidence of Reconstituted Limestone Blocks in the Great Pyramids of Egypt," Michel Barsoum

"Materials Letters" , July 14, 2011, "Were the casing stones of Senefru's Bent Pyramid in Dahshour cast or carved? Multinuclear NMR evidence."

Journal of Applied Physics, February 21, 2018, "Electromagnetic properties of the Great Pyramid: First multipole resonances and energy concentration," Mikhail Balezin and Andrey B. Evlyukhin

Infinite Energy, Issue 73 of 2007, "The Pyramidal Electric Transducer: A DC to RF Converter for the Capture of Atmospheric Electrostatic Energy," Peter Grandics

Article entitled "Surface luminescence dating of some Egyptian monuments," by Ioannis Liritzis and Asimina Vafiadou, of the Department of Archaeometry of Aegean University, Greece, appeared May 14, 2014, in the Journal of Cultural Heritage.

"Sphinx ARCE Project 1979-83," available at opencontext.org and arce.org. The following scholars participated: Ulrich Kapp, photogrammetric surveyor at the German Archaeological Institute in Cairo; Egyptologist Christiane Zivie-Coche, then director of the Wladimir Golenischeff Centre, École Pratique des Hautes Études; surveyor Attila Vas; surveyor Susan Allen (now employed at the Museum of Fine Arts, Boston); archaeologist Peter Lavovar (then employed at the Museum of Fine Arts, Boston, while now working at the Ancient Heritage and Archaeology Fund); archaeologist and surveyor Cynthia Schartzer; geologist K. Lal Gauri of the University of Louisville; geologist Thomas Aigner, of the University of Tübingen; and Dr. Mark Lehner.

The archaeology of an image - the great Sphinx of Giza, published in May 1991 by Mark Lehner

Update from ARCE, published in the November-December 2019 issue, edited by Mark Lehner

"A recent bottleneck of Y chromosome diversity coincides with a global change in culture," by Monika Karmin and colleagues, Genome Research, Feb. 13, 2015

"Der Bau der Cheops-Pyramide, Nach der Rampenzeit," by Heribert Illig and Franz Löhner, ISBN 3-928852-17-5

Encyclopedia of Ancient Egyptian Architecture (2003, Princeton University Press, ISBN 0-691-11488-9)

The Pyramids and Temples of Gizeh, Petrie Online Book, 1883

Howard Vyse, Operations Carried on at the Pyramids of Gizeh in 1837 (ISBN: 0938818309)

Studies on the illustrated Theban Funerary Papyri of the 11th and 10th Centuries B.C.,by Andrzej Niwinski, Year 1989, Zurich Open Repository and Archive, Zurich University

Giza Plateau Mapping Project, edited by Mark Lehner

"Ancient Egyptian mummy genomes suggest an increase of Sub-Saharan African ancestry in post-Roman periods," Nature Communications, by Verena J. Schuenemann, Alexander Peltzer, Beatrix Welte, W. Paul van Pelt, Martyna Molak, Chuan-Chao Wang, Anja Furtwängler, Christian Urban, Ella Reiter, Kay Nieselt, Barbara Teßmann, Michael Francken, Katerina Harvati, Wolfgang Haak, Stephan Schiffels & Johannes Krause, Nature Communications volume 8, May 30, 2017

"Le papyrus hiéroglyphique de Kamara et le Papyrus hiératique de Nesikhonsou," by Edouard Naville, Ernest Leroux Editeur, 1912

Building in Egypt, Pharaonic Stone Masonry (1991, Oxford University Press ISBN 0-19-506350-3).

"The Giza Project," Harvard University

"Etude géologique et géomorphologique de la colline originelle à la base des monuments de la quatrième dynastie égyptienne," which appeared on researchgate.net in August 2008, by Henri De La Boisse, Suzanne Raynaud, F. Makroum and Joël Bertho

Site en-nz.topographic-map.com

For translation of "Timaeus" and "Critias": site "perseus.tufts.edu"

Mysterious sudden increase of carbon-14 in coral caused by a comet, Science, Jan. 16, 2014

Genetic evidence for two founding populations of the Americas - Nature, September 3, 2015, Ponto Skoglund, Swapan Mallick, Maria Cátira Bortolini, Niru Chennagiri, Tábita Hünemeier, Maria Luiza Petzl-Erler, Francisco Salzano, Nick Patterson, and David Reich.

A genetic view of America's populations - Nature, August 6, 2016, Ponto Skoglund and David Reich.

Eden in the East: the drowned continent of Southeast Asia - Stephen, Oppenheimer (1999).

Independent Origins of Cultivated Coconut (Cocos nucifera L.) in the Old World Tropics - Plos One, June 22, 2011, Bee F. Gunn,Luc Baudouin, Kenneth M. Olsen

Denisovian DNA in the inhabitants of Melanesia - (March 20, 2016) Focus.it, Elisabetta Intini

New dating hypothesis for Denisova Cave, crossroads of human species - (February 2, 2019) Focus.it, Elisabetta Intini

Excavating Neandertal and Denisovan DNA from the genomes of Melanesian individuals - (April 8, 2016) science.sciencemag.org, Benjamin Vernot, Serena Tucci, Janet Kelso, Joshua G. Schraiber, Aaron B. Wolf, Rachel M. Gittelman, Michael D

Ancient genome reveals its secrets - (August 30, 2012), Max Plank Institute, Mpg.de, Matthias Meyer, Svante Pääbo, Sandra Jacob

Quantifying the legacy of the Chinese Neolithic on the maternal genetic heritage of Taiwan and Island Southeast Asia - Human Genetics, April 2016, Volume 135, Issue 4, pp 363-376, Andreia Brandão, Ken Khong Eng, Teresa Rito, Bruno Cavadas, David Bulbeck, Francesca Gandini, Maria Pala, Maru Mormina, Bob Hudson

Resolving the ancestry of Austronesian-speaking populations - Human Genetics Volume 135, Issue 3, pp 309-326, March 2016, Pedro A Soares et al

Evolutionary History of Continental Southeast Asians: "Early Train" Hypothesis Based on Genetic Analysis of Mitochondrial and Autosomal DNA Data - Society for Molecular Biology and Evolution, June 2012, Timothy A. Jinam, Lih-Chun Hong, Maude E Phipps, Mark Stoneking, Mahmood Ameen, Juli Edo, HUGO Pan-Asian SNP Consortium and Naruya Saitou,

Genomics of chicken domestication and feralization - IFM Biology, Department of Physics, Chemistry and Biology, Linköping University, Sweden, 2015, Martin Johnsson

Guanches, lanzaroteinformation.co.uk,

Investigating the Global Dispersal of Chickens in Prehistory Using Ancient Mitochondrial DNA Signatures - PLoS ONE, Storey AA, Athens JS, Bryant D, Carson M, Emery K, et al.

Out of southern East Asia: the natural history of domestic dogs across the world - Peter Savolainen et al

The Myth of the Pillars of Hercules - In Search of Knowledge Beyond All Limits, No. 86 - February 2015 (CXVII), Paola Scollo

The Pillars of Hercules: an investigation - by Sergio Frau, 2002 Nur Neon, Rome

Treatise On the Cosmos for Alexander - by John Reale/Abraham P.Bos, ed. Vita e Pensiero, Milan 1995

Herodotus "Stories"- edited by Luigi Annibaletto, Arnoldo Mondatori editore, Milan 2009

Polybius "Histories" - edited by Roberto Nicolai, 1998 Newton & Compton publishers, Rome

Plato, Complete Works - Editori Laterza, Rome 2003

Black Sea Odyssey? - Gianni Bassi - Val de l'Agno Archaeological Group

Indie Archaeology - YouTube Channel

"Sundaland. Atlantis in the Java Sea - Irwanto, Dhani (Sept. 29, 2015)

367

Borneo and Indochina are Major Evolutionary Hotspots for Southeast Asian Biodiversity - Systematic Biology

Palaeoenvironments of insular Southeast Asia during the Last Glacial Period: a savanna corridor in Sundaland? - Quaternary Science Reviews, Bird, Michael I.; Taylor, David; Hunt, Chris (November 1, 2005)

Response of Western Pacific marginal seas to glacial cycles: paleoceanographic and sedimentological features - Marine Geology. Wang, Pinxian (March 15, 1999).

Rapid Flooding of the Sunda Shelf: A Late-Glacial Sea-Level Record - Science, Hanebuth, Till; Stattegger, Karl; Grootes, Pieter M. (2000)

Modelled atmospheric temperatures and global sea levels over the past million years - Nature, Bintanja, Richard; Wal, Roderik S.W. van de; Oerlemans, Johannes (2005)

On the Forests of Tropical Asia: Lest the memory fade - Kew, Richmond, Surrey, UK: Royal Botanic Gardens, Ashton, Peter (2014).

Temperature and Size Variabilities of the Western Pacific Warm Pool - Science, Yan, Xiao-Hai; Ho, Chung-Ru; Zheng, Quanan; Klemas, Vic (1992).

Contributions to the Physical Geography of South-Eastern Asia and Australia - H. Bailliere. p. 40. Retrieved 2 December 2017. Earl, George Windsor (1853).

The Sunda Shelf, Southeast Asia - Zeitschrift für Geomorphologie, Tija, H.D. (1980).

Sedimentation in the Sunda Trench and forearc region - Geological Society, London, Special Publications. Moore, Gregory F.; Curray, Joseph R.; Emmel, Frans J. (1982)

The status of the Indo-Pacific Warm Pool and adjacent land at the Last Glacial Maximum - Global and Planetary Change, (January 1, 2003). De Deckker, P; Tapper, N. J; van der Kaars,

Vegetation on the Sunda Shelf, South China Sea, during the Last Glacial Maximum - Palaeogeography, Palaeoclimatology, Palaeoecology (July 15, 2009). Wang, XiaoMei; Sun, XiangJun; Wang, PinXian; Stattegger, Karl

Historical distribution of Sundaland's Dipterocarp rainforests at Quaternary glacial maxima - (November 25, 2014) Proceedings of the National Academy of Sciences. Raes, Niels; Cannon, Charles H.; Hijmans, Robert J.; Piessens, Thomas; Saw, Leng Guan; Welzen, Peter C. van; Slik, J. W. Ferry

"New research forces U-turn in population migration theory." EurekAlert - (May 23, 2008), University of Leeds

First identification of drugs in Egyptian mummies - (August 1992) Naturwissenschaften, S Balabanova, F Parsche, W Pirsig

Presence of drugs in different tissues of an Egyptian mummy - (January 1995), Fresenius' Journal of Analytical Chemistry, Franz Parsche and Andreas Nerlich

Article from "Nature Ecology & Evolution" that appeared on November 26, 2018

Article "Discovery of organic grains in comet Halley," which appeared in the renowned journal "Nature" on September 6, 1986

Article by Matthew S. Dodd that appeared in March 2017 appeared in the famous journal "Nature"

Article "Evolution of the human-specific microRNA miR-941," appeared Oct. 23, 2012, in "Nature"

June 28, 2016, article by journalist Nir Hasson that appeared in Ha'aretz

"The Thomson Review," July 19, 1922.

The Papyri of Elephantine, by Arthur Ernest Cowley

"Late Pleistocene Human Population Bottleneck, Volcanic Winter and the Differentiation of Modern Humans," published by Professor Stanley H. Ambrose in 1998

"Life Cloud. The origin of life in the universe," by Fred Hoyle and Chandra Wickramasinghe.

"Panspermia, octopuses and comets," by Michele Diodati.

"Astrobiology, the Origin of Life and the Death of Darwinism," Rhawn Joseph.

Potential Consequences of the YDB Cosmic Impact at 12.8 kya: Climate, Humans, and Megafauna - James P. Kennett

Advances.sciencemag.org - A significant impact crater beneath Hiawatha Glacier in northwest Greenland - Kurt H. Kjær

Genome.cshlp.org - A recent bottleneck of Y chromosome diversity coincides with a global change in culture - Monika Karmin

"Late Pleistocene Human Population Bottleneck, Volcanic Winter and the Differentiation of Modern Humans," published by Professor Stanley H. Ambrose in 1998

Animals in the symbolic world of Pre-Pottery Neolithic Göbekli Tepe, south-eastern Turkey: a preliminary assessment - Joris Peters, Klaus Schimdt

Mattias Oskarsson, Analysis of the origin and spread of the domestic dog using Y-chromosome DNA and mtDNA sequence data, Division of Gene Technology, School of Biotechnology, Royal Institute of Technology (KTH), Stockholm, Sweden, 2012

Stephen Oppenheimer, Out-of-Africa, the peopling of continents and islands: tracing uniparental gene trees across the map, Philosophical Transactions of The Royal Society B (2012)

Tatiana M Karafet, Fernando L Mendez, Herawati Sudoyo, J Stephen Lansing and Michael F Hammer, Improved phylogenetic resolution and rapid diversification of Y-chromosome haplogroup K-M526 in Southeast Asia, European Journal of Human Genetics (2015)

Using Ancient Mitochondrial DNA Signatures, PLoS ONE 7(7).

Images

P. 14 - Artistic depiction of String theory. Graphic elaboration.

P. 17: Artistic representation of DNA traveling through space. Graphic processing.

P. 21 -Bacteria. Graphic processing.

P. 28 - Viruses under the electron microscope. Graphic processing.

P. 48 - Diagram of the genetic bottleneck that occurred 75,000 years ago. Graphic processing.

P. 57 - Symbol of Zoroaster. Graphic elaboration.

P. 62 - Native American leader Geronimo. Drawing and graphic elaboration of an ancient photo of Chief Geronimo.

P. 74 - Woman belonging to the Neanderthals. Drawing and graphic elaboration of the possible face of a Neanderthal woman.

P. 89 Sundaland. Image processed from a Google Earth photo and other processing.

P. 102 - Geoglyphs of the Nazca. Graphic processing.

P. 114 Geoglyphs of the Nazca. Graphic processing.

P. 118 South American walls of Ollantaytambo. Graphic elaboration.

P. 128 Saharan Lakes. Image processed by drawing from Google Maps, "Seas of the Sahara" by YNot1989, source DeviantArt, and other processing.

P. 131 Tamanrasett River. Image processed by drawing from Google Maps, "African humid periods triggered the reactivation of a large river system in Western Sahara," Nature Communications, Nov. 10, 2015, and other processing

P. 133 Island formed by the Tamanrasett River. P. 96: Image processed from a Google Maps photo, from a photo included in "African humid periods triggered the reactivation of a large river system in Western Sahara," Nature Communications, Nov. 10, 2015, and other processing.

P. 135 - Canary Islands - Image processed from a Google Maps photo and other processing

P. 137 - Location of the "Continent" of Atlantis - Image processed from a Google Maps photo and other processing

P. 141 Stylization of the town of Nan Madol - Page 216: Drawing based on the processing of an online video of "Allora Picture," Green Park, 200 Brook Drive, Reading RG2 6UB

P. 143 - Artistic reconstruction of the city of Nan Madol. Graphic processing.

P. 155 - Reconstruction of the Djehutihotep painting - Elaboration based on a drawing by Sir John Gardner "ilkinson - "A popular account of the ancient Egyptians," Jan. 1, 1854

P. 167 - Denisova woman's face - Drawing and graphic processing of an image of a Denisova woman created Maayan Harel/ Maayan studios

P. 177 - Thermal overhang during the Younger Dryas. Graphic processing.

P.180 - Areas affected by meteoric bombardment. Graphic processing.

P. 194 - Circle structure of the Göbekli Tepe settlements. Graphic elaboration.

P. 196 - Side view of the central monoliths of Göbekli Tepe. Graphic processing.

P. 198 - Probable wooden covering of the circular settlements of Göbekli Tepe. Graphic elaboration.

P. 200 - Stratification over time of the settlements of Göbekli Tepe. Graphic elaboration.

P. 204 - Monolith B of Göbekli Tepe. Graphic processing.

P. 208 - Vulture Stele of Göbekli Tepe. Drawing and graphic processing of a photo.

P. 211 - Stylization of the Vulture Stele of Göbekli Tepe.

P. 219 - Stars of the Cranes of Göbekli Tepe. Drawing and graphic processing of a photo.

P. 226 - Positioning of the Sahara Eye. Graphic processing.

P. 228 - Three-dimensional reconstruction of the water-filled Sahara Eye. Image processed from a Radio Canada video by Norman Grondin and Jean-Francois Woods.

P. 252 - Dating of the "Small Pyramid." Excerpted from the 'article entitled "Surface luminescence dating of some Egyptian monuments," edited by Ioannis Liritzis and Asimina Vafiadou, of the Department of Archaeometry of Aegean University,

Greece, which appeared May 14, 2014, in the "Journal of Cultural Heritage."

P. 275 - Synthetic rocks of the Rhomboidal Pyramid. Drawing and graphic processing from a photo by Michel Barsoum, Drexel University.

P. 279 - Land levelling under the Pyramid. Graphic processing.

P. 281 - Perimeter and apothem of the Grade Pyramid. Graphic elaboration.

P. 283 - Angle widths at the base of the Great Pyramid. Graphic elaboration.

P. 285 Inclination of the Great Pyramid. Graphic elaboration.

P. 287 Eight visible faces in the Great Pyramid. Graphic elaboration.

P. 292 Inclination of the Great Pyramid with respect to the star Alpha Draconis. Graphic processing.

P. 303 - Graph of Dr. Monica Karmin's study group.

P. 327 - Stylization of a bust of Akhenaten. Graphic processing.

P. 329 - Stylization of the bust of Queen Nefertiti. Graphic elaboration.

P. 333 - Stylization of the head of a woman from Akhenaten's family, either his wife or daughter. Graphic elaboration.

P. 334- Stylization of Akhenaten's hand. Graphic processing.

P. 336 - Family of Akhenaten. Graphic elaboration.

P. 337 Timeline graph of Egyptian history. Graphic elaboration.

P. 352 - Light effect on a cloud. Graphic processing.